cirencester
college
a beacon college

The Short Oxford History of Europe

The Central Middle Ages

The Short Oxford History of Europe

General Editor: T. C. W. Blanning

NOW AVAILABLE

Classical Greece
edited by Robin Osborne

The Early Middle Ages
edited by Rosamond McKitterick

The Seventeenth Century
edited by Joseph Bergin

The Eighteenth Century
edited by T. C. W. Blanning

The Nineteenth Century
edited by T. C. W. Blanning

Europe since 1945
edited by Mary Fulbrook

IN PREPARATION, VOLUMES COVERING

The Romans
The Late Middle Ages
The Sixteenth Century

The Short Oxford History of Europe

General Editor: T. C. W. Blanning

The Central
Middle Ages
Europe 950–1320

Edited by Daniel Power

OXFORD
UNIVERSITY PRESS

*This book has been printed digitally and produced in a standard specification
in order to ensure its continuing availability*

OXFORD
UNIVERSITY PRESS

Great Clarendon Street, Oxford OX2 6DP

Oxford University Press is a department of the University of Oxford.
It furthers the University's objective of excellence in research, scholarship,
and education by publishing worldwide in

Oxford New York

Auckland   Cape Town Dar es Salaam   Hong Kong   Karachi
Kuala Lumpur Madrid Melbourne Mexico City   Nairobi
New Delhi Shanghai Taipei Toronto
With offices in
Argentina Austria Brazil Chile Czech Republic France Greece
Guatemala Hungary Italy Japan South Korea Poland Portugal
Singapore Switzerland Thailand Turkey Ukraine Vietnam

Oxford is a registered trade mark of Oxford University Press
in the UK and in certain other countries

Published in the United States
by Oxford University Press Inc., New York

ISBN 978-0-19-925312-8

General Editor's Preface

The problems of writing a satisfactory general history of Europe are many, but the most intractable is clearly the reconciliation of depth with breadth. The historian who can write with equal authority about every part of the continent in all its various aspects has not yet been born. Two main solutions have been tried in the past: either a single scholar has attempted to go it alone, presenting an unashamedly personal view of a period, or teams of specialists have been enlisted to write what are in effect anthologies. The first offers a coherent perspective but unequal coverage, the second sacrifices unity for the sake of expertise. This new series is underpinned by the belief that it is this second way that has the fewest disadvantages and that even those can be diminished if not neutralized by close cooperation between the individual contributors under the directing supervision of the volume editor. All the contributors to every volume in this series have read each other's chapters, have met to discuss problems of overlap and omission, and have then redrafted as part of a truly collective exercise. To strengthen coherence further, the editor has written an introduction and conclusion, weaving the separate strands together to form a single cord. In this exercise, the brevity promised by the adjective 'short' in the series' title has been an asset. The need to be concise has concentrated everyone's minds on what really mattered in the period. No attempt has been made to cover every angle of every topic in every country. What this volume does provide is a short but sharp and deep entry into the history of Europe in the period in all its most important aspects.

T. C. W. Blanning
Sidney Sussex College
Cambridge

Editor's Preface

When Timothy Reuter accepted the invitation to contribute one of the chapters in this volume, he wrote, 'I find the impossible task of summarizing the political development of 370 years almost irresistible.' As the editors of the other volumes in this series have acknowledged, writing a short collaborative history of Europe poses many challenges. All seven contributors to this volume would nevertheless agree with the late Professor Reuter that the difficulties of capturing the essence of the period are outweighed by the intellectual satisfaction of such an exercise. For me as editor, it has been a privilege to have the opportunity to bring together the work of six outstanding scholars whose chapters comprise the main part of this book.

In common with the early medieval volume of the Short Oxford History of Europe edited by Rosamond McKitterick, five chapters in the present collection examine the social, economic, political, religious, and intellectual and cultural history of (mainly western) Europe in the chosen period. The sixth chapter approaches the history of Europe's relations with the wider world by focusing upon by far the most important aspect of that topic between 950 and 1320, namely the expansion of Latin Christendom at the expense of its Greek Orthodox, Muslim, and pagan neighbours. Such a division of labour requires justification: a decade and a half after the fall of the Berlin Wall and in the aftermath of the admission of most of east-central Europe into the European Union, it may seem perverse that the first five chapters of this volume appear to perpetuate the divisions of the Cold War, which for much of the twentieth century encouraged the view of the eastern half of Europe as 'other'. Yet, since the shift in the relationship between western Europe and the rest of the continent between the mid-tenth and early fourteenth centuries was so dramatic and since it varied so greatly in its dynamics, nature, and outcome, the absorption of northern and east-central Europe and much of the Mediterranean littoral into Latin Christendom in the central Middle Ages surely justifies special treatment. As in the early medieval volume, military history has not been discussed in a separate chapter, since the aristocracy of the central Middle Ages was heavily militarized (although by the end of the period its warrior character was declining in some parts of Europe). It is also inevitable that some other topics—music and visual arts, to take two obvious examples—and some regions of the continent have not been discussed in the detail that they deserve. It is nevertheless hoped that the reader will find the following chapters and accompanying apparatus an informative and thought-provoking introduction to a fascinating period.

In general, dates given for monarchs and bishops are for their reigns or pontificates; for others, dates of birth and death are given (where known). For names, it is difficult to apply a single standard for the whole Continent and period (Comnenus or Komnenus? William, Guillaume or Guglielmo?), but standardization has been attempted where possible. Quotations from primary sources have usually been taken from widely available English translations. In common with most volumes in this series, no illustrations have been included. (An asterisk indicates an entry in the Glossary.)

I wish to express my gratitude to the authors of the six main chapters for their participation in this project, to Catherine Holmes and Julian Haseldine, both of whom kindly read the whole draft and made many penetrating comments, and to my medievalist colleagues at the University of Sheffield for answering numerous queries.

Tim Blanning's encouragement in his capacity as series editor proved invaluable. I wish to thank Fiona Kinnear of Oxford University Press for her assistance in the project's early stages, and her successor Matthew Cotton for his guidance and considerable patience as the book neared completion. The miniature of the 'three orders' on the front cover is reproduced with the kind permission of the British Library from the L'Ymage dou Monde of Gautier de Metz (Sloane MS 2435, fo. 85r). I am also indebted to the hundreds of Sheffield undergraduates who have taken my course 'Europe in the Central Middle Ages' in its various guises since 1996; the experience of teaching them assisted me greatly when I came to write the introduction and conclusion, and I dedicate those sections to them.

As noted above, Timothy Reuter agreed to write Chapter 3 of this book. His untimely death in 2002 deprived medieval scholarship of one of its most imaginative and knowledgeable practitioners. On Professor Reuter's own recommendation shortly before his death, Björn Weiler kindly agreed to write this chapter instead; he thereby earned the lasting gratitude of the editor and of everyone else involved in the publication of the present work.

Daniel Power
Sheffield
November 2004

Contents

List of Maps

List of Contributors

ANNA SAPIR ABULAFIA is Vice-President and Lecturer in History at Lucy Cavendish College, Cambridge. Her field of research is twelfth- and thirteenth-century intellectual history with particular emphasis on the medieval Christian–Jewish debate. She is the co-editor (with G. R. Evans) of *The Works of Gilbert Crispin, Abbot of Westminster* (*Auctores Britannici Medii Aevi*, 8) (Oxford, 1986), the author of *Christians and Jews in the Twelfth-Century Renaissance* (London, 1995) and *Christians and Jews in Dispute: Disputational Literature and the Rise of Anti-Judaism in the West (c. 1000–1150)* (Aldershot, 1998), and the editor of *Religious Violence between Christians and Jews: Medieval Roots and Modern Perspectives* (Basingstoke, 2002).

MARTIN AURELL is Professor of Medieval History at the Centre d'Études Supérieures de Civilisation Médiévale, University of Poitiers, and member of the Institut Universitaire de France. He is the editor of the review *Cahiers de Civilisation Médiévale*. He has written several books on nobility, kinship, and power in Catalonia and Provence: *Une famille de la noblesse provençale au Moyen Age: Les Porcelet* (Avignon, 1986), *La Vielle et l'épée: Troubadours et politique en Provence au XIIIᵉ siècle* (Paris, 1989), *Les Noces du comte: Mariage et pouvoir en Catalogne (785–1213)* (Paris, 1995), *La Noblesse en Occident (Vᵉ–XVᵉ siècle)* (Paris, 1996), and *Actes de la famille Porcelet d'Arles (972–1320)* (Paris, 2001). He currently works on western France and Britain in the twelfth century and on the political and social implications of the Arthurian legends. His most recent book is *L'Empire des Plantagenêt (1154–1224)* (Paris, 2003; English translation in preparation).

JULIA BARROW studied at St Andrews (MA in Medieval History, 1978) and at Corpus Christi College, Oxford (D. Phil., 1983). Since 1990 she has taught Medieval History at Nottingham, where she is now Reader. She has edited *English Episcopal Acta VII: Hereford, 1079–1234* (Oxford, 1993), *St Davids Episcopal Acta, 1085–1280* (Cardiff, 1998), and *Fasti Ecclesiae Anglicanae, 1066–1300, viii: Hereford* (London, 2002), and has written numerous articles on ecclesiastical history of the period c.900–c.1215, in particular on English and German clergy, on the late Anglo-Saxon Church, and on forged charters. She is currently writing a book on the secular clergy in northern Europe.

NORA BEREND is Lecturer at the University of Cambridge and Fellow of St Catharine's College. Her publications include *At the Gate of Christendom: Jews, Muslims and 'Pagans' in Medieval Hungary c. 1000–c. 1300* (Cambridge, 2001); *Medieval Frontiers: Concepts and Practices*, co-edited with David Abulafia (Aldershot, 2002), and numerous articles.

DAVID NICHOLAS is Emeritus Professor of History at Clemson University. After beginning his career as a historian of the Flemish cities in the fourteenth century, he has more recently studied broader patterns of comparative urbanization and specifically the linkages of the urban and rural economies and the impact of geography on city formation and structure. Professor Nicholas is the author or editor of fifteen books and numerous scholarly articles, including *Town and Countryside: Social, Economic, and Political Tensions in Fourteenth-Century Flanders* (Bruges, 1971); *The Domestic Life of a Medieval City: Women, Children, and the Family in Fourteenth-Century Ghent* (Lincoln, NE, 1985); *The Metamorphosis of a Medieval City: Ghent in the Age of the Arteveldes, 1302–1390* (Lincoln, NE, 1987); *Medieval Flanders* (London, 1992); *The Growth of the Medieval City: From Late Antiquity to the Early Fourteenth Century* (London, 1997); *The Later Medieval City 1300–1500* (London, 1997); *Urban Europe, 1100–1700* (Basingstoke, 2003).

DANIEL POWER is Senior Lecturer in Medieval History at the University of Sheffield. He is the author of *The Norman Frontier in the Twelfth and Early Thirteenth Centuries* (Cambridge, 2004) and editor (with Naomi Standen) of *Frontiers in Question: Eurasian Borderlands 700–1700* (Basingstoke, 1999). He has also published a number of articles concerning France in the central Middle Ages, especially Normandy and the Angevin 'empire'. He is currently preparing a study of the Anglo-French aristocracy between 1204 and 1259.

BJÖRN WEILER is Lecturer in Medieval History at the University of Wales, Aberystwyth. He has published on images of kingship and on political culture in the twelfth and thirteenth centuries, and is the author of *Henry III and the Staufen Empire: Politics and Diplomacy in Thirteenth-Century Europe* (Woodbridge, 2005). He has edited (with

Ifor Rowlands) *England and Europe in the Reign of Henry III (1216–1272)* (Aldershot, 2002) and (with Simon MacLean) *Representations of Power in Medieval Germany, 700–1500* (Turnhout, 2005). He is currently completing a book comparing the political culture of England and Germany in the thirteenth century, and is preparing a textbook on ritual and politics in England, 1100–1250. He also coordinates a British Academy-sponsored project on the political culture of Norman and Angevin England within its broader European context.

Introduction

Daniel Power

The 370 years discussed in this book represent a period of momentous change in Europe. Between the mid-tenth and early fourteenth centuries, the population of the continent increased vastly, and European society became more urbanized, more literate, and more complex in both economic and cultural terms. In particular, 'Latin Christian' (Roman Catholic) culture grew to be more assertive and outwardly homogeneous and came to cover a much greater area, but simultaneously it acquired deep and enduring political divisions. Its aggressive character was expressed most forcefully in the Christian holy wars known to history as the Crusades. Its homogeneity grew from the 'reform' of the Roman Catholic Church, bequeathing Europe its great Romanesque and Gothic cathedrals and its universities; the Church came under the vigorous direction of the papacy, which grew immensely in pretensions and in power. Latin Christendom's hardening internal divisions are apparent in the emergence of dynastic kingdoms in France, the British Isles, southern Italy, the Iberian peninsula, east-central Europe, and Scandinavia, from which the modern European system of nation states is descended, and in the fragmentation of Germany and northern Italy into numerous principalities and autonomous 'city states'.

Although modern Europeans owe much to the Europe of 700 or 1,000 years ago, they may well regard it as alien and primitive. Twenty-first-century Western culture is urban, globalized, and highly secular. It emphasizes the individual over the community and treats all people as free and equal—in theory at least—regardless of race, sex, birth, or beliefs. Its world of work is characterized by bureaucracy, mechanization, global communications, specialization, and near-universal literacy; its inhabitants are protected against all but the most virulent diseases by antibiotics and professional health care. In the popular imagination, the central Middle Ages seem like the very opposite of everything that today's Europeans know and value. Medieval Europeans are conventionally depicted as inhabiting a deeply religious world in which adherence to the Christian Church was often brutally enforced, and learning was constrained by inflexible doctrine that made original thought dangerous. The clerical elite's near-monopoly of literacy served to maintain its position. The interests of the community and kin group prevailed over the interests of the individual at all levels of society, and social as well as religious dissent was often ruthlessly punished. The organization of society under kings and princes who claimed to rule by the grace of God ensured grave social inequalities: power and status were usually determined by birth, which brought rights to control land and the people who worked on it; a great many people were unfree, which meant that their lords restricted where they might live, where and when they might work, and whom they might marry. The economy was dominated by labour-intensive, poorly mechanized agriculture, and towns and industry remained very small by modern standards. Recurrent famines and epidemics devastated whole populations, and life expectancy was short. Few people travelled beyond their immediate region, and little was known of the non-European world: distant lands were believed to be populated by fabulous creatures and subhuman savages. Depicted like this, medieval Europe seems strange and repellent.

Some modern feelings of repugnance are due to misunderstanding. It is simply not true, for instance, that the Church taught that the world was flat and persecuted as heretics those who believed it was round; on the contrary, it was well known in the Middle Ages that the world was spherical. Nevertheless, no medievalist would deny that there is much about medieval culture that seems unattractive. No doubt our thirty-first-century descendants will be equally scathing about the primitive nature of our own technology and ideas. A remote period may be of great historical significance, even though it lacks smoking factories or good dentistry, and the central Middle Ages were formative both in European and world history; its consequences still have profound resonances today.

The following set of essays is intended to introduce the history of Europe between c.950 and c.1320. Five of the six chapters below consider the nature of western European civilization from political, social, economic, religious, and intellectual perspectives, and the sixth chapter shows how this culture expanded into northern, east-central, and southernmost Europe, and attempted to incorporate parts of south-east Europe, the North African coast, and the Near East as well. All six essays emphasize that medieval society was far from static. The period of nearly four centuries discussed in this volume is a long time even for a premodern, 'traditional' society; and medieval Europe altered almost out of recognition between the mid-tenth and the early fourteenth centuries. This introductory chapter will explain why the period may be considered a distinctive era, which English-speaking historians frequently describe as the 'central Middle Ages'. It will then describe medieval Europe's main geographical limitations as well as its political and cultural divisions, and introduce some of the ways in which historians have attempted to sum up and explain the great changes of the period.

Why the 'central Middle Ages'?

All historical periodization has an element of arbitrariness, but the division into 'ancient', 'medieval', and 'modern' has proved the most enduring scheme of all for analysing European history. Of course, the peoples of eleventh-century or thirteenth-century Europe cannot have known that they inhabited the 'Middle Ages' (in Latin *medium aevum*, from which the word 'medieval' was coined in the eighteenth century). That concept was invented by the thinkers of the so-called Renaissance, influenced by the fourteenth-century Italian poet and humanist* Petrarch (1304–74). The Renaissance scholars came to the conclusion that they were separated by a 'dark' or 'middle' age from a glorious Classical past, the world of the ancient Greeks and Romans. Although refined and refashioned, this view of the Middle Ages has proved remarkably durable. Before and after the French Revolution, it became a weapon with which the critics of Europe's *anciens régimes* could denounce its monarchies and the Roman Catholic Church. Hugely influential works as diverse as Edward Gibbon's *The Decline and Fall of the Roman Empire* (1776–88), Karl Marx's *Communist Manifesto* (1848), and Jakob Burckhardt's *The Civilisation of the*

Renaissance in Italy (1860) all reinforced the view of the Middle Ages as an undifferentiated era of ignorance, superstition, and political and religious oppression.

With the emergence of a more specialized historical profession, however, the notion of a single 'Middle Age' between 500 and 1500 has come to seem an overgeneralization of magnificent proportions. Since the late nineteenth century historians have sought various ways of subdividing those ten centuries. German historians, generally followed by their English-speaking counterparts, have tended to differentiate between the *Früh-*, *Hoch-*, and *Spätmittelalter*, or 'early', 'high', and 'late' Middle Age(s). In contrast, historians in Romance-speaking countries prefer to distinguish between the 'high' (early) and 'low' (late) Middle Ages (in French, for instance, *haut* and *bas Moyen-Age*). Hence, although in English usage 'high Middle Ages' usually corresponds to the period covered by the present book, in the context of continental historiography it is a very ambiguous phrase. The current volume follows standard Anglo-American practice in dividing the Middle Ages into three, but has adopted a well-established alternative phrase, 'central Middle Ages', for the middle period, in order to avoid any confusion.

There are several reasons why the history of Europe from the mid-tenth to the early fourteenth centuries may be regarded as a defined period. First, at the outset western Europe emerged from a period of sustained pressure from neighbouring peoples. Since the 790s the coastlines of the North Sea and Atlantic Ocean had been subject to periodic Viking raids from Scandinavia, and the northern shores of the Mediterranean Sea had long suffered comparable attacks from Muslim fleets. Already intermittently assaulted from the north, west, and south, from the 890s onwards western Europe faced a new threat from the east. From the Eurasian steppes, so often a source of nomadic invasions of Europe, the Magyars migrated into the Hungarian plain, from where they launched raids far and wide across the continent. However, for a variety of reasons, most of these raids subsided after 950, although the British Isles experienced further bursts of Scandinavian activity between the 980s and 1070. It is true that relations between early medieval Christians and their neighbours before 950 were by no means always hostile, and the assaults themselves had some positive effects; it is also true that occasional external assaults were rarely as disruptive as strife amongst

Christians. Nevertheless, the late tenth century marks the beginning of a new phase in European history, since Latin Christendom ceased to be on the defensive against neighbouring cultures and began to expand aggressively against them.

Secondly, Latin territorial expansion was accompanied by a demographic and economic transformation, vastly increasing the continent's population, number of settlements, and cultivated land. The tenth and eleventh centuries also witnessed some radical changes to settlement patterns, often through aristocratic direction, which transformed the social and economic structures of the countryside (see below, pp. 22–5, and Chapter 1). Conversely, by the late thirteenth century the demographic expansion was faltering, and by the 1320s, after a series of famines and livestock plagues, the population of western Europe may even have been in decline; soon after it was devastated by the Black Death (1347–51) (see Conclusion).

Thirdly, the second half of the tenth century witnessed several events that recast the framework of western European politics for several centuries. Since the eighth century, much of the European continent had been dominated by the Frankish or 'Carolingian' Empire, but by the mid-tenth century it had effectively disintegrated: in its stead its central and eastern territories were being welded into an 'Ottonian empire' (from which the better-known Holy Roman Empire would later emerge), an event marked by the coronation of Otto I, king of the east Franks (933–72), as emperor in 962. Meanwhile, in 987 the Carolingians were formally replaced by the Capetian dynasty in the kingdom of the West Franks (or France); and, quite independently, the unification of the kingdom of England under the kings of the West Saxons was achieved in the 950s. At the same time, however, the leading noble dynasties of western Europe were increasingly rooting themselves in particular regions, thereby laying the foundations of the patchwork of duchies, counties, and lordships that would form many of the chief building blocks of European politics until the French Revolutionary wars of the 1790s. The end of the period was also marked by several major political developments, notably the beginning of chronic conflict between several of the western European monarchies and crises for the two 'universalist' powers in the continent, the Holy Roman Empire and the papacy (see Conclusion).

So the period covered by this book may be regarded as a single era, differentiated from the early and late Middle Ages by political, economic, and social conditions. The periodization is most appropriate from a western European perspective, since population increase and the reclamation of marginal land continued apace in eastern Europe in the fourteenth century, when they had largely ceased in the West. Yet the virtual end to the expansion of Latin Christendom in the late thirteenth and early fourteenth centuries affected the whole continent and the adjacent parts of the Near East.

This periodization inevitably has its limitations. Romance-speaking historians have generally preferred a twofold Middle Ages because of certain profound changes that occurred midway through the period covered by this book, between c.1060 and c.1230. The significance of this 'long twelfth century' will be apparent in most of the following chapters. Many of the most important political changes discussed by Björn Weiler (Chapter 3) were concentrated in this shorter period, including the rise of accountable government and of extraordinary taxation, and a growing shift from oral customary law to written law proclaimed through princely ordinances; the period also witnessed the spread of the influence of Roman Law upon notions of rulership. Martin Aurell's survey of western European society (Chapter 1) shows how these institutional changes contributed to the hardening of social divisions, in particular the reinforcement of the status of the nobles precisely when the weakening of manorial structures were undermining seigneurial controls over their peasants—a trend discussed by David Nicholas (Chapter 2), who emphasizes the qualitative shift in the European economy either side of the year 1180.

The 'long twelfth century' was also the most important phase in the transformation of the Roman Church, often dubbed the 'reform movement' by historians (discussed in Chapter 4 by Julia Barrow), which now enforced much tighter moral control over both clergy and laity and embarked upon a heightened search for religious order and orthodoxy. This political and religious revolution is marked by the crusaders' capture of Jerusalem from the Muslims in 1099 and of Constantinople from the (Greek Christian) Byzantine Empire in 1204; the codification of canon law in Gratian's *Decretum* (*c.*1140), of feudal law in the Italian *Libri Feudorum* (late twelfth century), and the justification of temporal power by John of Salisbury in his *Policraticus* (1159). The emergence of universities at Bologna, Salerno, Paris, Montpellier, and Oxford formed part of a new intellectual flourishing often now called the 'Twelfth-Century Renaissance'. As Anna Sapir Abulafia (Chapter 5) remarks, many scholars in this period sensed that they were living in a new age.

The mid-twelfth century also witnessed what has traditionally been regarded as one of the most fundamental shifts in the history of architecture (although nowadays architectural historians tend to be more cautious), as heavier Romanesque traditions began to be super-seded by lighter and more graceful Gothic forms. Lester K. Little has even taken this change as emblematic of an entire shift in Christian culture:[1] what he calls 'Romanesque' Christianity, informal in character and dominated by Benedictine monasticism and liturgy, was superseded by a far more regulated 'Gothic' Christianity; the dynamic forces within Christianity were no longer Benedictine monks but the church hierarchy (the pope, bishops, priests, and diocesan officials such as archdeacons), new religious orders, and the universities. Karl Leyser described the transformation of the Roman Catholic Church as the 'first European revolution'; compar-ing European society to other Eurasian cultures of the same period, R. I. Moore has used the same phrase for the whole set of social, economic, religious, and political developments in western Europe in the eleventh and twelfth centuries.[2] Hence the 'long twelfth cen-tury' marks a significant shift within European (particularly western European) history, yet, like one Russian doll inside another, it also fits into a much broader age of demographic, social, and religious expansion that we know as the central Middle Ages.

Europe in the central Middle Ages: climate and environment

When examining the history of Europe between the mid-tenth and early fourteenth centuries, it is helpful to consider some basic aspects

[1] L. K. Little, 'Romanesque Christianity in Germanic Europe', *Journal of Interdisciplinary History*, 23 (1992–3), 453–74.
[2] K. Leyser, 'On the Eve of the First European revolution', in his *Communications and Power in Medieval Europe. Part II: The Gregorian Revolution and Beyond*, ed. T. Reuter (London, 1994), 1–19; R. I. Moore, *The First European Revolution c.970–1215* (Oxford and Malden, MA, 2000).

of the continent's geography as well as its main political, religious, and cultural divisions. Geography has always exerted a strong influence upon European societies. Variations in climate, the physical landscape, and soil quality have largely determined land use, which in turn has had a huge impact upon political, social, and even religious organization. Arable cultivation tends to encourage the growth of nucleated settlements, as the population clusters together for mutual support in labour-intensive cultivation; however, such settlements are also easier to dominate, for farmers cannot afford to abandon their crops when threatened by military might. In European history, arable societies have typically experienced strong political control, and have also usually been wealthier and more populous than pastoral societies. Tending livestock, by contrast, is often a more solitary occupation, so that areas of primarily pastoral farming tend to be characterized by scattered hamlets or temporary settlements, weak political control, and relatively poor populations.

Europe has three main climates: temperate, Mediterranean, and continental. In the temperate zone a huge belt of potentially good farmland forms the North European Plain, which extends from the modern Baltic republics (Estonia, Latvia, and Lithuania) and Poland through northern Germany and the Low Countries to western France. The Mediterranean climate is relatively arid, and most of the countries surrounding the Mediterranean Sea are also very mountainous, but despite their physical drawbacks many of these lands were already densely populated in 950 and more prosperous than their counterparts in north-west Europe. Muslim regions such as Valencia and Sicily benefited from complex irrigation systems that had been developed with Arab technology. However, forest clearances and marsh drainage were transforming the northern European landscape for several centuries before 950, and in the central Middle Ages they intensified, bringing vast tracts of land into cultivation and greatly increasing the prosperity of these regions. Ultimately some of the reclamation also had disastrous consequences, for by the late thirteenth century much of western Europe was dangerously overpopulated and relying ever more heavily upon poorer marginal soils for its sustenance, a situation that engendered terrible famines in the 1310s and 1320s. Further east, the great zone subject to a continental climate extends eastwards from the Great Hungarian Plain or Alföld towards the Russian forests and central Asian steppes. These regions, which experience the most extreme climatic variations in Europe, remained far more sparsely populated, although a steady stream of warriors, farmers, and traders migrated there from western Europe; the same regions also underwent periodic influxes of nomadic populations from the east.

The European mainland is broken up by several major mountain ranges, of which the most important are the Alps, Pyrenees, Carpathians, Apennines, and Balkans (see Map 1). Although they served as important landmarks and obstructed communications, they did not hermetically seal off societies from one another. Each range was crossed by several passes, and transhumance* was common. In the central Middle Ages the Alps, which today mark the frontiers between several European states, lay within a single political entity, the (Holy Roman) Empire. Even though north Italian cities frequently exploited their strategic position at the southern end of the main Alpine passes to thwart imperial ambitions, their prosperity also depended upon those same routes. In the Iberian peninsula (Spain and Portugal), the central plateau was always sparsely populated, and the Christian kings and lords who wished to dominate it repeatedly attempted to attract settlers from further north. The impact of the environment was even more significant for water-based transport. Europe is not strictly speaking a continent at all, but rather one of several peninsulas of the Eurasian land mass. The relative proximity of seas, fed by a series of navigable river systems, provided a viable network of communication: until the invention of the railways, water transport was invariably the easiest, cheapest, and—if the winds allowed—fastest means of travel.

Although the Byzantines, Muslims, and Mongols used systems of beacons or carrier pigeons for more rapid transmission of news, it is a truism that, until the invention of telegraphy in the nineteenth century, news in Europe could not travel over land faster than relays of horses. A late-twelfth-century example reveals both the possibilities and the limits of land communications. On 20 December 1192 Richard I 'the Lionheart', king of England, was taken prisoner near Vienna while returning from the Third Crusade. Word of his capture reached the Emperor Henry VI in central Germany by 28 December, and the king of France, Philip Augustus, in or near Paris, by c. 7 January 1193. This exceptionally weighty news had travelled about 630 miles as the crow flies within eighteen days, an average of 35 miles a day. That was an impressive rate of travel for an overland journey in the depths of winter, but it also shows that the peoples and rulers of medieval Christendom were too remote from one another to respond quickly to distant events.[3] In 1215, Pope Innocent III wished to support King John of England against English rebels, but in central Italy he was always hopelessly out of touch with events in England, and his ill-informed interventions helped to plunge that country into a bitter civil war.

The limited nature of medieval communications meant that, throughout this period, the local symbols of authority—the castle on the hill, the parish church, the town wall or bridge—remained the chief symbols of authority to most of the population. Local networks also retained an overriding significance, whether ties of kinship or arrangements for trading and bartering. Yet there were also huge advances in improving communications (see p. 78). On land, the burgeoning population and the concern of princes and towns for order and trade encouraged improvements to roads, causeways, bridges, and ports. At sea, the longship, seaworthy but small, and the galley, unsuited to Atlantic storms, gave way to the much larger cog, which allowed merchant fleets to make annual trips from Italy to Southampton. The magnetic compass, already known in Europe in the twelfth century, was being used for navigation before the end of the thirteenth. So, too, were charted maps. In the tenth and eleventh centuries maps of the world were primarily representations of religious thought. They were based upon Classical Roman maps that organized the world into a simple tripartite scheme of Asia, Africa, and Europe, to which medieval mapmakers added the main sites, peoples, and creatures of the Bible and Classical mythology. These so-called *mappae mundi* (literally 'cloths of the world') were not intended to be mathematically accurate charts, but they have often led modern observers to exaggerate medieval ignorance of science and geography. In fact, some of the finest *mappae mundi* were produced around 1300, by which date relatively accurate charts or 'portolans'* were being used in Mediterranean navigation, for they served very different purposes.

---

[3] L. Landon, *The Itinerary of Richard I* (London, 1935), 71–2; cf. 184–91, 203.

The faultlines of European culture

While the natural environment is an important consideration for understanding the course of central medieval history, so, too, were the continent's major cultural divisions. In the tenth century Europe was divided between four main religious blocs: Latin Christianity (Roman Catholicism), Eastern Orthodox Christianity, Islam, and paganism. In the West most of the population were 'Latin' Christians who recognized the religious authority of the pope, at least in name. Greek and other Eastern Orthodox inhabited the Balkans as well as some adjacent parts of the Near East, and from the late tenth century Rus´ (approximating to modern European Russia, Belarus, and Ukraine) was being converted to the Orthodox Church as well. The Latin and Greek Orthodox churches were not formally divided by a schism* until 1054, but, although there were few doctrinal differences between them, they had long since grown apart in matters of religious practice. Nevertheless, whereas 'Europe' was rarely anything more than a geographical expression, 'Christendom' represented a genuine community: the defence of eastern Christians inspired warriors from as far away as Denmark and Scotland to journey to Palestine during the crusades.

It is important to remember that Europe also had significant groups of non-Christians. In the north-east and far north of the continent the majority of the population in the tenth century were pagans of various sorts, and paganism persisted in some regions until the end of the Middle Ages, particularly in Lithuania, which covered a much larger area than the modern Baltic republic of that name. In 950 most of the Iberian peninsula and many of the Mediterranean islands had Islamic rulers, and the majority of the populations of these regions were Muslims. Although Islam had begun to retreat from the high-watermark of its expansion into south-west Europe in the seventh and eighth centuries, it was still prominent as far north as Provence, where a group of 'Saracens' terrorized the Alpine passes until local Christians expelled them in c.972. As Muslim power gave ground in western Europe over the next three centuries, new Christian kingdoms emerged in its wake. Nevertheless, there were several major revivals in Spain of Muslim power, which was still far from negligible in 1300; the lands conquered by Christians also usually retained Muslim inhabitants. Finally, across much of the continent were scattered Jewish communities, whose distribution and size would vary enormously in the course of the period (see Chapter 4).

The expansion of Latin Christendom, described by Nora Berend in Chapter 6, meant that Latin relations with the Eastern Orthodox, Muslim, and pagan powers worsened almost everywhere; by the early fourteenth century most of the northern pagan tribes had vanished from the map and the Jews were being expelled from much of western Europe. Latin Christians also developed a stronger sense of non-Christians as the 'Other' against which they identified themselves. In a cycle of Old French poems that relate the deeds of the semi-mythical hero William of Orange, his Muslim enemies are sometimes called 'Slavs'.[4] Perhaps these texts preserved a dim memory of the Slavonic slaves who had fought in early medieval Spanish Muslim armies; it is equally possible, however, that they were fusing the non-Christians of the Mediterranean (the Muslims) and those of north-central Europe (pagan Slavs), for were they not all the enemies of Christ? In the twelfth century Latin Christian armies in the Baltic regions justified their aggression against pagans in terms derived from the crusades to Jerusalem (see pp. 193, 205–6).

Another of the great cultural demarcators was language. Europe has several main linguistic groups; then as now the Romance, Germanic, and Slavonic languages, which all belong to the Indo-European 'family', were predominant. Romance, derived primarily from Latin, included not only the precursors of modern French, Spanish, Catalan, Portuguese, Italian, and Romanian, but also Occitan (less accurately called Provençal), the chief language of southern France that in the twelfth century served the flourishing 'troubadour'* culture. Germanic languages extended from Old (later Middle) English in the British Isles to Middle High German in southern Germany and Austria; they also included the Scandinavian languages, which at the height of Viking power were spoken from Greenland to Kiev, although they retreated thereafter. German spread through migration into east-central Europe, while French warriors

---

[4] *Guillaume d'Orange: Four Twelfth-Century Epics*, trans. J. M. Ferrante (New York, 1974), e.g. 205 (l. 850), 208 (l. 1199), 212 (l. 1647).

exported Old French to the British Isles, Sicily, Greece, and Palestine. Slavonic languages retreated from eastern Germany, but otherwise their range remained remarkably static: linguists customarily divide them into western Slavonic (nowadays including Polish, Czech, and Slovak), southern (the languages of Bulgaria and Former Yugoslavia), and eastern (which now includes Russian and Ukrainian). In addition, the Celtic tongues in the British Isles and Brittany, Basque in northern Spain and south-west France, and the Baltic languages represented by modern Latvian and Lithuanian were all more widespread than today. Magyar or Hungarian formed (and forms) a 'Finno-Ugric' island in an ocean of Indo-European languages, with which it has no affinities. Further south, medieval Greek was one of the main languages of southern Italy, Turkey, and Syria.

In most modern European nations, language is the single most important determinant of identity. In the Middle Ages, in contrast, bilingualism was part and parcel of ordinary life for many of Europe's inhabitants, and the political repercussions of language were often far from straightforward. In 1295 King Edward I of England accused the French (in a letter written in Latin) of wishing to destroy the 'English language', meaning the English people; but the Anglo-Norman dialect of French was then the dominant language of the English court.[5] At the thirteenth-century Bohemian court, Czech, German, and Latin literature all flourished. The most significant linguistic divide was between the vernacular of ordinary people and Latin, the chief language of learning and of power. Knowledge of Latin in western Christendom was never confined to clerks, and it is now recognized that early medieval lay elites made much use of Latin; nevertheless, one of the main developments of the central Middle Ages was the growth of the educated laity who knew and used this far from dead language in everyday affairs. Moreover, outside the British Isles vernacular tongues had hitherto been primarily oral across Latin Europe, but from the twelfth century onwards writing in the vernacular became ever more possible and popular (see Chapter 5).

Modern science has discredited the notion of 'race', but medieval writers usually worked on the assumption that the peoples of Europe were distinct, and to each one they attributed a distinguished ancestor

[5] *Select Charters and Other Illustrations of English Constitutional History*, ed. W. Stubbs, rev. H. W. C. Davis (9th edn., Oxford, 1913), 480.

in antiquity. The myths and legends that developed may seem laughable to a modern audience: by 1200 the French, Danes, and Welsh amongst others were all claiming Trojan ancestry, while the Scots began to allege that they were descended from a daughter of Pharaoh called Scota. What these stories attested was not the inherent gullibility of medieval authors—plenty of writers treated the more outlandish origin myths with scepticism or disdain—but a desire to prove the antiquity of one's 'people' (*natio* or *gens*) and use this 'history' to foster political unity. When the diverse origins of a *gens* could not be ignored, it could still be turned to advantage: in the 1050s a monastic historian at the abbey of Saint-Wandrille near Rouen commented that Rollo, the Viking whom tradition regarded as having founded the duchy of Normandy in 911, 'united in a short time men of all origins and different occupations . . . and from the different races he made one people'. This statement was evidently meant to allay anxieties amongst the Normans about their mixed Scandinavian and Frankish origins.[6]

Such tales of national origins were not intended only for drinking halls or monastic scriptoria*. In 1301 a letter of Edward I to the pope justified his claim to lordship over Scotland by describing the exploits of Trojan refugees who had divided Britain between them, the most senior receiving England with royal authority over the whole island.[7] Did Edward know, and did it matter, that most of this account had been invented in the twelfth century by the author Geoffrey of Monmouth? The famous Scottish rebuttal of English claims to overlordship, the Declaration of Arbroath (1320), stated that the ancient Scots had 'journeyed from Greater Scythia [modern Ukraine] by way of the Tyrrhenian Sea [in the western Mediterranean] and the Pillars of Hercules [Straits of Gibraltar], and dwelt for a long course of time in Spain among the most savage tribes'. Scottish unity in the face of external threat is instructive because the Scots were a particularly heterogeneous people, formed from the fusion of Gaelic, Pictish, Norse, Anglo-Saxon, British (Welsh), French, and Flemish elements. Origin myths were no less powerful in the opening years of the fourteenth century than in the tenth; if anything, the spread of learning and literacy encouraged their elaboration.

---

[6] C. Potts, '*Atque unum ex diversis gentibus populum effecit*: Historical Tradition and the Norman Identity', *Anglo-Norman Studies*, 18 (1996), 139–52.
[7] *Anglo-Scottish Relations: Some Selected Documents*, ed. and trans. E. L. G. Jones (London, 1965), no. 30.

For the sake of convenience historians may refer to 'French', 'German', 'Italian', or 'Spanish' and talk of kingdoms as political entities, but, as Björn Weiler notes in Chapter 3, the nature of communications and political organization meant that regional and local identities often counted for far more than allegiance to a distant monarch or abstract concepts of regnal solidarity. Bishop Liudprand of Cremona, on an embassy from the western Emperor Otto I to the Byzantine emperor in 968, described Otto's subjects as 'we Lombards, Saxons, Franks, Lotharingians, Bavarians, Swabians and Burgundians'.[8] Deep-seated regional sentiment would remain an abiding theme in the history of the western Empire, where it was both a force for local cohesion and an obstacle to many emperors' designs. The peoples of the kingdom of France might all acknowledge the authority of the Capetian kings by 1300, but preferred to define themselves as Poitevins, Angevins, Normans, and so on: 'French' usually denoted only the inhabitants of the region around Paris. Perhaps most striking of all was the fierce loyalty that developed amongst Italians towards their minuscule city states. 'Among all the regions of the earth, universal fame extols, distinguishes and places first Lombardy [the North Italian plain],' wrote Bonvesin de la Riva, an inhabitant of Milan, in 1288, 'and among the cities of Lombardy, it distinguishes Milan as the rose or lily among flowers . . . the lion among quadrupeds and the eagle amongst birds'.[9]

The political divisions of Europe

If the world known to tenth-century Europeans was divided into four main religious zones, it was far more fragmented in political terms. No regime then inspired greater awe in Christendom than the Byzantine Empire. As the heirs of the eastern half of the great Roman Empire of antiquity, the Byzantines usually thought of themselves as Romans, although their empire was far more Greek than Latin in character. Under Justinian I (527–65), whose legal codes later formed

[8] Liudprand of Cremona, *The Embassy to Constantinople and Other Writings*, trans. F. A. Wright, ed. J. J. Norwich (London, 1993), 183.

[9] Bonvesin de la Riva, in *The Towns of Italy in the Later Middle Ages*, trans. T. Dean (Manchester, 2000), 11.

the basis of 'Roman' law in the West, the empire had extended from southern Spain to Mesopotamia, but vicious maulings by the Lombards, Persians, Arabs, and Bulgars had greatly reduced it in size and power. In the mid-tenth century Byzantine and Arab power rubbed shoulders in an uneasy equilibrium along the eastern fringes of Anatolia (modern Asiatic Turkey), as they had done for over two centuries.

The central Middle Ages would be an era of repeated catastrophe for the Byzantine Empire, but its opening decades actually witnessed significant Byzantine expansion in the Balkans, Armenia, and in the Mediterranean from southern Italy to Syria. In the mid-eleventh and the late twelfth centuries, however, it underwent two periods of sustained internal rupture, marked by provincial revolts and recurrent usurpations of the imperial throne. In the 1070s and 1080s the Seljuk Turks overran most of Anatolia, hitherto the heart of the empire. Meanwhile, 'Franks' from western Europe repeatedly troubled the Byzantines, expelling them from Italy and attempting to conquer parts of the Balkans and Greece. In 1204, a Frankish crusading army captured Constantinople itself, and its leaders parcelled out the empire amongst themselves: for two generations a 'Latin' emperor sat on the imperial throne. Although the Greeks of Nicaea eventually expelled the Latins in 1261, irreparable damage had been done to this ancient and venerable state.

To the Byzantines the territorial extent of their empire mattered less than their view of themselves. This is how the Byzantine princess Anna Comnena, writing in the 1140s, envisaged her 'Roman' world: 'There was a time when the frontiers of Roman power were the two pillars at the limits of east and west—the so-called Pillars of Hercules in the west and those of Dionysos not far from the Indian border in the east. As far as its extent was concerned, it is impossible to say how great was the power of Rome.'[10] Anna's description conveys the Byzantines' consciously unchanging view of themselves as the true heirs of ancient Rome. For the same reason, she frequently referred to the Franks, as the inhabitants of western Europe, as 'Celts'. Two generations later, the Byzantine official Niketas Choniates dismissed the crusaders whom he witnessed sacking Constantinople in 1204 as

[10] *The Alexiad of Anna Comnena*, trans. E. R. A. Sewter (Harmondsworth, 1969), 205–6.

'beef-eating Latins'.[11] Such defiant self-confidence helps to explain the respect that the 'Celts' still paid to the Empire in the twelfth century. One of those same 'beef-eating' conquerors of Constantinople marvelled at the city's wealth shortly before its capture: 'Many of our men, I may say, went to visit Constantinople, to gaze at its many splendid palaces and tall churches, and view all the marvellous wealth of a city richer than any other since the beginning of Time. As for the relics, these were beyond all description; for there were at that time as many in Constantinople as in all the rest of the world.'[12]

The Byzantine Empire was not the only power that claimed to be the heir of ancient Rome. In 800 the pope had awarded the imperial title to Charles the Great (Charlemagne), king of the Franks and Lombards, the most powerful man in the West. This event was the culmination of over 400 years of integration of the Germanic and Roman heritage of western Europe. This Carolingian Empire included modern France, the Low Countries, western Germany, Switzerland, Austria, most of Italy, and north-east Spain. By 888 Charlemagne's warring descendants had irrevocably shattered the unity of his empire, but the imperial ideal lived on, as Otto I's coronation as emperor demonstrates. Smaller in extent but equal in pretension to its Carolingian predecessor (see Map 3), Otto's empire was destined to last in one form or another until 1806; historians usually refer to it as the Holy Roman Empire from the twelfth or thirteenth century.

Although the Empire comprised only the kingdoms of Germany, Italy, and (from 1032) Burgundy, to the biographer of Frederick I Barbarossa (1152–90) the imperial crown conferred 'sole rule over the world and the City [of Rome]' (*orbis et urbis*), and far away in Normandy a monk referred around 1200 to Otto IV's throne as 'empire of the whole world'.[13] It was believed that an emperor would play a role in the apocalyptic events at the end of Time: since the Prophet Daniel had foretold that there would be four empires in human history, and scholars had calculated that Rome must be the

[11] *O City of Byzantium: Annals of Niketas Choniatēs*, trans. H. J. Magoulias (Detroit, 1984), 326.

[12] Geoffrey de Villehardouin, 'The Conquest of Constantinople', *Joinville and Villehardouin: Chronicles of the Crusades*, trans. M. R. B. Shaw (Harmondsworth, 1963), 76.

[13] Otto of Freising, *The Deeds of Frederick Barbarossa*, trans. C. C. Mierow (New York, 1953), 135; *Les Annales de l'Abbaye Saint-Pierre de Jumièges*, ed. J. Laporte (Rouen, 1954), 77.

fourth and last, did not Scripture (reinforced by late Classical and early medieval prophetic texts) ordain that the Roman emperor would be the final ruler on earth? Yet even the strongest emperors could appear weak in much of the Empire. In 1155, when Frederick Barbarossa went to Italy, an integral part of his empire, he had to fight his way down to Rome, was crowned emperor by the pope in the teeth of the citizens' armed opposition, then beat a hasty retreat northwards. Frederick's subsequent attempts to control Italy met with greater success, but he was defeated by a league of Italian cities in 1176, and few other emperors matched his power. The Empire comprised a patchwork of duchies, counties, lordships (both lay and ecclesiastical), and fiercely autonomous cities; even as the emperors pursued their goals of universal rule, the princes were consolidating their rule over their territories within the Empire. Imperial power and authority likewise tended to be at their strongest in the regions of the emperors' hereditary domains: for the Ottonian dynasty (962–1002), this meant in Saxony in northern Germany; for the Salians (1024–1125), the middle Rhineland around Worms and Speyer, while Frederick Barbarossa's Hohenstaufen dynasty (1138–1254) had its greatest concentration of estates in Swabia in south-west Germany and in Alsace (now in eastern France).

The other main successor to the Carolingian Empire was the kingdom of the West Franks, which evolved into the kingdom of France. At the outset of our period, it notionally included most of the modern French Republic apart from the regions east of the Rivers Rhône, Saône, and Meuse. In reality, its kings exerted less influence in much of the kingdom than magnates or local lords. One of the most significant developments of the period was the growth of French monarchical power, aided by the misfortunes or folly of many of these great subjects, by quite remarkable dynastic community, and by the growing prosperity of its main powerbase, the Paris Basin. In addition the intellectual currents of the period heightened respect for kingship, as scholastic theories of the organization of society emphasized the place of the monarch at its head, and the revival of Roman Law popularized the maxim that the ruler's will had the force of law. The chief obstacle to the monarchy's rise was the power of the territorial princes, notably the kings of England, who became dukes of Normandy and Aquitaine and counts of Anjou (see below, pp. 19–20). By 1214, however, the Capetian kings had established their hegemony within northern and central France. Throughout the period the kings of France also periodically attempted to make their presence felt in the vast Occitan-speaking southern regions of their kingdom, and when the so-called Albigensian Crusade (1209–29) against the Cathar heretics shattered local power structures, the Capetian kings intruded themselves into the vacuum.

Given their competing claims to be the heirs of the immortalized figure of Charlemagne, the kings of France and the Emperors might be expected to have been in constant rivalry. In fact, the reverse was true, precisely because neither monarchy wielded a great deal of influence along their common borders, where a vast buffer zone dominated by dukes, marquises, and counts extended from the Netherlands to Provence. Indeed, across the whole of Latin Christendom, the power of the nobility was vast and, as Martin Aurell shows below (pp. 37–40), it developed and refined a distinctive ethos during the twelfth and thirteenth centuries. The contrast between monarch and nobles should not be drawn too sharply. They shared a similar desire to promote their dynasties; royal and noble families constantly intermarried, and the great noble families regularly supplied monarchs when royal lines failed. Conversely, many of the great noble families were descended from junior branches of royal houses.

The kingdom of England was a novel creation in the mid-tenth century, emerging from the kingdom of Wessex (south-west England). In 950 the British Isles were largely subsumed into the North Sea world of the Northmen or Vikings from Scandinavia. Until 954 there was a Viking king at York; in 1014, King Swein of the Danes conquered the whole of England, and his son Cnut III the Great (1016–35) ruled over an empire that included Denmark, England, and Norway. Yet, despite this Scandinavian influence, for most of the central Middle Ages England was dominated by French, not Danish culture. In 1066 the duke of Normandy, William the Conqueror, famously conquered England and had himself crowned king. Over the next 150 years nobles, knights, merchants, and clerics exported northern French culture across the Channel, while the kings of England tried to balance their monarchical duties in England with princely aspirations in France (although they never aimed for the French crown itself). From 1154 to 1204 the 'Angevin'* or 'Plantagenet' kings of England ruled a motley collection of provinces known to historians as the 'Angevin Empire'. Its rulers struggled to make their authority respected in much of this territory, particularly south of the River Loire; eventually, internal dissensions enabled Philip Augustus of France to add Anjou, Maine, Normandy, and much of Poitou to his domain between 1202 and 1204. Successive kings of France worked hard to erode the surviving Angevin possessions in Aquitaine; by 1328 these comprised little more than a small coastal strip in Gascony.

Other parts of the British Isles felt the consequences of the Norman Conquest of England. Neither Wales nor Ireland had previously achieved political unity, although rulers such as Brian Bóruma (or Boru, d. 1014) in Ireland and Gruffydd ap Llywelyn (d. 1063) in Wales had achieved temporary hegemony. Soon after 1066 the Norman invaders of England began making inroads into Wales, although some Welsh princes successfully resisted Anglo-Norman power until the 1280s. In 1169 Anglo-Norman adventurers entered Ireland, initially as mercenaries but soon as conquerors, and the king of England soon followed. After a high point in the mid-thirteenth century, English fortunes in Ireland began to decline in the face of resurgent Gaelic power. The Scots, meanwhile, quickly established peaceable relations with the Normans of England, many of whom migrated to Scotland at the behest of its kings.

The other Latin Christian kingdoms outside the former Carolingian lands are discussed in Chapter 6. They include the Scandinavian kingdoms of Denmark, Norway, and Sweden; in east-central Europe, the realms of Poland, Hungary, and Bohemia; and, in the Mediterranean, numerous new polities formed at the expense of the Muslims and Byzantines. The Iberian peninsula underwent the greatest political transformation of any region in Europe. In the tenth century it mostly lay under the rule of the Muslim Umayyad Caliphate based at Córdoba, the most sophisticated and cosmopolitan culture in western Europe. Although there were many Christians under Muslim rule, known as 'Mozarabs' (literally the 'Arabized'), independent Christian powers were confined to the northern fringes of the peninsula. After the disintegration of the Caliphate in 1031, al-Andalus (Muslim Iberia) contracted in the face of Christian advances. Further east, the Muslim retreat also enabled the establishment of the kingdom of Sicily in 1130, which survived in some form until the unification of Italy in 1860. Placed at the nodal point of Mediterranean communications, it became the hub of a series of dynastic rivalries that drew in the Holy Roman Emperors, the kings of France and Aragon and the papacy. More transient were the new kingdoms and principalities in the eastern Mediterranean founded in the wake of the Crusades; only the island states such as the kingdom of Cyprus (founded 1191–2) and the Venetian and Genoese acquisitions such as Crete proved longlasting.

The borders of kingdoms mattered, but we should not assume that they were sovereign in any modern sense of the term. Kings of one kingdom might be active in another on account of their dynastic lands: at various times the kings of England, Aragon, Navarre, and Castile all had lands and rights in France, for instance. In any case, monarchy was far from the only form of political organization: city communes, principalities, ecclesiastical lordships, and semi-independent castellanies all had a crucial role to play. The central Middle Ages were not a period of monarchy so much as an age in which monarchy began to prevail over these other polities (except in the Holy Roman Empire). Even so, with no standing army or police except bands of household knights, most rulers remained reliant upon the aristocracy for military support—the alternative of mercenaries, paid for through taxation, had a high financial and political cost—and so noble power remained deeply entrenched in 1320 as in 950. This reliance meant that the norm for royal–noble relations was not conflict but cooperation, which was reinforced through political rituals that are vividly characterized by Björn Weiler in Chapter 3.

In addition to the continent's temporal rulers, the Church was of immeasurable significance to European society throughout the central Middle Ages, when its power and authority were transformed out of all recognition. The tenth century was possibly the nadir of the papacy's fortunes; like most bishoprics of the time, it was controlled by local nobles, notably the Roman senatrix Marozia and her family, and several popes were even deposed and murdered. Between the 1040s and the mid-thirteenth century, however, the papacy rose from relative feebleness to the moral leadership of Christendom, with ambitions even to depose emperors and with influence over the daily lives of all Catholics. Yet the transformation of the Church reached far beyond the papacy; as Julia Barrow shows in Chapter 4, it mobilized the whole populace. The parish system was already developing long before 950, but only in the central Middle Ages did it become comprehensive. The physical fabric of the institutional

Church, its cathedrals and parish churches, was established across most of Europe in the eleventh and twelfth centuries.

It would be a mistake to assume that the Church was a monolithic institution: so vast and diverse an organization was bound to be brimming with competing interests and rivalries. The archdeacon Walter Map, who frequented the late-twelfth-century English court, had caustic words for religious orders, observing that 'Monks recognize their prey as the hawk spies the frightened lark'.[14] Conversely, the numerous conflicts between individual European rulers and the papacy or local prelates should not mask the fact that rulers normally cooperated closely with their bishops and clergy. Although the hierarchy professed to speak on behalf of everyone, all Christians were 'sons of the Holy Mother Church'. To be outside this community, as heretics and excommunicates, Muslims, Jews, and pagans were, was increasingly to be an outcast who might be tolerated but was rarely trusted. By tightening its definitions of orthodox belief and creating a system of ecclesiastical courts and canon law, the Church made exclusion of dissenters both more likely and more terrible, although temporal rulers jealously guarded their monopoly of the death penalty in heresy trials.

Europe around the year 1000: a continent transformed?

> A thousand years after the Lord was born on earth of a Virgin
> Men are become prey to the gravest errors . . .
> Fraud, theft and all infamy reign supreme in the world,
> Saints are not honoured nor the sacred worshipped.[15]

With these words Rodulf Glaber, writing in the late 1030s, bemoaned the state of the kingdom of France around the year 1000. Although this monk's complaints related to very specific conditions at the French king's court, his opinions have exerted a deep influence over historical writing, for he wrote with a pervasive sense that the coming

---

[14] Walter Map, *De nugis curialium: Courtiers' Trifles*, ed. and trans. M. R. James, rev. C. N. L. Brooke and R. A. B. Mynors (Oxford, 1983), 85.
[15] Rodulfus Glaber, *Opera*, ed. and trans. J. France (Oxford, 1989), 166, 168.

of the second millennium signalled an unparalleled crisis of authority. Historical scholarship, particularly in France, has tended to agree with him that the late tenth and early eleventh centuries witnessed great social crisis, sometimes called the 'transformation of the year 1000' (*mutation de l'an mil*).

It was not the year itself that mattered very much. Although some people regarded the date 1000 as ominous, for most Christians who knew the Bible and its conventional interpretations the year 1033 was far more likely than 1000 to herald the end of the world, for, according to accepted calculations, it marked the thousandth anniversary of Jesus' crucifixion, resurrection, and ascension into heaven. Rodulf Glaber wrote expressly to interpret the history of the 'Roman world' (by which he meant the former Carolingian lands) in the context of these two millennial dates; for instance, he linked 1033 with the councils known to historians as the Peace of God (see Chapter 4), during which 'bishops, abbots and other devout men' sought to restrain the violence of the warrior class. Yet the calendar-based anxieties of one Burgundian monk do not prove that there was a crisis of authority across Europe. Historians now recognize, for instance, that the Peace 'movements' were far from coherent and responded to local issues. Yet other factors have convinced many historians that the opening decades of the eleventh century saw radical social change. Monastic writers had long bewailed the violence of warrior-landowners, but across much of western Europe their complaints seem to increase dramatically after 1000. Around the same time, heresy became an issue of great concern and provoked a forceful response from the Church authorities. Did millennial anxieties, aristocratic violence, and rising religious dissent together constitute a grave social crisis?

A particularly influential interpretation was Georges Duby's study (1953) of the county of Mâcon, an area located, like Glaber's monasteries, in Burgundy. Duby concluded that, although the Carolingian Empire had been divided in the ninth century, the public order that it had established persisted until around 1000. Only then, he maintained, did the emerging castellans overturn the old Carolingian order: these castle-lords forced all the local freemen to acknowledge their authority by surrendering their allods* and receiving them back conditionally from the lord as fiefs*. The castellans exerted their oppression through the recruitment of bands of warriors from whom the knights emerged. Duby's theories were carried much further by

Guy Bois in 1989: examining a single village in the same region, he concluded that the ancient socio-economic system of slavery had persisted until the rise of the castellans rudely overturned it at the turn of the millennium.

Since 1990 there has been an extensive reaction against these 'mutationist' theories. Greater sensitivity towards the sources has suggested that the 'transformation of the year 1000' was essentially a *mutation documentaire*: a change in the way that documents were produced. After 1000 the style of producing charters in the former Carolingian lands became more informal, allowing monastic scribes greater freedom to narrate how nobles atoned for their 'violence' by piously endowing the scribes' monasteries. Many denunciations of aristocratic violence may therefore be largely rhetorical. The leading exponent of this interpretation, Dominique Barthélemy, has argued that the new types of charter unmasked social changes that had already taken place a century or more earlier: there was no social 'revolution' around 1000, merely a 'revelation' of slower, long-term trends. Barthélemy also argues that there is little evidence of a free peasant class before 1000 and that knights were not a new phenomenon: no one doubts that early medieval magnates had also surrounded themselves with retinues of ambitious warriors. It has also become clear that models of abrupt social change based upon regional studies cannot be applied to the whole of Europe, or even all of France. The 'transformation' model requires the collapse of princely rule and 'public' order; yet in England this happened only temporarily during dynastic strife (for example, 1138–53), while in Germany royal power was undermined not by deep-seated structural changes but by a series of civil wars from the 1070s onwards—in other words, what could be called 'high' politics.

And yet, if the sources are really so subjective, it is equally difficult to argue that they prove social continuity. Even in England, recent comparative work suggests that the continuing strength of the monarchy masked massive aristocratic violence and profound religious anxieties. There can be no doubt that there were far more castles in Europe in 1150 than in 1000, and that individual aristocratic families, organized into lineages (see pp. 48–54), regarded these as the cornerstones of their inheritance; in most regions, they also asserted 'bannal'* authority over the neighbourhood, in a more concerted and coherent manner than 200 years earlier. If some regions clearly do not fit the Duby model, it does not mean that all Europe avoided social upheaval, nor that these changes did not sometimes seem bewildering and frightening to contemporaries, especially if they accompanied disorder or dissent. Martin Aurell argues below (pp. 41–2) that free peasants with the right to bear weapons were abundant in the Mediterranean regions around 1000: their numbers were destined to fall precipitously over the course of the next 200 years. The vast increase in both the number and the type of written sources produced during this period may testify to social, economic, political, and religious revolution. All in all, the debates surrounding the 'transformation of the year 1000' remain controversial, but their importance should not be underestimated, for they concern one of the key problems for the historian of central medieval society: how it differed from early medieval structures, and why.

An age of expansion

For the period as a whole, a rather different set of interpretations has come to the fore in recent years. As long ago as 1958, Archibald R. Lewis described the slowing-down of Latin expansion between 1250 and 1350 as the 'closing of the medieval frontier'. With the historical parallel of the American West in mind, he asserted that 'Few periods can be better understood in the light of a frontier concept than western Europe between 800 and 1500 AD . . . From the eleventh to the mid-thirteenth century Western Europe followed an almost classical frontier development,' adding: 'The [most] important frontier was an internal one of forest, swamp, marsh, moor and fen.'[16] More recently, Robert Bartlett has identified the territorial expansion of Latin Christian society as the defining characteristic of the central Middle Ages. He partly attributes this process to three technological advantages enjoyed by the 'Franks' of western Europe: castles, archery (especially crossbowmen), and heavy cavalry. The physical expansion of the frontiers of Latin society were accompanied by great cultural change, as the aristocracy of north-west Europe in particular

[16] A. R. Lewis, 'The Closing of the Mediaeval Frontier, 1250–1350', *Speculum*, 33 (1958), 475–83, at 475, 476.

exported its ethos in almost all directions, and combined this with a strong religious ideology. These warriors also found justifications to treat some avowedly Catholic regions at the peripheries of Latin Christendom, such as Ireland, as ripe for settlement and conquest, while elsewhere, such as in Scotland, Bohemia, and Byzantium, native rulers eagerly sought the services of warriors from western Europe. There could be a direct connection between the 'transformation of the year 1000' and the ensuing expansion of Latin Christendom, a hypothesis that Bartlett cautiously proposes: if the aristocracy was now monopolizing both military and economic resources as never before, and the concentration of its resources in castles was excluding the younger sons of the nobility (see pp. 48–50), it might explain the aggressiveness, cupidity, and rootlessness of the 'Frankish' warriors who migrated to the frontiers of Christendom.[17]

Bartlett's thesis has not received universal acceptance. It risks blurring the differences between very different types of expansion: crusades to the Holy Land, for instance, occurred in a highly specific ideological context and brought financial ruin, not prosperity, to most participants. Many of the identifiable crusaders were rich heads of families, not impoverished 'cadets'. It is also true that demographic growth had begun long before 950; that the Christian cause had often been invoked to justify territorial expansion (for instance, by Charlemagne against the Saxons in the late eighth century); and that the enlargement of Christendom through missionary activity had long been assisted by the attractiveness of Christian cultural concomitants to pagan rulers. Nor did Latin Christian expansion wholly cease around 1300 (see p. 210). Nevertheless, there can be no doubt that a peculiar combination of military superiority and religious enthusiasm dominated the fortunes of Latin Christendom in the central Middle Ages. In Chapter 6 Nora Berend discusses the conversion and integration of east-central and northern Europe into Latin Christendom, as well as the forceful expansion of Christians in the Mediterranean at the expense of Byzantium and Islam; she also considers these regions on their own terms, for many of these 'new' polities were also quite capable of aggressive expansion, and, as she shows, their experiences were very diverse.

[17] R. Bartlett, *The Making of Europe: Conquest, Colonization and Cultural Change 950–1350* (London, 1993), especially 24–51.

Latin society did not expand at its geographical fringes alone. In Germany, there were about 200 towns in 1200; by 1350 there were about 2,000.[18] Seigneurial enterprise often fostered rapid development: the eleven-fold increase in the population of Stratford-upon-Avon between 1086 and 1252 was largely due to the foundation of a new town there by the bishop of Worcester in the 1190s.[19] The reclamation of uncultivated land constituted a different sort of 'frontier': William TeBrake has used this term for the Rhine delta in Holland in this period, for, although it lay in the geographical heart of Latin Christendom, the draining of the wilderness of peat bogs and polders had a dynamic effect upon Dutch society, much as many historians have argued that the great American wilderness influenced the formation of American society.[20] While such an interpretation is as controversial for medieval Europe as it is for the nineteenth-century United States, there can be no doubt that vast tracts of the continent were brought into permanent cultivation.

These economic and demographic changes have led R. I. Moore to describe the more urbanized societies of north-west Europe in the eleventh and twelfth centuries as a genuinely new civilization, radically different from its early medieval predecessors in structure, economy, and belief.[21] The following six chapters seek to characterize the Europe that evolved between c.950 and c.1320, and the Conclusion will consider the end of this period.

[18] J. Gillingham, 'Elective Kingship and the Unity of Medieval Germany', *German History*, 8 (1991), 124–35, at 127.
[19] E. M. Carus-Wilson, 'The First Half-Century of the Borough of Stratford-upon-Avon', *Economic History Review*, 2nd series, 18 (1965), 46–63.
[20] W. H. TeBrake, *Medieval Frontier* (College Station, TX, 1985).
[21] Moore, *First European Revolution, passim.*

Society

Martin Aurell

Around the year 1000, European society underwent a number of major changes. Chris Wickham's chapter in the early medieval volume of the *Short Oxford History* identifies several of them:[1] the aristocracy came to monopolize all military activity, from which the peasantry was henceforth excluded; in judicial matters seigneurial courts replaced village assemblies; the nobles no longer sought the protection of kings, dukes, or counts, and began to profit more from new types of seigneurial exaction; and the theory of the 'three orders' reached ideological maturity. Taken together, these were far-reaching changes. On the Continent, it marked the end of the administrative and cultural structures of the Carolingian world, the heir of the classical Roman Empire. Instead, social relations would henceforth be organized around fiefs, lordship, or lineage.

This interpretative framework developed from the 1950s onwards, particularly following the works of Georges Duby, but it no longer commands universal acceptance amongst medievalists.[2] Since 1990 the debate concerning the 'Transformation (or "Mutation") of the Year 1000' (see Introduction) has highlighted the flaws in the *mutationniste* model and introduced important qualifications. Those who deny that there was radical social change have argued instead that dramatic changes to the documentary evidence (dubbed by French historians a *révélation documentaire*) have misled us into believing that there was a 'feudal revolution' that, they claim, never really happened.

Translated by Daniel Power.
[1] C. Wickham, 'Society', in R. McKitterick (ed.), *The Early Middle Ages: Europe 400–1000* (Oxford, 2001), 90–4.
[2] G. Duby, *La Société aux XIe et XIIe siècles dans la région mâconnaise* (Paris, 1953).

In their eyes, the *mutationniste* historians have failed to recognize the implications of the new ways of producing charters that the Gregorian reform movement (see Chapter 4) propagated in monastic scriptoria*. For in the eleventh century scribes began to write long 'notices', phrased in the past tense and listing a plethora of details about aristocratic oppression, rather than more traditional acts that had been couched in the present tense and that had had little to say about military affairs; this new genre of document allowed them to condemn violence far more than before and to exaggerate the social disorder that had in fact been rocking west European society for decades.[3] Accordingly, there must have been social continuity, not transformation. The anti-mutationist school argues that the old Carolingian nobility could never have bolstered its power with knights drawn from the allod-holders, who had full property rights over their lands; nor could the peasants have been enserfed at this point, since they were already subject to a form of servitude before the year 1000. As for the theory of the 'three orders', this had already been clearly formulated by the ninth century.

This historical debate has certainly not yet been resolved. Two lessons can be drawn from it, however. First, we see the realities of medieval society through the distorting prism of the discourses of contemporary authors; and, secondly, these transformations were characterized by great regional diversity, varying from principality to principality and extending from the late ninth century to *c.*1170.

Scholarly discourses versus social realities

Between the ninth and eleventh centuries, clerks described society in terms of the ancient Indo-European model, which since the earliest historical times had classified people according to the tripartite religious myth of war, priesthood, and fertility. This scheme divided people into three social groups: 'those who fight' (*bellatores*), 'those who pray' (*oratores*), and 'those who toil' (*laboratores*). This tripartite model was extremely widespread, being found, for instance, in the

[3] D. Barthélemy, *La Société dans le comté de Vendôme de l'an mil au XIVe siècle* (Paris, 1993), 19–83.

work of Alfred the Great (849/71–99), king of Wessex; Remigius of Auxerre (*c.*841–*c.*908); Aelfric (d. 1020), abbot of Eynsham, and around 1025–30 in the writing of Adalbero, bishop of Laon (977–1030), and Gerard, bishop of Cambrai (1013–51). According to these authors, warriors, clerks, and peasants had complementary functions. Hence it was natural that the warriors whose blood was shed on the battlefield should be fed by the peasants whose sweat was spilled in the fields. The reciprocal nature of their roles was indispensable to the smooth functioning of society.[4] From the twelfth century onwards, however, scholars increasingly regarded the notion of three orders as an inadequate way of describing their world. The Parisian master Peter the Chanter (d. 1197) still used it, but subdivided the *laboratores* into 'peasants', 'the poor', and 'artisans'. By then scholars recognized that the tripartite model no longer served as a means of analysing a society that had become far more complex because of increasing urbanization and demographic and economic growth. Nevertheless, the model was not abandoned completely: an illuminated miniature in a manuscript of the mid-thirteenth-century, *L'Ymage dou Monde* of Gautier de Metz, employs this archaic motif (see front cover).

Once the 'trifunctionalist' model had become obsolete, writers preferred to compile long lists that confused social ranks, professions, legal status or functions, and even ages. In northern Italy, a relatively urbanized, mercantile land, as early as the tenth century we find Ratherius (*c.*890–974), bishop of Verona, cataloguing some nineteen different groups: civilians, warriors, artisans, physicians, merchants, lawyers, judges, witnesses, 'procurators', employers, mercenaries, counsellors, lords, serfs, (school)masters, pupils, the rich, those of modest status, and beggars.[5] Similar classification is found later in the *Elucidarium* of Honorius *Augustodunensis* (*c.*1080–*c.*1157): clerks, knights, merchants, artisans, minstrels, penitents, the 'poor in spirit', labourers, children, pilgrims, judges, executioners, and the victims of torture. Such categorization became ever more refined: the *Libre de contemplació* (1270) of the Catalan author Ramón Lull adds doctors, sailors, painters, and manual workers. It was generally found in moral

---

[4] G. Duby, *The Three Orders: Feudal Society Imagined*, trans. A. Goldhammer (Chicago, 1980).

[5] J. Le Goff, *Medieval Civilisation*, trans. J. Barrow (Oxford, 1988), 257.

treatises, preachers' manuals, or confessional works, in which priests carefully adapted their advice to suit the different social 'estates' (*status*). From John of Salisbury's *Policraticus* (1159) onwards, works written with a more overtly political purpose used the metaphor of the different parts of the body to assign a specific social place and function to each estate; their unity around the ruler, who represented the head, became a necessary condition for the survival of the body politic.

Although described by the clerks of the period primarily for pastoral reasons, these social divisions also developed their own codes and symbols, which everyone could easily recognize. In a society in which reality and appearance were easily confused, clothes neatly embodied social difference. This can be seen in the contemptuous reproach that Jean de Joinville (1225–1317), the biographer of (Saint) Louis IX of France (1226–70), once delivered to the king's chaplain Robert de Sorbon:

Master Robert, I am, if you will allow me to say so, doing nothing worthy of blame in wearing green cloth and squirrel fur, for I inherited the right to such clothing from my father and mother. But you, on the other hand, are much to blame, for though both your parents were villeins, you have abandoned their style of dress, and are now wearing finer woollen cloth than the king himself.[6]

At that time nobles wore tunics and capes, long, full robes that eventually, in the fourteenth century, were superseded by more closely fitting garments: furs and fine-quality cloth in resplendent colours set them apart from ordinary people.[7] Other external signs symbolized aristocratic rank, such as riding an expensive horse, sporting a falcon on one's wrist, or displaying one's coat of arms. Manners conferred further subtle distinctions, since they were a code by which the elites distinguished themselves from the rabble. The hero of Gottfried von Strassburg's *Tristan* (1200–30) reveals the antiquity of his lineage merely through the dexterous way in which he carves meat in the presence of strangers. Extravagant feasts and liberal largesse also characterized the aristocracy, whose rites of

---

[6] Adapted from Jean de Joinville, 'The Life of Saint Louis', *Chronicles of the Crusades*, trans. M. R. B. Shaw (London, 1963), 164–353, at 171.

[7] E. Jane Burns, *Courtly Love Undressed: Reading through Clothes in Medieval French Culture* (Philadelphia, 2002).

passage (baptism, knighting, marriage, and funerals) were crucial occasions for noble sociability and ostentatious display.

Those who belonged to the less affluent sections of society were marked out quite differently. Peasants wore short, worn-out, and ill-fitting garments; courtly romances, which aimed to flatter the nobility, depicted them as hideous in appearance: weather-beaten, filthy, and stooped. Those excluded from mainstream society were also distinguished by external symbols, such as the badge stitched on the clothes of Jews or the uncovered, unkempt hair of prostitutes. In short, someone's place in society could be known at a glance. In towns the identity of each social category was regularly displayed through grand processions: each group would parade in the appropriate attire with its distinctive insignia, in an order of precedence that reflected its place in the social hierarchy.

The castellan aristocracy in the eleventh and twelfth centuries

There can be no doubt that, as in previous centuries, the nobility clung on to its dominant position at the top of the pyramid of power. The disintegration of the Carolingian Empire even served to reinforce noble power: in the Western Empire and Capetian France, the established aristocracy progressively shook off the authority of the emperor or king, whose court they no longer attended and whose orders they rarely obeyed (see Chapter 3). Moreover, they also acquired vast 'private' domains from the imperial lands that had once been 'public'. In the midst of these virtually independent lordships they constructed castles, which had a great many functions—as permanent residences, as symbols of the exercise of regalian powers, as centres for levying seigneurial dues, and, of course, also as military strongholds.

From around 1000 onwards, Latin charters contain far more references to these fortifications: the texts abound with terms—often newly coined—such as *dungio* ('donjon'), derived from *dominus* ('seigneur'), *munitio* ('fortification'), *firmitas* ('firmness', hence 'strongpoint'), *turris* ('tower'), *forcia* ('force', hence 'fortress'), and *castellum* ('castle'). Historians have deduced from these texts that a dense network of castles was rapidly coming to embrace much of Europe. Their view has been confirmed by archaeologists, who have taken advantage of advances in the study of ceramics to date excavated sites precisely. Some examples witness to the explosive character of the spread of castles. In Provence, which lay in the kingdom of Burgundy until the absorption of the kingdom into the Empire in 1032, a mere twelve castles are attested around 950, but there were thirty by 1000 and over 100 by *c*.1030. In the kingdom of France, there were no more than three castles in Poitou before the Viking invasions, but thirty-nine in the eleventh century; in Auvergne there were eight fortresses in 1000 and between twenty-one and thirty-four by 1050. The density of this network may be seen in Catalonia, where some 800 fortresses existed by *c*.1050—an average of one per 45 square kilometres (17 square miles). In the region of Lazio in central Italy, we find a similar development, but it occurred somewhat earlier, beginning in the 950s. From the beginning of the eleventh century the number of castles per county tripled, and sometimes quintupled, every fifty years.[8]

These constructions varied in design from region to region and also altered over time. At the beginning of the eleventh century the motte was the most widespread form of castle in northern Europe (except the British Isles and Scandinavia). It usually consisted of a round wooden tower surrounded by a palisade and built on an artificial mound with a ditch dug around it; sometimes it also had an 'outer bailey', an extensive area enclosed by a protective line of stakes. The motte continued to be one of the principal means of control in England and Wales after the Norman Conquest of 1066 and in Ireland after the English invasions which began in 1169, but on the Continent simple donjons were developing into more complex fortifications from the mid-eleventh century onwards. During the twelfth century castle architecture continued to reach new levels of sophistication. The number of towers increased; square towers began to be built again, often with walls 3–4 metres thick. Larger, cut stones were used, in imitation of Romanesque churches; on some donjons fine double windows, similar to those on bell towers, were added. In general the

---

[8] P. Toubert, *Les Structures du Latium médiéval: Le Latium méridional et la Sabine du IXe siècle à la fin du XIIe siècle* (Rome and Paris, 1973).

buildings for the lord and his family became more spacious and luxurious. All in all, castles benefited from the period's flourishing architecture, improved living standards, and artistic and cultural progress. Their imposing character also underlined their symbolic importance, which may even have outweighed their military functions: dominating the village and surrounding countryside, these superb fortresses dramatically demonstrated the power of their masters to everyone who saw them.

During the eleventh and twelfth centuries, the heightened part played by castles across the European landscape testified to the ubiquity of warfare, which all too often was waged at a local level, between neighbouring nobles. Here, too, the Anglo-Norman realm appears exceptional, together with some other kingdoms where strong monarchical power maintained the peace such as Castile or some parts of Scandinavia; nonetheless, in times of crisis, such as the wars of succession in Normandy (1087–1106) between the sons of William the Conqueror or the civil war in England in the reign of King Stephen (1135–54), the aristocracy resorted as elsewhere to the untrammelled construction of what chroniclers called 'adulterine' castles. In their struggles the *nobiles*, most of whom hailed from families of great antiquity, swelled the ranks of their forces with other warriors whom the charters call *miles** (pl. *milites*, a generic term for a warrior that increasingly came to mean 'knight'), *caballarius* ('mounted warrior') or *castellanus* ('defender of a castle'). These men were often of much humbler origin. The historian William of Poitiers (d. *c.*1101), archdeacon of Lisieux, happily referred to *milites gregarii*, meaning 'common soldiers' or 'knights of the common herd'; Orderic Vitalis (1075–1142), an Anglo-Norman monk writing in the Norman abbey of Saint-Évroult, talks of 'mounted peasants' (*pagenses equites*).[9] Such evidence emphasizes the renewal of the ranks of the nobility, which in practice was always ready to welcome people of inferior origin into its ranks. These sources are nonetheless compatible with the nobles' fascination with the ideology and practice of knighthood, which would push them eventually to adopt the epithet of *miles*, since it laid emphasis upon their military function.

---

[9] *Ecclesiastical History of Orderic Vitalis*, ed. and trans. M. Chibnall (6 vols, Oxford, 1968–80), e.g. iii., 334; iv., 104.

There were, of course, geographical variations in the 'rise' of the knights, such as in England after 1066, where Anglo-Saxon 'thegns' mingled with *milites* from France.

The ceremonies of fealty and homage made the knights dependants of a *nobilis*, whose vassals they became, and who rewarded their military service by investing them with a fief*. However, this was an honourable act of submission that even increased the knights' prestige, for it was restricted to mounted warriors and never involved ordinary peasants. The shared sense of belonging to a single warrior elite explains why in the course of time knightly families came to merge with the old nobility. Combined with the demographic growth of older families, the social ascent of the knights meant that the nobility of western Europe increased almost ten times in size between 1000 and 1300.

In the German Empire, these mounted retinues were called *ministeriales* or *Dienstleuten*, terms that literally mean 'servants'. In the tenth and early eleventh centuries, most of them were constrained by the obligations of servitude: they were bound to their lord's lands and were required to marry there, they could not buy or sell lands outside the lordship, and they did homage to their lord on terms comparable to those of serfs. From the 1050s onwards, however, their condition improved. Private wars and the imperial–papal conflicts of the 'Investiture Contest' brought these experienced warriors to the fore. Whether fighting for the emperor or for ecclesiastical lords, the most fortunate or shrewd *ministeriales* might amass considerable fortunes: Werner von Bolanden, a *ministerialis* of Emperor Frederick Barbarossa (1152–90), obtained lands from forty-six different lords! The acquisition of a *freies Eigen**, or a 'free' fief, made them much the same as the aristocrats: their new liberty was manifested in the assemblies that they held from 1140 onwards without the express permission of their lords, and in 1159 the *ministeriales* of Utrecht even formed a league to preserve their privileges. Thereafter they were generally deemed to belong to the lesser nobility. Hence in 1160 the abbot of Ebersheimmunster alleged that, after Julius Caesar had conquered the Germans, he had converted their princes into senators and their *ministeriales* into Roman citizens, also ordering the former to employ the latter in high office and to protect them and grant them fiefs. In thirteenth-century Germany those who were noble by descent, the *Freigeboren* ('free-born'), coexisted with those who had become noble through service, the *Dienstherren* ('service-lords') and *Ritter* (knights).[10]

The dramatic rise of such knights of peasant origin was made possible by a radical technical change. In most of the former Carolingian territories, military activities were henceforth to be the preserve of the warrior elite, and general summons of all freemen were abandoned (although the latter persisted where strong state structures survived, such as in England and Normandy, demonstrated in Henry II's 'Assize of Arms' of 1181). Saddles and stirrups, which had become widespread in the West since the mid-ninth century, increased the military capacity of horsemen and from then on they often had a decisive effect in battle. They allowed warriors to wield their swords and spears more forcefully on horseback. Spears were still used as a thrusting weapon overarm or thrown like a javelin, however, and the true technological revolution came later with the couched lance. It first appears in the Bayeux Tapestry, embroidered around 1080, which depicts some of William the Conqueror's horsemen using their spears as lances, couched under their armpits; they are galloping straight at their enemies with the aim of unhorsing them with the sheer shock of the impact. This charge at full speed would be carried out in *conrois*, compact groups comprising twenty or so warriors who would break through the fray of battle together. No foot soldier could resist them; popular levies of infantry tended to disappear from the battlefield as a result (even though trained men-at-arms or dismounted knights could still repulse horsemen, as happened at Bourgthéroulde in 1124 and Gisors in 1188). As a result the cost of warhorses rose substantially. It has been calculated that a late-twelfth-century French warhorse cost as much as seven ordinary horses, whereas in the eighth century it had been worth only four. Swords, helmets, hauberks*, and shields were equally expensive. Henceforth only the members of a wealthy aristocracy or their household knights, whom they had equipped at their own cost, could afford to fight on horseback.

So during the eleventh and twelfth centuries the aristocracy underwent profound changes. Its appropriation of the public 'ban'*—the power to command, punish, and commit violence— made it a warrior aristocracy before all else, as if the profession of

---

[10] B. Arnold, *German Knighthood 1050–1300* (Oxford, 1985).

arms was henceforth the chief characteristic defining nobility. In many Mediterranean principalities, the emergence of independent lordships increased the numbers of nobles, whose ranks were swelled with new members, often drawn from the humbler ranks of allod-holders. Elsewhere, especially in the kingdoms of England, Castile, and León, no such transformation took place, since the king prevented the creation of autonomous castellanies beyond his effect-ive control. Yet, even where central power remained strong, the aristo-cracy continued to be a social group with fluid legal boundaries, continually modified as some rose in society and others lost their noble status. The evolution of this group was accompanied by the 'christianization' of its warrior ideals, which became less aggressive and paid more respect to the rights of those who did not bear arms. The heightened role of the clergy in the ceremony of dubbing attests to this evolution of the warriors' ideology into the codes known as 'chivalry'.

A 'nobility of privileges' in the thirteenth century

A still more important transformation took place in the thirteenth century, when social hierarchies became more organized and insti-tutionalized. In France, the revival of royal power and the birth of the 'State' served to structure society (see Chapter 3). These factors locked each individual into a personal legal status, which was endorsed by institutions and laws that the higher legal authorities applied with rigour. In short, the 'State' consolidated the 'estates', and a hierarchical social stratification emerged that was more rigid than previously. Each social group acquired a collective consciousness and became, in effect, an order. The nobles were most affected by this new legal demarcation, since it accorded them the highest of the new ranks. The aristocracy therefore became more defined by its claims to nobility, even if significant social differences persisted within its ranks.

Article 10 of the *Usatges de Barcelona*, an important legal text com-piled around 1150 in Catalonia, describes a noble as someone who 'eats wheaten bread daily and rides a horse'.[11] For the author of the *Usatges*, lifestyle and the profession of arms determined who belonged to the aristocracy. A century later, in contrast, the *Coutumes de Beauvaisis* of Philippe de Beaumanoir (1252–96) emphasized birth: 'We call gentlemen those who come from a free lineage, such as kings or dukes or counts or knights.'[12] In the space of a few decades, heredity in the strictest biological meaning of the term had become the chief distinguishing mark of nobility.

Being born into a noble lineage brought 'privileges', a concept that needs to be understood in its literal meaning of a 'private law' restricted to a particular order within society. At a time when monarchies and the increasingly powerful urban communities were taxing their subjects heavily, the most desirable privileges to have were fiscal exemptions. From the twelfth century onwards, the kings of Castile exempted from direct taxation any armed knights who were ready to fight the Muslims, as the franchises for the towns of Cuenca (1180–94) and Soria (1195–6) make clear. In effect, taxation was seen as a commutation of military service: the dues that the noble warriors paid in blood were worth as much as the dues that commoners paid in cash. Everywhere else, noble status entailed other legal privileges: a noble should be judged only by his peers; he could not be tortured or hanged; he could avoid imprisonment by giving sureties; his residence was an inviolable refuge and neither his horse nor his arms could be confiscated; his possessions, even if mortgaged, were protected by royal respites and so could not be used to pay debts. Gentlemen also enjoyed special privileges in the laws of inheritance and for dower and dowry.

From then on the nobles enjoyed legal, fiscal, and social privileges by virtue of royal or princely confirmation. The same administrative machinery that created more efficient law courts and bodies for raising revenue also helped rulers to gain tighter control of the aristocracy. The king now oversaw personal status; as the supreme member of the nobility, he decided who else should belong to this group and should thereby enjoy tax exemptions and the right to be judged separately from the common herd. He reserved the right to ennoble a

---

[11] *The Usatges of Barcelona*, trans. D. J. Kagay (Philadelphia, 1994), 67.
[12] *The* Coutumes de Beauvaisis *of Philippe de Beaumanoir*, trans. F. R. P. Akehurst (Philadelphia, 1992), 518 (§1451).

commoner and dub him a knight, and prevented other nobles, however important they might be, from doing the same: 'No one, however gentle [i.e. noble] he is through his mother, can be a knight if he is not gentle through his father, unless the king grants him special permission,' asserted Beaumanoir in his customarily laconic way.[13] In France, one of the earliest examples of such an ennoblement concerned a burgess of Tours whom the *bailli* of Saint Louis knighted in 1239, and from 1285 onwards letters of ennoblement issued by the king himself conferred this privilege. Philip IV (1285–1314) handed them out liberally in return for much-needed cash to refill his treasury, in the wake of the defeat of the French nobility by Flemish urban militias at Courtrai (1302).

Owning a noble or 'free' fief could entitle the fiefholder to do homage directly to the king. The ceremony was no longer regarded as humiliating: at his coronation the prince received the allegiance of the heads of the aristocratic families who had gathered in his palace in celebration, and lists of the nobility of his realm would be compiled during the ceremony. This custom is first attested in May 1199, when the newly crowned King John of England received the homage of his barons and the fealty of the English bishops.[14] Those who held a fief in the king's name were also periodically required to render him military service. In addition, feudal law, first drafted by Italian lawyers in the twelfth century, associated fiefs with the exercise of judicial power within the lordship.[15] As associates of princes, as knights in the royal army, and as judges of their own peasants, fiefholders were implicitly noble.

Even after it had coalesced into a single order, the nobility remained very hierarchical. Ancient and new dynasties continued to remain largely distinct; so did well-endowed families and impoverished landlords. In the thirteenth century the noble hierarchy became fixed through the adoption of titles. German legal texts such as Eike von Repgow's *Sachsenspiegel* and the *Schwabenspiegel* compared these gradations to the seven ages of the world: kings; ecclesiastical princes; lay princes; counts and lords without any title (*Edelfreien*, literally the

---

[13] Ibid. 518 (§1451).
[14] H. G. Richardson and G. O. Sayles, *The Governance of Mediaeval England from the Conquest to Magna Carta* (Edinburgh, 1963), 147.
[15] S. Reynolds, *Fiefs and Vassals: The Medieval Evidence Reinterpreted* (Oxford, 1994).

'noble free'); vassals of counts, lords, and aldermen (*Schöffenbare*); vassals of vassals and *ministeriales*; and finally *Semperfreie*, the lowest rank of knights. These titles recalled the ancient offices of the Roman and Carolingian empires but had almost nothing except honorific value.

In practice the chief demarcation almost everywhere still lay between the great and lesser nobility. The differences between them were manifested in political assemblies, where they sat separately, and in public ceremonies through orders of precedence and contrasting insignia. In England from 1295 onwards the greater aristocracy or 'peerage' sat with the bishops in the upper chamber (the House of Lords), separated from the lower chamber, the House of Commons, which comprised the lesser aristocracy or gentry and representatives of the urban oligarchies. Sumptuary laws* forbade the lower ranks to dress in the same style as the upper ranks; the Peace and Truce of God* assemblies held in Catalonia in 1235 forbade the lesser nobles to wear red hose, which were the privilege of the barons alone. In the Namurois (in modern Belgium), only the nobles were permitted to seal their charters with equestrian seals (that is, one that depicted the issuer as a mounted warrior), excluding knights from using them as they did elsewhere in Europe. The dichotomy between the greater and lesser aristocracy prolonged the ancient division between *nobiles* and *milites*: we find Lords and gentry in England, *ricos hombres* and *hidalgos* or *infanzones* in Castile, and *barones* or *magnates* as against *milites*, *popolares*, and *cavalerotti* in Italy.

The peasantry: servitude and freedom

The overwhelming majority of the European population—about 90 per cent—were peasants. Even if the urban revival encouraged many of them to migrate to the towns, especially in the Mediterranean regions, it remains true that most people lived on and worked the land. Their laborious daily tasks in the fields had barely altered in thousands of years, although iron tools and mills that aided their work were becoming more widespread. Between 950 and 1320 favourable climatic conditions increased agricultural production and improved the peasants' quality of life, so that they became better fed, housed, and clothed than ever before (see Chapter 2).

This general growth in prosperity had varying consequences for the rural population. At the top of the village hierarchy were those peasants who owned their own plough and enough animals to draw it, which means at least eight oxen or four horses. Village upstarts of this sort might lend money to other peasants and even to impoverished petty landowners, from whom they might one day be able to buy 'free' fiefs, or with whom they might form marriage alliances, thereby breaking into the ranks of the nobility. The second and probably the largest category of peasants comprised those who barely possessed enough to support their family or pay their dues to their lord: perhaps a house with a vegetable patch, a field, and some livestock grazing on the common fields. Finally, at the bottom of the social scale were the labourers, farmhands, and shepherds who had no land at all, but relied upon daily wages and resorted to seasonal migration to sell their labour. From the thirteenth century onwards abundant English manorial records reveal that this underclass represented up to half the peasant population.

Craftwork played an important part in villages (see Chapter 2), involving at least a fifth of the peasantry. Althought there was certainly an elite of full-time artisans with their own workshops, such as blacksmiths and glassmakers, most craftwork was done by peasants who supplemented their income from farming with small-scale work such as pottery or tile making. They might employ some labourers to help them with the hardest tasks such as extracting clay, chopping firewood, or making charcoal. These wage-labourers dwelt at the fringes of society, frequenting the forest, which consequently became the focus of repeated friction and conflict, for it provided the peasants with lands to clear, grazing, and an indispensable source of energy for artisans' ovens. Like some agricultural produce, artisans' wares were sold in town markets: such commercialization furnished the more affluent peasants with extra income, serving to increase the social differences within village communities.

In the West the legal status of peasants was still more problematic because of significant regional differences. Around the year 1000 the class of allod-holders, who had freedom of movement and controlled their own lands, paying no taxes except to 'public' authorities, was in steep decline. The members of this upper level of the peasantry, which was particularly abundant in the Mediterranean regions, were numerous enough for some of them to become mounted warriors and to force their way into the nobility; the less fortunate amongst them succumbed to seigneurial domination.

At the other extreme, servitude underwent a major transformation in the thirteenth century, becoming institutionalized. Like nobility, which became an 'estate' or 'order' with specific privileges, serfdom was influenced by the revival of Roman Law in the universities, which affected legal thought and legislation. Jurists compared the status of serfs to that of the ancient Roman *coloni*, while charters referred to them with terms such as *colonus*, *servus*, or *adscripticius*. Just as nobility was largely defined by the fief, servitude became increasingly bound up with the plot of land to which a particular peasant was attached, and which he could not leave without his master's express grant of manumission*. Lords exercised tight legal controls over both the person and the possessions of serfs. Various humiliating taxes denoted this dependence: a poll tax or *chevage*, paid in a ceremony of submission; *formariage*, which demonstrated that a serf's offspring were also dependants of his master; and *mainmorte*, which reflected the serf's inability to pass on his inheritance. Nevertheless, it is important not to confuse legal status with landed income: in return for being dependent on their lord, some serfs enjoyed a level of agricultural success that many freeborn labourers would have envied.[16]

Like the German *ministeriales*, serfs could even rise spectacularly up the social scale. Hugh of Fleury (d. 1122) tells the improbable but suggestive story of Stabilis ('Steadfast'), a serf of the abbey of Saint-Benoît-sur-Loire, who fled his village out of poverty: he sought his fortune in a remote village of the county of Troyes (in Champagne) called Auxon, where he toiled until he grew rich; he then devoted himself to the profession of arms, learning to ride, hawk, and hunt, employing pages, and eventually marrying an aristocratic lady; when the monks of Saint-Benoît demanded the customary rent that was the badge of his servile status in the court of the count of Troyes, the nobles of Champagne pleaded his cause. Stabilis was a truly self-made man, largely thanks to his military skills. In *The Murder of Charles the Good* (*c*.1128), Galbert, a notary of Bruges, related a similar story concerning Bertulf, a man of very

---

[16] A. Raftis, *The Estates of Ramsey Abbey: A Study in Economic Growth and Organization* (Toronto, 1957).

obscure origin who became the chancellor of the count of Flanders and provost of the collegiate church of Saint-Donatien de Bruges: he propelled his relatives into the highest positions in the count's court, entrusting them with castles, granting them prebends at Saint-Donatien, and marrying his nieces to nobles. The members of his Erembald clan began to bear the title of *nobilis* but still bore the stigma of servitude: it was in order to prevent a court case that would prove its servile ancestry that the family assassinated the count in 1127.[17] The condition of the peasantry was still far from fixed and could be evaded, as numerous examples show. This is true both for individuals and for groups: from the 1250s onwards there are numerous continental examples of whole communities of serfs purchasing their freedom.

Proud to be merchants

Merchants may have been excluded from the concept of the three orders, but they were certainly not excluded from society. Medievalists no longer accept the traditional view that the Church or even the whole of society rejected merchants.[18] Usury* and loans to strangers had certainly aroused much mistrust in the past, as had the sworn associations and guilds that were sometimes treated as conspiracies to overthrow the social order. By the end of the twelfth century, however, a quite different situation prevailed: Omobono, a draper of Cremona in northern Italy, was one of the first saints to be canonized by the papacy (rather than by popular veneration). Bernard of Clairvaux (d. 1153), despite his reputation for religious rigour, incited people to join the Second Crusade (1147–9) with these words: 'To those of you who are merchants, men quick to seek a bargain, let me point out the advantages of this great opportunity. Do not miss

---

[17] Galbert of Bruges, *The Murder of Charles the Good*, trans. J. B. Ross (2nd edn., New York, 1967), 96–119.

[18] J. Baldwin, *Masters, Princes and Merchants: The Social Views of Peter the Chanter and his Circle* (Princeton, 1970). For the thirteenth century, see R. De Roover, *San Bernardino de Siena and Sant'Antonino of Florence, the Two Great Economic Thinkers of the Middle Ages* (Cambridge, MA, 1967).

them!'[19] So Western thought was disposed to recognize the existence of a category of people whose fortune and prestige were due to their mercantile activities alone. In the thirteenth century the mendicant orders or friars (see Chapter 4), even though at the outset they represented a rejection of such values, appreciated the new economic realities in the towns, and so they helped to promote this new way of thinking. From then on capitalism could develop.

From the end of the eleventh century a genuine merchant class established itself in the great maritime cities of northern Italy: Venice, Genoa, and Pisa. The ports of Provence, Languedoc, and Catalonia followed them, as did those of England and Flanders (see Chapter 2). A merchant was rarely the marginal, rootless figure, half pedlar, half brigand, to whom nineteenth-century historiography paid so much attention.[20] In the Mediterranean, they sometimes belonged to the old nobility, which controlled the forests providing the wood and iron that were indispensable for constructing boats; their military training did not deter them from the gambles of long-distance trade. They were undoubtedly attracted to business at first by the taste for adventure, the acceptance of risk, and the ability to adapt to hostile or foreign environments. More often, merchants came from the urban patriciate, which had its own rudimentary legal, literary, and mathematical culture, which made mercantile activity possible. Often the necessary capital first came from land, and it was in land that merchants invested their profits from commerce since it could guarantee the security, leisure, and social recognition that they desired.

In the thirteenth century merchants tended to abandon a travelling lifestyle in favour of a sedentary one, directing the family company from the offices of mercantile palaces. At a technical level this development was made possible by new types of contracts (see Chapter 2), but the successes of the merchant class also had great political consequences: in many Mediterranean cities, they not only formed an urban oligarchy that controlled the municipal council but also extended the city's *contado** far and wide, forcing the rural nobility to do homage to the city commune, and waging war against rival cities in the neighbourhood. Even in Paris the upper bourgeoisie, which

---

[19] *The Letters of St Bernard of Clairvaux*, trans. B. S. James (2nd edn., London, 1998), no. 391.

[20] H. Pirenne, *Les Villes du Moyen Age* (2nd edn., Paris, 1971).

supplied luxury commodities to, and maintained cordial relations with, the king and princes, disdained ennoblement because it would deprive it of its municipal power, since no noble could sit on the city council. Merchants devoted much of their fortune to making their towns grander. They desired little more than the prestige and renown that money brought them.

The poor and marginalized

Material deprivation was the usual fate of most members of medieval society. It was certainly a structural problem and affected whole sections of the population who could never escape it. But the welfare of peasants and labourers could change overnight into outright destitution: sickness, infirmity, old age, being widowed or orphaned could make them 'poor', a term that had a vast array of meanings. References to 'poverty' certainly implied a precarious existence that bred hunger and destitution, but they could also describe the oppression of the poor by the powerful. Before 1200 this poverty was primarily a rural phenomenon, where it was widespread. Poverty was not yet synonymous with social exclusion, however, since destitute peasants could always benefit from the support of relatives, neighbours, or other members of the village community. In the thirteenth century, in contrast, it seems to have become a primarily urban phenomenon. Many of the rural poor abandoned the little they had in the country in order to take advantage of the emerging welfare institutions in the towns, while urban artisans and workers were vulnerable to economic crises and rapidly ended up unemployed. There were also many who outwardly attempted to disguise their decline into poverty but who were still willing to profit from their neighbours' charity.

In the face of poverty, the Church, municipal authorities, and private benefactors responded by founding almshouses, which distributed food amongst the needy; hospitals, which welcomed the destitute, sick and dying, and pilgrims; and lazarhouses*, where lepers were locked up in isolation, even though, as the poorest of the poor, they merited the special respect that Saint Francis of Assisi, Saint Louis, and others accorded them. In the twelfth and thirteenth centuries, evangelization and voluntary poverty became very popular, heightening townspeople's awareness of the poor and needy. The 'poor' should not therefore be confused with those marginal figures whose degrading professions (*mercimonia inhonesta*, literally 'dishonest trades') invariably led to them being excluded from society. Butchers, slaughtermen, and executioners typically dwelt on the outside of the town walls and could not engage in normal social relations with their fellow citizens, owing to their contact with blood; the same was true to a lesser extent for all those who did dirty work—for example, dyers of cloth. Usurers and prostitutes faced still greater condemnation.

Minstrels and performers are a special case. They were certainly the object of ecclesiastical censure and much deplored for their unstable, itinerant lifestyle and lewd performances: 'What hope is there for minstrels? None, for in the depths of their soul they are the servants of Satan. It is said that they have never known God and that God will spurn them: he shall laugh at those who now laugh,' wrote Honorius *Augustodunensis* in the twelfth century.[21] Some decades later, however, minstrels began to be rehabilitated, not least thanks to the mendicant orders (see Chapter 4), whose way of life and preaching to audiences had parallels with those of performers. Even Saint Francis of Assisi sang in public like a troubadour* and pretended to imitate a hurdy-gurdy player. When Thomas Aquinas (1224/5–74) sought to establish whether a minstrel's life was moral, he reached a nuanced conclusion. It was a legitimate profession, he concluded, because its specific function was to enhance rest, when all those who worked could recuperate; it deserved to be reimbursed adequately; but it needed to be practised with moderation so that it did not excite unwholesome pleasures. This discourse was a world away from the doctrinaire condemnations of earlier ages that depicted minstrels as the devil's henchmen. The reflections of Franciscan and Dominican theologians prepared the way for more general social acceptance of professional performers, who began to form confraternities, religious associations for mutual support, and guilds. Henceforth a place was reserved for them in the hierarchy of estates and the orders of Christian society. They even acquired their own training schools: one of the first to be attested was held by a certain Simon at the fairground of Ypres in Flanders in 1313.

---

[21] E. Faral, *Les Jongleurs en France au Moyen Age* (3rd edn., New York, 1970), 277.

The family

Amongst the peasants the nuclear family reigned supreme. The average household has been calculated as containing between three and seven people. Arranged marriages and endogamy* were far less common amongst peasants than nobles; the age for marriage was typically about 16 years old for girls and 27 for boys. Children tended to be weaned late, around eighteen months, and since peasants could ill afford to use wet-nurses, this ensured a greater interval between births. After a period of playing without cares, a child would be put to work at 12, chiefly to watch over the flocks; at this point his father would take over his upbringing.

Apart from preparing children for society, the family, as the basic economic unit, supplied the material needs of its members, beginning with food. With a small herd and a vegetable patch, a household might well achieve autarky* by practising mixed farming and avoiding undue expenses, but payments to the lord were likely to prevent it saving any money. Married couples shared out their tasks neatly between them: since a wife came from another family, she had difficulty making her presence felt in a predominantly patriarchal environment. Mothers took charge of the upbringing of young children and household tasks such as keeping the fire going, cooking, grinding, fetching water, washing clothes in the river, and spinning with a spindle or, in later centuries, with a spinning wheel. Many of these tasks were carried out as a group, encouraging female sociability. Peasant women also took part in many rural pursuits such as haymaking, milking, shearing sheep, and grape picking. Their husbands were more likely to dig the vegetable patch, work in the fields, or sow and harvest the crops.

From the twelfth century onwards peasant homes were more and more frequently built in stone, but people and animals were not separated, since the latter were a valuable source of heat. Hearths and chimneys also became more common, fostering the family's social interaction as they spent evenings together, and so preserving the oral culture of folklore. Furniture was still rudimentary, consisting of a larder in which to store food, a trunk that doubled up as chair and represented a certain level of material comfort, and a single bed or straw mattress for the whole family.[22]

In contrast to those of the peasantry, the kinship structures of the aristocracy underwent a major transformation. Around the end of the tenth and the beginning of the eleventh century, a new system, the lineage, came to replace the clan (known in German historiography as the *Sippe*), as well as the equality of inheritance between brothers and the semi-nomadic lifestyle that had existed previously. In the former Carolingian lands, the fragmentation of regalian powers amongst a multitude of independent 'castelries' and the replacement of wars conducted under imperial leadership by private conflicts forced each noble family to reorganize itself in order to survive in this context of violence and insecurity. Elsewhere, the evolution of the family varied according to local political circumstances. In England, aristocratic family structures did not experience this transformation until the end of the eleventh century, under Norman influence. In Castile-León it happened even later, since the nobility, organized around the monarch to combat the Muslims, did not form into clearly defined lineages centred upon family castles, which were of recent construction, until the thirteenth century.[23] In central Europe and the 'Celtic' parts of the British Isles families continued to be organized into tribes, reminiscent of the Germanic *Sippe*, in which women retained a greater political role than elsewhere. In general, though, the lineage had triumphed by the 1050s. The solidarity of the aristocracy became stronger than ever, as members of families strengthened their ties with one another in order to fight rival dynasties.

In these war-torn conditions, the authority of the eldest son grew stronger: he was now the head of the family and leader of a miniature army composed of his close relatives and loyal warriors. He therefore came to enjoy the lion's share of the family inheritance. He enjoyed a special relationship with his father, as agnatism, which privileged male ancestry and descent, prevailed over cognatism, which took equal account of relationships through the female line. In this situation younger sons and women were the chief losers, although they were very numerous as the aristocracy enjoyed vigorous demographic

---

[22] R. Fossier, *Peasant life in the Medieval West*, trans. J. Vale (Oxford, 1988).
[23] S. Barton, *The Aristocracy in Twelfth-Century León and Castile* (Cambridge, 1997).

growth in this period. Noble children were better fed and better cared for, and so more likely than peasants to reach adulthood. Nevertheless, the era had now past in which they had equal prospects within their families to their elder brothers.[24]

All in all, younger brothers had less access to their families' wealth and power than in the past, and so they often had to leave their homes to try their luck elsewhere. They would form warrior bands that roamed on horseback in tireless quests for glory and riches, robbing merchants and peasants, hiring themselves out to castellans, or winning riches in tournaments. United from the outset by their unbridled pursuit of booty, they squandered or shared out their gains, for in their eyes generosity was the highest virtue. These wandering knights, unstable, violent, and predatory, were called *juvenes* ('youths'), a term that referred less to their age than to their inferior status as unmarried, landless warriors.

Their elder brothers sought to channel their violence into distant adventures. Orderic Vitalis relates how Tancred de Hauteville, whose two wives had together given him twelve sons as well as several daughters, granted his patrimony in the Cotentin (in western Normandy) to his eldest son Geoffrey, in the early eleventh century; he then 'advised the others to seek their living by their strength and their wits outside their native land'.[25] They therefore set off for southern Italy, where their descendants became rulers of Sicily and eventually even of Antioch in the Near East. For its part, the Church frequently excommunicated the 'youths' for their breaches of the Truce of God and obliged them to atone for their sins by fighting in holy wars or, from 1095 onwards, in crusades.

The principal aim of these migrant warriors was to gain a secure home, usually by marrying a rich heiress who would give them domains and children in order to establish their own lineage. They did not always succeed. The frustration of some eternal bachelors is apparent in the literature written for them, notably in the topos of the demeaning marriage. In the Occitan* romance *Flamenca* (*c.*1270–1300), Archambaut de Bourbon falls into bestiality and becomes a wild, unkempt greybeard on his wedding day; he is then

---

[24] M. Aurell, 'La Parenté en l'an mil', *Cahiers de Civilisation Médiévale*, 43 (2000), 125–142.

[25] *Ecclesiastical History of Orderic Vitalis*, ii. 98–100.

overcome with violent jealousy towards his wife, whom he shuts up in a tower until the hero, the young Guillaume de Nevers, arrives and seduces her. *Érec et Énide* (*c*.1170), the first known work of the author Chrétien de Troyes, is constructed around the *recreantise* or cowardice to which, it is rumoured, the hero has succumbed as a result of his marriage; Érec must become young again, and sets off in quest of adventures that will restore his valour. Ultimately, through denigrating married life in this way, the younger sons were expressing their desire for the lot of the elder son, who monopolized the inheritance. It has even been argued that *fin'amors** or 'courtly love' developed as an outlet for youthful frustrations of this sort, although many historians now believe that the coherence of this supposed code of honour has been exaggerated.

It was not only younger sons who lost out because of the growth of the eldest son's power within the lineage. It also undermined the privileges of women, who had previously enjoyed considerable freedom and inheritance in the *Sippe*: they controlled a sizeable dower or morning gift conferred upon them by their husbands. Women were also guardians of the family memory, which ensured their prestige. The hagiographers* of the Ottonian queens Matilda and Adelaide depicted them as pious widows who preserved the memory of their dead relatives and secured prayers for their souls from religious houses. With the emergence of the lineage, women's status declined to some extent: its chief effect was to diminish the importance of the dower, and the revival of Roman Law in the thirteenth century led to its complete replacement by the dowry, which the bride's father provided. Thereafter, the new legal culture tended to reduce women to the status of minors: a woman could not make contracts or plead in court without a male representative, usually her husband, who was effectively her guardian. Some courts even denied widows the wardship of their own children, granting it instead to a third party. This decline in female status did not take place until the thirteenth century, though.

Be that as it may, what we can say is that the power of aristocratic women progressively increased as they passed through the three stages of life: childhood, marriage, and widowhood. Unmarried girls were at the mercy of the head of the lineage, who could marry them off as his shifting political needs and family strategies dictated. They were usually educated at home amongst the women in the castle, often in a more learned environment than their brothers, who were absorbed in being trained to fight. The rich and diverse work of Hildegard of Bingen (1098–1179) is a fine example of the learning that some women could acquire in convents: many were educated there before leaving to be married. After marriage, a woman enjoyed much more power, but it is difficult to discern exactly how much, since it was largely domestic and informal: much depended upon her influence upon her husband, which has left few traces in the sources. In lands prone to war, women bore much responsibility for the administration of the family inheritance, for their husbands were often campaigning far away. Moreover, women had to organize the defence of the family castle in time of siege: several famous passages in Orderic Vitalis's *Ecclesiastical History* depict these fearsome *châtelaines* as far apart as the Anglo-Norman realm of Henry I (1100–35) and the frontiers with Islam in Spain (for instance, at Tarragona) and in the Holy Land.

It was as widows, however, that women asserted most power, especially if their children were minors. A widow could issue charters in her own name; she administered her husband's inheritance freely and controlled its revenues. She could also command the men of her lordship. The hagiographer of Bishop Arnulf of Soissons (d. 1087) lambasted Evegerdis, lady of the castle of Veurne (Furnes) in Flanders, who made war on an enemy lineage to avenge the slaying of her husband and son.[26] In this traditional society, a widow's authority was reinforced by her age—a strong contrast with the absolute dependence of a young marriageable woman upon her kin.

Apart from the *juvenes*, the nobles of the early eleventh century were more settled than their ancestors. The remorseless wandering of members of the kin group had ceased, for primogeniture prevented the dispersal and fragmentation of the inheritance across vast regions; the evolution of the lineage made a family more established in a particular locality but also caused its zone of influence to contract. The eldest became the master of a castle and the surrounding countryside. A castle had both military and symbolic functions and would be passed from father to son, as the rock on which the lineage's fortunes were founded. The lord of the castle and his kin would usually be buried in a nearby chapel or monastery, and this family mausoleum would preserve the memory of the lord's ancestors: the

[26] *Acta Sanctorum*, Aug. III, p. 249, paras. 88–9 (BHL 704).

prayers of the clerks or monks there would ensure the salvation of the deceased members of the lineage, and the same churchmen would often compile genealogies that traced the lord's descent from a mythical ancestor who had established both the lineage and the castle.

This sense of belonging to an ancient dynasty attached to a particular fortress also encouraged the adoption of surnames, a revolution in naming patterns that coincided with the emergence of the lineage. Early medieval naming systems, whereby people normally had a single name, gave way to the new practice of coupling a Christian name with a toponymic* surname, the latter preceded by 'of' (for instance, in Provence we find Uc des Baux, that is, 'Hugh of Les Baux') or by the possessive form of the name (for instance, Guillaume *Porcelleti*, that is, 'William [son or kinsman of] Porcelet'). Most surnames referred to the lineage's chief property: between 1080 and 1100, twenty-four of the thirty-one patronyms* used by the nobility of the Mâconnais, a region of southern Burgundy, were derived from the family lordship; only seven were nicknames.[27] Here, too, the spread of hereditary surnames demonstrated the extent to which lineages entrenched themselves around their castles. The practice of using two names rather than one served the practical purpose of connecting an individual to his lineage, but it also acquired strong cultural prestige: from the twelfth century onwards, it came to be imitated at all levels of society and in parts of Europe to which the dominant French culture spread. In England, Domesday Book refers to some Anglo-Saxon landholders in a similar fashion (for instance, Thorkell of Warwick); in early thirteenth-century Wales, descendants of the royal dynasty of Glamorgan abandoned Welsh naming traditions in favour of French practice by calling themselves Hywel and Morgan of Caerleon.

The emergence of the lineage also led dynasties to use a decreasing number of forenames as another way of emphasizing their distinctiveness. In the late tenth century the practice began of naming the eldest son after his father or paternal grandfather; the second son typically received another name from his father's side, whereas younger sons might be given names from their mother's side, another indication that they, like women, had been downgraded. The stock of male names contracted because of these new rules based upon

[27] G. Duby, *Hommes et structures du Moyen Age* (Paris and The Hague, 1973).

primogeniture: in the eleventh and twelfth centuries, by far the commonest names amongst French nobles were William, Robert, Hugh, Geoffrey, or (in the south) Raymond. New religious trends meant that a number of saints' names were added to the stock of baptismal names: the success of Peter and its feminine form, Petronilla, reflects the progress of the Gregorian reform and of the centralization of the Roman church (see Chapter 4). Epic poetry popularized Roland, Oliver, Aeneas, and Alexander. Despite such fashions, inheritance practices remained the chief determinant of aristocratic forenames.

Another consequence of the triumph of the lineage was the emergence of heraldry. In the early twelfth century nobles began to paint symbols with strong genealogical significance upon their shields, to aid recognition in the confusion of battle. Coats of arms invoked the name, history, or mythology of their owners' families. 'Canting' arms alluded directly to the lineage's surname, so that the shield of the Porcelet, lords of Arles in Provence, bore a pig (Fr. *porc*). Other arms drew upon more complex family traditions: the chains on the shields of some noble lineages in Navarre referred to their capture of the fortified camp of the Muslim emir of Córdoba at the battle of Las Navas de Tolosa (1212); the six-pointed star of the Les Baux family in Provence alluded to the Star of Bethlehem because Balthasar, one of the Three Wise Men, was a mythical founder of the dynasty. Like the new naming patterns, heraldry reflected a noble's dynastic consciousness, and his pride in belonging to an ancient, honourable, and renowned dynasty.

All in all, an eleventh-century lineage was markedly different from the kinship structures that had preceded it. It was founded upon patrilineality* and agnatism; it was dominated by an all-powerful eldest son; it demoted younger sons; it linked each noble family with a castle; it received spiritual expression in the form of a mausoleum; it developed a strong awareness of its ancestry; and it flaunted its superiority through its surname and coat of arms. This system of kinship was so effective in assuring the success of noble families that it was even adopted by kings, whose dynasties were strengthened by the primogeniture which regulated succession to the crown.[28] It is true that in some regions the system changed: in France, when the

---

[28] A. W. Lewis, *Royal Succession in Capetian France: Studies on Familial Order and the State* (Cambridge, MA, 1981).

revival of the monarchy in the late twelfth century curtailed private warfare, the reimposition of order tested the old familial solidarities to the limit, since they had been developed as a means of making war on rival kin groups. The return of more general peace encouraged lineages to splinter into several branches, as each younger son wished to found his own 'sub-lineage' and to build his own fortified house.[29] Nevertheless, the lineage's values were already so deep-rooted that they left a permanent impression upon the noble mindset.

The village and the lordship

The locations for castles were chosen for both strategic and economic reasons. Standing at the confluence of two rivers, on the slopes of a steep-sided valley, at the top of a mountain pass or on the edge of a forest that formed the frontier between two principalities, eleventh-century castles controlled the principal routes. Since these places were favourable from both a political and a military perspective, they had often been occupied for centuries: hence a castle frequently occupied the site of an Iron Age fort (*oppidum*), a Gallo-Roman *villa*, or a Carolingian palace (*palatium*). They were also invariably built in regions with fertile soil or near woods inviting clearance, except in Italy and the Iberian peninsula, where the populations had already made much progress in clearing forests by the ninth century.

With so many advantages, such sites inevitably attracted numerous peasants. In the Mediterranean lands, their dwellings began to cluster around an aristocratic fortress on a hilltop rather than being scattered across the adjacent plain. The word *castrum* came to signify both a castle and its fortified village, and indeed the future of noble residences became inextricably linked to the peasant dwellings grouped around them. Historians refer to this migration as *incastellamento** or *enchâtellement* (literally 'encastlement') or *encellulement** ('breaking up into cells'); some have even described these processes as the 'birth of the village'.[30]

---

[29] D. Barthélemy, *Les Deux Âges de la seigneurie banale: Coucy aux XIe–XIIIe siècles* (Paris, 1984).

[30] Toubert, *Structures du Latium médiéval*; M. Bourin-Derruau, *Villages médiévaux en Bas Languedoc (X–XIVe siècle)*, 2 vols. (Paris, 1987).

This transformation of the landscape depended to a large extent upon the initiative of lords who forced the peasants to congregate in villages so that they could control and tax them more easily. In charters, the territory that a lord dominated around his castle is called the *districtum* (from the Latin verb *distringere*, meaning 'to constrain' or 'to punish') or *potestas* (literally 'power'). This system of lordship was partly inherited from the great estates of the early Middle Ages: it required the peasants, particularly in England, to perform *corvées** (labour services) on the lord's domain and to pay him a proportion of their crops as well. Other exactions, such as tallages levied directly on each peasant household, had probably originated more recently, as the castellans appropriated public courts and brought villagers under their power and authority. Lordship over land therefore went hand in hand with control of justice and economic resources (termed 'bannal'* lordship by historians).

Nevertheless, the success of these communities was largely due to decisions made by peasants, not lords. Living in the village enabled peasants to cooperate in such activities as crop rotation, the use of common land, draining marshes, or irrigating gardens. This collective organization gave rise to village assemblies, held in the place most associated with their collective identity such as the churchyard or an elm in the centre of the village. It overlapped with forms of religious association such as the parish or confraternities*. These forms of fellowship aided the appearance of communes or sworn associations, thanks to which villagers could negotiate effectively with the castellans to have their exactions reduced. In the thirteenth century many charters of enfranchisement granted villages self-government or reduced taxes, or commuted labour services for cash. Most of the time these documents were secured peacefully from the lords.

There was some violent resistance to lordship, however, such as the great uprising of the *Stedinger*, who assaulted the castles of Lower Saxony and the North Sea coast of the Continent between 1207 and 1234. Similar revolts broke out in the great cloth towns of Flanders and northern Italy at the turn of the thirteenth and fourteenth centuries. They were the work of the artisans, who were vulnerable to financial crises and who aspired to participate in the decisions of the town commune, which were invariably monopolized by the urban patriciate. On the eve of the great crises that lasted from the 1320s to the 1350s, these conflicts between different social groups heightened the tensions within the cities of western Europe.

This brief survey of European society in the central Middle Ages shows the importance of the transformations in this period. In the tenth and eleventh centuries regalian power shifted to castles and lordships, while in the thirteenth century these arrangements became permanently established in law across most of western Europe. In general, from the late twelfth century (although the exact chronology and forms varied from country to country), each social group acquired a precise status. Emerging royal administrations hardened these stratifications through laws, judicial inquests, and ceremonies. From then on these legal categories and badges of identity would precisely define each social 'estate'. The social orders of the *Ancien Régime* were thereby established and in most of Europe they would endure until the great revolutions of the nineteenth century.

2

Economy

David Nicholas

A strongly market-driven economy emerged during the central Middle Ages. Population increased significantly, but the extent of the growth is debated. Virtually all demographic reconstructions face the problem of converting heads of households, who are listed in surveys, into a total population figure through the use of a multiplier that can somehow average out everything from ten-child families to celibates. J. C. Russell has calculated a population of Europe around 1000 at 38.5 million, nearly doubling to 73.5 million by 1340, an exercise described by Norman Pounds as 'nothing more than intelligent guesswork'.[1] The rate of relative population increase can be estimated more reliably than total population. It was most marked in France and the Low Countries, followed by Germany and Scandinavia, the British Isles and Italy, but was slower in Greece, the Balkans, Iberia, and the Slavic East. Anecdotal evidence and fragmentary statistics tend to confirm Russell's rates of increase, but his overall population figures are almost certainly too low: overpopulation everywhere, and thus the press on resources, were more severe by 1300 than Russell admitted.

While the population of Europe south of the Alps and Pyrenees exceeded that of the north in 1000, the balance had shifted by the fourteenth century. Thus, although Italians still dominated finance, banking, and long-distance trade, a fundamental change had occurred: the economic development of the north, with market relations and concomitant urbanization and production of goods.

---

[1] J. C. Russell, 'Population in Europe 500–1500', in C. M. Cipolla (ed.), *The Middle Ages* (The Fontana Economic History of Europe; London, n.d.), 36, a slight upward revision of Russell's calculations in earlier publications; N. J. G. Pounds, *An Economic History of Medieval Europe* (2nd edn., London, 1994), 146.

Two phases of economic growth can be detected, with expansion quickening in the late twelfth century. Population was distributed unevenly, which necessitated trade between villages with an agricultural surplus and those that needed to import food to feed a population that in turn had to support itself at least in part by exchanging the marketable skills of its labour force. Thus villages, towns, and regions were developing specialities of goods and services, in some cases dictated by the limitations of the natural environment, so that exchange at central points became a matter of survival. Finally, exchange became more demand- than supply-driven. While this had always been the case for luxury goods, it became true of food and other necessities after about 1180. The cities as well as lay and ecclesiastical lords constituted a powerful demand market for the goods of their environs.

The first phase of rural economic expansion (to *c*.1180): an agricultural revolution?

The essential change in the agrarian economy during the central Middle Ages was the expansion and eventual intensification of land use in response to population growth. In the older settled and most densely populated parts of Europe, demand for food prompted agrarian clearance and changes in land management. Hamlets and dispersed farms yielded in most regions to villages. Previously forested land on the edge of villages and between villages was brought under the plough. Inducements were offered to skilled technicians in the densely populated Low Countries to move east and drain swamps along the Baltic coast. The resulting land was used first for pasture, then for farmland as the soil was desalinized. The most famous reclamation occurred in Flanders, Artois, and the Pas-de-Calais, but diking and drainage of the Po delta in northern Italy also created considerable new arable land. By 1180 the density of place names in Picardy and parts of England was as high as it would be in the nineteenth century, although this does not mean that the locations bearing these names were as intensely settled as later.

There is also an external component to the expansion of arable land. Entirely new villages were established, first in 'old' Europe, then in the German/Slavic East. In England twenty-one new towns were founded between 1066 and 1100 and another nineteen by 1130; only eight were established before 1150 in the German areas, but some 3,000 small towns were founded there in the thirteenth century. Lords, eager to attract labourers to clear land that was bringing them no profit, vied to found markets that would lure settlers and trade to their domains, not only by giving privileges to make their new villages attractive, but also by trying to centralize trade in their chief towns. Massive German and Flemish colonization extended east of the River Elbe in the thirteenth century. Colonization in the Iberian peninsula happened in tandem with conquest from the Muslims, as it was associated in the East with Christianizing the Slavs and the Baltic peoples.

Reclamation and the consequent growth of the food supply have been associated with the ending of serfdom, and this equation works in parts of continental Europe, particularly in the more economically developed areas. Lords gave freedom from many labour services and payments to their colonists, and in some cases complete legal emancipation (see Chapter 1). But 'freedom' is essentially a legal and social issue that must be divorced from economic questions, which are concerned with the delivery of goods and services.

The most prosperous agricultural regions of Europe were England and the German/Slavic East, both of which had numerous serfs (in the latter case the Slavs), and the southern Low Countries and northern France, where most peasants were free by 1200. Economically there was often little difference between free and unfree peasants, who lived side by side in the same village. In some English villages in the late thirteenth century the serfs (villeins) held more land on average than the free tenants.

On the 'classic' manor the tenant farmer paid his landlord rent for the land that he occupied by doing labour services on his 'demesne', the portion of the estate that the lord did not lease to tenants. This was an efficient organization, in which the larger estates were centres of administration for smaller farms and places where the lord's power was less extensive—for example, when he held only part of the village. As lords' powers grew, these estates were enlarged, and peasants whose ancestors had lived on the outskirts were brought under the 'ban'* (the power of command over free persons) of the lords.

But the classic manor began to weaken in the eleventh century and was almost gone by 1300 except in England and eastern Europe. In the Low Countries, Germany, and the economically developed parts of northern France, labour services, which initially had been owed throughout the year, were normally confined by charters to planting and harvest, the peak seasons of the year, and lords hired occasional labour for the rest of the year as needed. The practical distinction between serf and freeman was reduced further as the serfs' obligations to do labour services on the demesne were reduced in favour of rent. Thus, although there are plenty of exceptions, by 1180 the bonds of most peasants to their lords were expressed most cogently in rent rather than in legal subjection, and this change would be accelerated in the thirteenth century.

The expansion of the food supply has been associated with an 'agricultural revolution', but recent research has weakened this thesis. It was associated principally with Lynn White and Georges Duby,[2] who thought that three-field agriculture expanded at the expense of two-field: with only one-third, not half, of the land lying fallow, it theoretically increased the amount of land under cultivation on a given estate by 33 per cent. They also thought that the diffusion of the heavy northern plough, with coulter and ploughshare that raised the soil to the mouldboard that turned it, led to an increase in yields on grain and thus supported a denser population. The ox- or horse collar, which threw the weight of the plough to the animal's withers rather than to his neck, gave him more endurance.

There are problems with all of these hypotheses except for the collar. The heavy plough was not intrinsically superior to the 'sling' plough, which could plough adjacent furrows, while the mouldboard turned the soil to one side, creating a ridge. Given the difficulty of turning the wheeled plough, it was best suited to long strips of land. The sling plough dominated agriculture in the Mediterranean, where soils are thin, but it was also found elsewhere, including parts of the East and mountain areas, although the German colonists in east-central Europe preferred the wheeled plough. Thus the use of the heavy plough cannot explain the growth of farm productivity.

[2] L. White, Jr., *Medieval Technology and Social Change* (Oxford, 1962); G. Duby, *The Early Growth of the European Economy: Warriors and Peasants from the Seventh to the Twelfth Century* (Ithaca, NY, 1974).

Most importantly, the fact that a technique is known to have existed does not necessarily mean that it was widely practised. Although the new villages founded in the colonial east after the twelfth century usually had three fields, the transition was harder in Germany west of the Elbe and in France and England, for new fields had to be laid out and incorporated into an existing diversified structure of fields and hamlets. Rarely did villages once under a two-field structure convert to three. Some villages had more than three fields, particularly in the thirteenth century, as lords and some tenant farmers experimented with non-food crops that had industrial applications, including dyes such as madder. While three-field agriculture predominated in areas of intense grain cultivation, two fields remained the standard in the Mediterranean countries as well as parts of northern Europe.[3]

Furthermore, it is not entirely certain that yields on grain improved significantly in the first phase of the central medieval expansion. By the most optimistic calculations, in the ninth century wheat got 4:1–5:1 on good soil and when the weather was favourable; more often it was 3:1–4:1. Rye and maslin (a wheat/rye mix) got 6:1–8:1. Evidence from the twelfth century is within this range, suggesting that there was little amelioration of yields until the thirteenth century, when population pressure forced more intensive cultivation. Farmers had to hold back a substantial part of one year's crop to use as seed corn for the next year. This, combined with rent payments in kind, tithes, and work week and boon services, meant that per capita productivity was low and that it was difficult for an individual peasant to accumulate a surplus for sale.

Lords, however, could do so. The economic expansion of the central Middle Ages required considerable human and financial capital, which only lords could mobilize. Secular lords who wished to have land cleared would publicize their new foundations and the advantages that they were giving to tenants, on their own over-populated estates and also in partnership with churches, which could make the opportunity known on the estates of their affiliated houses. Clearing even a few acres of trees required a massive labour force.

---

[3] J.-P. Devroey, 'The Economy', in R. McKitterick (ed.), *The Early Middle Ages: Europe 400–1000* (Oxford, 2001), 116; W. Rösener, *Peasants in the Middle Ages* (Urbana, IL, 1992), 24, 51–4, 106–10.

Lords' powers remained substantial even in villages that had charters. They owned the watermills, which were numerous everywhere, the windmills, which appear around 1180 but could be used principally in coastal areas of the Low Countries and England, where winds were strong and relatively constant, and the machines that they powered. The village bakery and wine press required capital as well as a specialist to operate them. These *banalités*, or expressions of the lord's bannal power, are often considered abuses, and some charters ended the peasants' obligation to use his facilities, but in fact before the thirteenth century few village communities and fewer individuals were able to maintain such establishments on their own.

The lord's bannal power is critically important for understanding the production and extraction of surpluses. Most landlords collected more food as rent than could conceivably have been consumed in their households. The surplus was sold on markets, some of which developed at the gate of the castle, church, or monastery or around a storehouse. As population and production grew, the surpluses were taken to more distant localities. Very few individual tenants could afford the high transport costs; indeed, some charters of village liberties, such as the famous one given to the French village of Lorris, stipulated both that a market would be held in the village and that the tenants were obliged to provide cartage for the lord's goods to more distant places, usually a town or the lord's other domain centres, where they could be sold.

The market economy presupposes the intersection of supply and demand. Peasants who held too little land to feed their families could clear more land or move (either of which involved both permission of the lord and considerable risk), or they could sell their skills and services in return for food or for money, which could buy food on the village market, much of it coming from the lord's granaries. Through the late eleventh century the exchange economy fostered by the use of rents in kind operated mainly at a local level; but with improved transportation thereafter and the development of towns that could act as conduits for the re-export of goods, farm products came into interregional trade as well. The village clearly came to contain more wealthy but also more impoverished peasants as the market orientation of the rural economy quickened.

The towns and the development of a market economy

The urban market is distinguished from the rural by the greater variety of goods exchanged, the greater likelihood that exchange will be in monetary form or at least convertible to arithmetical terms, and the larger radius from which traders and goods come.[4] As the rural economy produced surpluses, trading settlements developed. The abbeys, bishoprics, and castles were also centres of seigneurial administration and markets for grain and wool. As princes increasingly tried to focus exchange operations in their chief places so that they could be controlled and taxed more effectively, they incidentally promoted urban growth. The presence of a bishopric (less often a monastery) or a princely residence entailed demand for goods and services, many of which could not be satisfied locally—for example, the demand for wine in northern regions that could not produce grapes—and thus required the development of links to more distant regions.

The central Middle Ages witnessed the birth of 'commercial capitalism', in which money was used to make more money but was not invested in substantial quantity in industry. But it was not *laissez-faire* capitalism, in which the 'free' market remains unregulated. As in the rural areas, exchange operations in the towns developed under the impulse generated by the bannal power of the princes. Rarely if ever did a city, however advantageously sited, grow without assuming monopoly functions over aspects of the trade of its environs, either through conquest or by a prince granting regional privileges. The statutes of the English kings restricting large commercial transactions and minting to places that they designated as 'ports' are well known, as were their efforts to centralize trade in the shire towns, efforts that were generally successful until the quantum growth of trade in the thirteenth century rendered them nugatory. On the Continent princes vied with one another in requiring transients to bring their goods to a specified local market, which thus was assured not only of a regular supply of goods but also of profits from reshipping goods

---

[4] For this section see D. Nicholas, *The Growth of the Medieval City: From Late Antiquity to the Early Fourteenth Century* (London, 1997), and literature cited.

and the entire development of a trade infrastructure. As early as the 1020s the western emperors as Lombard kings were making Pavia a commercial as well as a political capital. Pavia was also the great demand market of northern Italy at that time, dependent on Venice for luxury goods from Constantinople. Customs depots were fixed at the exits of Alpine valleys, which were very important in the local and long-distance trade of all north Italian cities.

Town markets grew at linkage points of supply and demand for goods and labour and thus on economic frontiers. Sometimes the economic frontier that gives rise to a town or an urban network is obvious: the Mediterranean is the junction of the west European, Byzantine, and Muslim economies. Often it is more subtle, as a town developed at the intersection of a poor farming area and a wealthier one, as happened in the southern Low Countries in the case of Ghent. The function of the city was thus to link local trade, which can be conducted in a network of small local markets, illustrated most clearly in England, and long-distance trade. For, while the cities derived most of their population from the immediate environs, their capital base was in long-distance trade, which in turn provided money that generated local demand and jobs. Before the late twelfth century, when the cities for the first time were producing exportable goods in large quantities, this capital base came almost entirely from importing goods for sale to those who had money from extra-urban sources.

The rural and urban economies were thus not discrete entities. Although they were generally in symbiosis until the late twelfth century, city-dwellers and farmers do not have the same market interests. Farmers benefit from high food prices and low prices for industrial goods, while people living in cities want the opposite. Competition in the rural economy was increasingly determined from the eleventh century by market considerations that involved the towns. The reclamation of coastal Flanders created swampy areas that were suitable for sheep, and thus clothmaking developed in the early Flemish towns. But, as the land dried out in the twelfth century, population pressure and demand for food meant that grazing lands were converted to agriculture. By that time, however, the Flemish cities had such a thriving textile industry that they had to create an infrastructure to get wool from outside their immediate region. Accordingly, they developed a profitable trade with England, which became Flanders' major supplier of wool and customer for luxury-grade textiles.[5]

The development of towns involves a very rough division of labour between commercial/industrial town and agricultural and pastoral countryside, although it was never absolute, given the extent of industry in the countryside and of food production in the towns. Clothmaking and construction, the chief industries of most cities, used significant amounts of rural labour. In the case of construction, irregular demand for buildings meant that the less skilled jobs were often given to persons who lived near the town and could work intermittently in the town while maintaining their principal agrarian establishments outside.

In the case of clothmaking, technological innovations allowed the production of a higher-quality product without the use of additional labour and thus enhanced both quality and quantity of production. The spinning wheel came into general use in the thirteenth century. The treadle-operated horizontal loom for weaving wool replaced the primitive vertical loom, then yielded in the thirteenth century to the horizontal broadloom, which had to be operated by two skilled weavers sitting adjacent to each other. The labour was present in the rural areas, but the process also necessitated a substantial capital investment, which was possible only in the cities. The diffusion of mills contributed substantially to the rural economic expansion, but except for mining and metallurgy the industrial application of mills is associated largely with the cities from the eleventh century. The fulling mill, for softening raw wool through the application of fulling earth, appeared in the late tenth century and spread before 1200 to most of northern Europe except Flanders. It was used in the rural areas, often by artisans who worked for city-based drapers, but also in the cities. The camshaft, which permits the detachment of a water wheel from the activity that its energy generates, appeared in the twelfth century, followed by the hydraulic saw in the thirteenth.[6]

The rise of the market economy is associated with the development

---

[5] D. Nicholas, *Medieval Flanders* (London, 1992), 164–8; *id.*, 'Of Poverty and Primacy: Demand, Liquidity, and the Flemish Economic Miracle, 1050–1200', *American Historical Review*, 96 (1991), 17–41; T. H. Lloyd, *The English Wool Trade in the Middle Ages* (Cambridge, 1977).

[6] E. S. Hunt and J. M. Murray, *A History of Business in Medieval Europe, 1200–1550* (Cambridge, 1999), 40.

of economic regions, which before the late twelfth century were definable in most places as the area required to feed the chief town. As population continued to expand, the area from which the towns attracted immigrants extended and more specialized occupations developed, a further stage was reached. While initially surpluses were exchanged mainly in the area where they were produced, by the twelfth century the development of urban industry, combined with the demand from the elites, rural but now also urban, for luxury goods obtainable only from distant locales, contributed to greater diversification on the urban markets. For the town is bound by its economic region but must transcend it if it is to continue to grow.

The expansion of the rural economy: the second phase (c.1180–c.1330)

As the urban economy became more diverse, jobs were available for peasants who could not support themselves on the land. The towns provided markets for agricultural surpluses, an infrastructure through which more specialized goods could be exported to markets outside the region, and a demand market for luxuries. But economic change became more rapid after 1180. While most towns before the mid-twelfth century must be seen essentially as outgrowths of a rural market economy, thereafter the towns became more active players, as more farmers were producing goods with a view towards sale on the urban market and townspeople were increasingly found as investors in rural land and organizers of farm production.

Until the late twelfth century agrarian expansion was basically linear, with extension of existing settlements and plantation of new villages. Although most of the best land had been cleared before 1200, population continued to rise, and clearances continued, in some areas even more rapidly than in the previous two centuries. In the thirteenth century population growth slowed relatively but was building on two centuries of steady increase. On most estates the number of heads of households, the chief indicator of population size, increased proportionally much more than did the amount of new arable. English population may have doubled in the thirteenth century, against an increase of cultivable land surface of less than 20 per cent. On the estates of the bishop of Winchester in the Vale of Taunton, the land, which was admittedly very fertile, was largely occupied by 1200; yet population increased by nearly 2.5 times between 1209 and 1311.[7] The population growth of the cities was modest until the late twelfth century, but many of them seem to have grown more strongly in the following century than in the previous three combined. Most of this increase was in the form of immigration from their immediate environs. Rents, real wages (the face value of the wage adjusted for inflation), and profit margins all grew during 1100–1250, but thereafter real wages stagnated or declined. The theory that the soil was becoming exhausted by overcropping has been criticized: yields on wheat, which was grown on the better soils, remained relatively strong, while yields on oats and barley, for which marginal soils were used, declined. This suggests that, while the best soil continued to produce, overall production of edible grain declined.[8]

We have no way of quantifying the portion of the caloric needs of the population that was met by fish or by the produce of gardens around private homes. More sophisticated farming techniques that had been developed in earlier centuries now became more widely used. There is some evidence in the thirteenth century of the use of chemical fertilizer in addition to manure and marling. The most important changes were probably the increased use of iron in ploughs and as horseshoes and the spread of the wheeled plough. Horses were increasingly used as draught animals in the thirteenth century and also for hauling, particularly in northern Germany and England, where they contributed substantially to capitalizing farm markets in the thirteenth century.[9] The sickle remained little changed, but it was yielding to the scythe in the more highly developed grain economies of northern France, Flanders, and the Rhineland.

Lords paid more attention to estate administration, which gave them greater financial resources and liquidity, and to more flexible

---

[7] M. M. Postan, 'Medieval Agrarian Society in its Prime: England', *The Cambridge Economic History of Europe*, i. *The Agrarian Life of the Middle Ages* (2nd edn., Cambridge, 1966), 550, 563.

[8] J. Z. Titow, *Winchester Yields: A Study in Medieval Agricultural Productivity* (Cambridge, 1972), 14–15.

[9] Rösener, *Peasants*, 111–14; J. Langdon, 'Horse Hauling: A Revolution in Vehicle Transport in Thirteenth-Century England?' *Past and Present*, 103 (1984), 37–66.

and efficient land use. In agriculturally advanced areas, demand in nearby cities led to more intense crop rotation, sometimes involving five or more fields, and planting more fodder and industrial crops. In the mid-twelfth century most lords still realized greater profits from their demesnes than from rents, tithes, and the *banalités*. But, except in the German–Slavic East and England, demesne farming virtually ended in the thirteenth century, and lords were actually leasing out large portions of their demesnes to prosperous local peasants. In England and Germany, however, the demesne economy actually was being revitalized, as lords sought to take advantage of high grain prices. In areas where grain was cultivated intensely, many lords preferred payments in kind to money rents. Some village charters prevented lords from adjusting rents to reflect market value, but the lords could raise entry fees when heirs succeeded to a tenement. On the Continent, term leaseholds, often for nine years, were emerging in the thirteenth century, after which the rent could be renegotiated upward.

Most lords found it advantageous to commute labour services for money rents, particularly as the money supply grew (see pp. 69–72). Most remaining manorial dues were abolished, except in England, but this did not automatically translate into better economic conditions for the peasants, who had less profit margin than the lords and were thus less able to take advantage of the high food prices in the cities. Given fragmentation of plots of land and a tendency for yields to decline even as prices rose, many poorer tenant farmers as well as landless labourers would work cheaply, as the continued growth of population created a supply of labour that exceeded demand.

The English kings permitted markets to be established every $6^2/_3$ miles, since this was the area within which a farmer could bring his goods to market and return home in the same day. Markets at this distance thus could not theoretically compete with one another, and recent work has shown that in central England this ideal situation was rather close to reality.[10] The thirteenth century thus witnessed the increased integration of the rural and urban economies, made possible by better distribution facilities and diversification both of demand and of production. This period was 'the turning point between the era of the relatively closed, autarkic household economy

[10] J. Masschaele, *Peasants, Merchants, and Markets: Inland Trade in England, 1150–1350* (New York, 1997).

and that of an exchange economy based on the division of labour'.[11] The thousands of new markets founded in the thirteenth century gave individual peasants better opportunities to market their grain, as infrastructural changes now made it feasible to market a smaller surplus than had been true before 1180.

Amongst the peasantry, impartible inheritance benefited usually the eldest son, occasionally the youngest, but made all other heirs dependent on whoever got the tenement. But in the thirteenth century partible inheritance became more common, particularly in regions such as the Rhineland and Flanders, which developed a strong urban life and market relationships. Better credit mechanisms and more liquidity in the economy made it feasible for owners of plots of land that were too small to support a household to sell them or convert them to profitable uses having nothing to do with grain agriculture. The options of the landless peasant included of course leaving the land for a town, but others sold their labour, as lords hired seasonal workers to replace the demesne services of emancipated tenant farmers. Still others developed second sources of income, notably in crafts such as iron- and woodworking and the less skilled branches of clothmaking. The overheating of the rural economy in the thirteenth century thus prompted changes in the labour market. Some peasants were able to purchase or sub-let enough land, in many cases from seigniorial demesnes, to make themselves into *de facto* village lords. The gaps in landholding between rich and poor tenants in the same village became much sharper in the thirteenth century than before: the great division was between those who inherited a complete large tenement in default of other heirs, those who had access to the capital necessary to buy land and build up large tenancies, and those who did not and had to leave the land or diversify their activities in order to survive.

The coinage revolution

During the central Middle Ages the amount of bullion increased exponentially, as gold and silver were dis-hoarded and new mines

---

[11] Rösener, *Peasants*, 22–3.

were opened.[12] In the late tenth century small-scale exchange had to
be by barter, for coin was scarce and was used mainly for large transactions. The early phases of the European economic revival were
accomplished without a sound coinage, but a stagnation that threatened in the late twelfth century was averted by new supplies of
metal, the expansion of the native silver coinages of Europe, and the
development of gold coinages that were suitable for large-scale and
international transactions.

Beginning in the late tenth century new silver mines were opened
in Germany, notably in the Harz mountains. The new supply of money
facilitated trade between Germany and other parts of Europe and
made it briefly the commercial centre of the north. The expansion of
the Germans into the Slavic East and the growth of trade in Scandinavia were accompanied by a spread of German coin in both regions.
But the Harz mines produced little after the mid-eleventh century,
and trade became more difficult. The English, for example, minted
about twenty million pennies c.1000, with the number rapidly rising
in the early eleventh century despite payments of vast tributes to
Danish invaders, but outputs declined to ten million by 1158.

Just as the agrarian expansion took a new and more capital-
intensive form in the late twelfth century, new silver mines were
opened after 1160 that fuelled the urban expansion. This was a more
broadly based development than its predecessor, for large quantities
of silver were produced not only in Germany, but also in Bohemia,
Tuscany, and Sardinia. By 1180 'silver worth hundreds of millions of
pfennigs' had entered the commercial and political economies.[13]

The consequences were profound. Heightened demand for goods
and services will naturally create some monetary inflation, but this is
fuelled immeasurably by an abundant supply of coin. Inflation thus
became severe in the late twelfth century. With increased bullion in
the economy came the growth of public demand and the transfer of
assets from towns and villages to territorial governments and regional
economies, since taxation was much easier in money than in kind. As
small market transactions could now be paid for in silver pennies that
were worth intrinsically less, larger silver coins, and eventually gold

[12] P. Spufford, *Money and its Use in Medieval Europe* (Cambridge, 1988), chs. 3–5, is
the most scholarly and convenient summary of a highly technical literature.
[13] Ibid. 111.

coins, became necessary. In 1172 Genoa issued a silver coin worth 4 pennies, and the other north Italian cities (Pisa, Florence, Venice) soon issued *grossi* (groats). The silver *tournois* of Louis IX in 1266 was the equivalent of 12 pennies (1 *sou*).

Peter Spufford has argued that the 'need for a larger denomination of coin was only reached when and where there was sufficient urban growth for there to be a large enough number of people living primarily on money-wages, and when those money-wages, in terms of the existing denari or deniers, required an inconveniently large number of coins to be paid on each of a large number of occasions'. This meant that the larger coins came into general use in the first half of the thirteenth century in Italy, in the second half in the Low Countries, and in the fourteenth century in most other places. Small coins were still used for individual purchases, such as loaves of bread, while the larger ones were used for bulk purchases.[14]

Most gold came to the West through trade with the Byzantine Empire and Egypt. The Muslims paid in gold; they sold cotton, spices, and luxury cloth to the westerners, receiving silver in exchange. The Muslim rulers of Spain, who also controlled much of North Africa, and some Italian princes were minting gold coins even in the tenth and eleventh centuries, and some Byzantine and Muslim gold coins circulated in Italy in the twelfth. But by the late twelfth century the West was exporting industrial goods and considerable grain to the Levant and Africa. A further source of payment in gold was the carrying trade, which the Venetians controlled in the eastern and the Genoese in the western Mediterranean.

In the West, the first gold coin that was used outside Italy since the Merovingian period, reflecting the newly favourable balance of trade, was the emperor Frederick II's gold *augustalis* of 1231, using gold obtained as tribute from Tunis and from Sicilian grain shipments to North Africa. It was followed by the Venetian ducat in 1248 and in 1252 by the Genoese januino and the florin of Florence, the most influential, which was worth 20 Florentine shillings or 1 pound. Louis IX of France (1226–70) and Henry III of England (1216–72) then issued gold coins, although the latter did not achieve wide circulation and was discontinued. The success of gold coinages suggests that western Europe had a positive balance of trade with the East in the

[14] Ibid. 236 for quotation.

early thirteenth century, probably attributable to the production of exportable manufactured goods. The Mongol conquests changed this, for they cut the Middle East off from its normal supplies of gold, through the Sahara and Morocco, and the Mongols dealt only in silver. Thus the Muslims came to need western silver, and by the mid-thirteenth century gold was overvalued in the West and silver in the East. Silver thus moved eastward, hurting the western economy by depleting stocks of silver in the West and leading to coinage debasement and inflation and the eventual 'bullion famine' of the late Middle Ages.

The commercial changes of the thirteenth century

Even as late as 1100 the major users of coin were lay and ecclesiastical rulers, but the expansion of the coin supply in the late twelfth century made the use of money normal also in towns. Virtually all large-scale transactions in Europe by 1300 used money. Urban artisans could now produce smaller quantities and goods of less value for export, where previously the cheaper items were feasible only for barter on the local market. Most services were now paid with a cash wage. The use of money then became generalized in the agrarian sector in the thirteenth century. In England, the best-documented case, mint output was less than one million pennies in the 1170s but rose to four million annually between 1180 and 1204, ten million between 1234 and 1247, and fifteen million in the 1250s. The total volume of coin in circulation was less than £125,000 in 1180, rising to £300,000 by 1218, £400,000 by 1247, and more than doubling again to £1,100,000 in 1311. This rate of increase meant the amount of coin per person more than trebled.[15]

Most cities of Europe reached their greatest population before the modern period at some point in the late thirteenth or early fourteenth century. The suburbs around the primitive Roman walls and princely fortifications were being walled, even before 1180, but there-

---

[15] R. H. Britnell, *The Commercialisation of English Society, 1000–1500*, 2nd edn. (Manchester, 1996), 102–3.

after the rate of territorial growth increased. The population of the largest cities at least tripled in the thirteenth century, against an overall doubling of the population. Pisa more than tripled, to about 38,000 in 1293, but it still lost position in Tuscany to Florence, which was smaller than Pisa in 1200 but more than twice its size by 1300, due to its control of the grain trade from southern Italy and its rapid development of industry and banking. Northern Italy had the largest cities of Europe except for Paris, which quintupled in size after 1180 to a population of 250,000 by 1328. Milan, Genoa, Venice, Naples, Florence, and Palermo probably had populations of over 100,000 by 1300, declining thereafter. The other major pole of urban development was in north-western France and Flanders. In England London had a population of about 80,000 by 1300, double its late-eleventh-century size, but it completely dominated its region, with York, the second largest English city, having only 10,000 inhabitants in the late thirteenth century.

Several economic variables play into these changes. First, the tertiary sector of the economy, which involves activities such as services that were not directly connected to the production of consumer goods, first became significant in the late twelfth century. The impact that the tertiary sector could have on the primary and secondary sectors constitutes an essential difference between the urban and village economies, linked by liquidity.

Secondly, the towns that grew significantly developed industry, in most cases textiles, that could be exported. Industry was a late development with most towns, with the result that most of the city centres were given over to markets and financial operations, while the artisans, who came later to the city, lived in the suburbs. Yet with the rapid growth of the cities in the thirteenth century and the progressive walling of suburbs, many artisans found themselves living within the walls.

Thirdly, the cities themselves became demand markets for consumer goods. Most persons who immigrated to the cities in the thirteenth century found jobs, not only in exportable industries such as clothmaking, but even more in most cities in provisioning the local market with buildings, comestibles, and transport services. Poverty became a much more serious problem with the downturn of the fourteenth century, even though the cities' populations by then were declining. Given that much more money was invested in commerce than in industry, even with the expansion of manufacturing, more profit went to the merchant who sold the product than to the artisans who produced it, and the cities in many areas, especially those that could be considered relatively developed economically, thus acquired an economic importance that exceeded both their percentage of population and their share of the wealth of the economic regions that came to be based on them.

Fourthly, since the cities were even less able to feed themselves after 1180 than before, the grain trade became critically important for them in the thirteenth century. Virtually all the larger cities—London is the conspicuous exception—had to develop a means to obtain food from outside the region, particularly in years of poor harvest. Ports such as Barcelona and Genoa, which had agriculturally poor hinterlands, were especially vulnerable but also had the coastal connections that facilitated grain importing. Inland towns had to rely on what could be brought by river and overland. The Flemish cities were fed by grain that came down the Leie and Scheldt rivers from Picardy and Artois in northern France. The Italian cities obtained considerable grain from North Africa and especially Sicily and Corsica. The inland cities tried to make their rural environs into granaries for the city, a policy that was pursued most effectively in Italy, but which often depressed the rural economy artificially to provide the city with cheap grain. The larger cities forbade grain exports from their 'country' (*contado**) and required the peasants to sell in the city, even at a loss. Virtually all Italian cities instituted grain offices during the thirteenth century, and the city governments worked with private companies to secure the grain supply.

The cities were characterized by a highly differentiated occupational structure and a diversity of demand. The larger cities had several markets, often distinguished from one another by the type of goods sold, but at least one of them would be open every day except for religious holidays. On market days the farmers from the environs and wandering pedlars would set up their stalls on the market, often prefabricated shacks carried on their backs. But in addition, considerable wholesale traffic came through merchant halls, most often grain and meat markets, that were established in the larger cities in the thirteenth century as control points, to ensure the proper accounting of imported raw materials and high quality for goods that were being exported from the city and would bear its seal of quality.

By the thirteenth century the bannal power of princes was even more important than earlier in fostering the growth of the major cities. England, which had a relatively undifferentiated economy and low level of urbanization, with much of the trade infrastructure in foreign hands, nonetheless posed fewer hindrances to commerce than any other region, with few of the internal tolls that still slowed trade elsewhere by raising transport costs. On the Continent, in contrast, princes still used the cities as centres of toll collection (see p. 79) and administration, but, more importantly, the cities' size now made them vulnerable to outside pressure, and particularly to interruption in the supply of food and industrial raw materials.

Thus virtually all cities either obtained from their lords or simply asserted a monopoly or 'staple' privilege. This might be over a specific profitable trade, such as the control of Bordeaux over the wine trade of the Garonne valley. The grain staple of Ghent obliged farmers of the environs to sell on the central town market and required all shipments of grain that passed by river through the city to stop, be taxed and be offered for sale on the market before being re-exported. Other staples were a coastal-intermediary trade involving many items, such as the famous example of Bruges (see p. 90). These monopolies were obtained only after the city was already large, but they characteristically involved both necessities for the local demand market and also goods for re-export.

The thirteenth century witnessed the critical transition to the urban manufacture of fine items that became the basis of the cities' export trades, as they gained access through the fairs and in some cases simply through pre-emptive buying to more distant sources of industrial raw materials. Urban manufacture was still directed towards princely courts, but now increasingly also to the urban wealthy. Occupations that were too esoteric to command a mass market, such as glassmaking and gold- and silversmithing, could survive in the cities because their products could be exported through the growing urban networks. Clothmaking became more highly specialized, in the case of luxury woollens involving the work of as many as twenty separate artisans.

Particularly in the larger cities, occupational guilds developed, initially as charitable fraternities, but during the thirteenth century many of them began regulating the technical specifications of the guild's product, labour conditions and wages, the importation of raw materials, and often the distribution of goods as well. Growing demand for silk after 1250 was met largely from the Italian cities, particularly Lucca before the fourteenth century, although Florence, Genoa, Venice, and Milan also had silkmaking. A virtual industrial zone developed in Flanders and north-western France, where the labour-intensive manufacture of fine woollen cloth enticed workers into the cities and gave them a valuable capital resource through export.

While before 1180 only the most expensive grades of cloth could be sold profitably outside the region of manufacture, in the thirteenth century the regional and international fairs made it feasible to sell medium grades to a broader demand market. The finest cloth was Flemish, but some of it was made in imitation of English export textiles (for example, the *estanfort*, named after Stamford), which began to lose ground to the Flemish products only in the second half of the century. Languedoc, Catalonia, and Lombardy also produced fine grades. The Italian cities bought 'undressed' northern cloth at the fairs and finished it, then sold it in the Levant and Africa. Linen manufacture, which used a simpler technology than woollens, became largely rural, although large quantities were marketed through the towns, particularly in south Germany and Switzerland. As quality-control regulations for cloth became more exacting in the thirteenth century, some Flemish statutes required given grades of cloth to use imported English wools. Less attention was given in the statutes to the cheaper grades, which were more mass-marketed than the luxury products, and to mixed fabrics, such as fustians, a mixture of linen and cotton.[16]

A few statistics can give some idea of the volume of trade in industrial raw materials and manufactured goods. In the early fourteenth century the English exported 35,000–40,000 sacks of wool annually, for a total weight of fifteen million pounds, and 50,000 cloths (each 28 yards long). At its peak, the Flemish industry produced three times this much cloth. The number of lead seals used to certify cloth at the hall at Ypres rose from 10,500 in 1306 to 92,500 in 1313. According to the chronicler Giovanni Villani, Florence produced 100,000 *pezze* of woollen cloth in the early fourteenth century, worth

[16] M. F. Mazzaoui, *The Italian Cotton Industry in the Later Middle Ages, 1100–1600* (Cambridge, 1961).

1,200,000 gold florins. The value of goods subject to toll at Genoa, both imports and exports, quadrupled in the two decades after 1274. Around 1280 Venice produced 60,000 pieces of cotton cloth from 140 tons of raw cotton.

Cloth, wool, and grain were not the only commodities that developed mass markets. Production and trade of metals increased, most obviously gold and silver but also utilitarian metals such as tin. A major expansion of iron-working occurred in the late thirteenth century, with Swedish osmund and Biscayan iron as the major items.[17] Olive oil, beer, building materials, and fuel are also found in interregional trade in the late twelfth century with the development of larger boats. The wine and salt trades were highly lucrative. The distributive networks of wool and wine were mirror images of each other, as wool moved south and wine north, virtually all of both going through the towns. Until the late thirteenth century most Atlantic trade was in the wines of Gascony and Poitou to England and the Low Countries, iron from the bay of Biscay and salt from the bay of Bourgneuf in western France. Once the kings of England had lost control of Normandy, which gave access through Rouen to southern French wines, Bordeaux became the major depot of wine for England from the second quarter of the thirteenth century, so that English demand led to increased grape cultivation in the Garonne valley. The wine trade was perhaps the most lucrative of all from the perspective of profit generated per unit of production. Labour costs were lower than for grain and the final product less heavy, and the price of wine, which was also heavily taxed everywhere, was quite high. The Burgundy and Rhine wine trade routes were essentially riverine but some overland connections had to be made. In the early fourteenth century 80,000–100,000 tons of wine were brought north annually. Wine accounted for 31 per cent of the value of all goods imported into England and 25 per cent of those brought to the Low Countries: Bordeaux's export peaked at 103,000 barrels in 1308–9. The wine ships also carried Mediterranean fruits, wood products, honey, and dyes northward.[18]

---

[17] R. Sprandel, *Das Eisengewerbe im Mittelalter* (Stuttgart, 1968).

[18] Statistics here and in previous paragraph from J. Bernard, 'Trade and Finance in the Middle Ages, 900–1500', in Cipolla (ed.), *The Middle Ages*, 281–2, 310; C. M. Cipolla, *Before the Industrial Revolution: European Society and Economy, 1000–1700* (2nd edn., New York, 1980), 209.

Improvements were also made in overland trade during this period. Roads were being paved, new bridges built, and older ones rebuilt in stone—for example, London Bridge. By the thirteenth century land routes were competing with rivers as arteries of commercial transportation. The four-wheeled cart was being used for hauling in the twelfth century but became dominant in the thirteenth. The construction of inland canals formed important commercial networks everywhere. Before 1200 Flanders was laced with canals that brought the major cities into contact with rural supplies and markets, and the commercial cities themselves were linked by canals by the mid-thirteenth century. Canals are particularly important for the development of Milan, which was between two river systems, the Ticino and Adda, but was never linked to the region's main river, the Po. While princes tried to attract merchants to their domains, their goal was more to enhance their own revenues than to promote the economic well-being of their subjects. Thus tolls were a problem everywhere except in England.

Until the thirteenth century the only pass through the Alps that was open throughout the year was the Brenner, but before 1300 the passes of Mont-Cenis, Great St Bernard, and Mont-Genèvre were discovered and began carrying substantial traffic (see Map 2). From there the great trade routes led up the Rhône valley, then overland to the Saône and Seine valleys, thence north through the toll at Bapaume to Artois and Flanders. The Champagne fairs were a short distance from Paris by land routes, canals, and the Aube. A major direct road ran from Bordeaux across Orléans to Paris and thence to Flanders. In the late thirteenth century direct seaborne traffic became more common from Germany and the East to Bruges and London, but most commerce on the east–west axis was still overland, from Flanders across Brabant to the Rhineland, thence down the Rhine and Danube, with a major overland route linking Frankfurt to the Danube valley. A trip between the Mediterranean coast and Paris required between twenty and twenty-four days in the thirteenth century, or half that time for a solitary person on horseback. The merchant caravans from Italy took about twenty days to reach the fairs of Champagne.[19]

---

[19] K. L. Reyerson, 'Commerce and Communications,' in *The New Cambridge Medieval History*, v (Cambridge, 1999), 54–8.

Merchants travelling to the fairs or domiciled in a foreign city often made interurban arrangements for mutual protection, including several German towns that had sponsored colonization in the East. Lübeck, originally a Slavic settlement, was refounded after 1159 on the isthmus of Holstein. Its location made it the logical link between the North and Baltic Sea trades, and it quickly cut into the profitable trade of the island of Gotland with Russia. German merchants established resident offices in Novgorod and Bergen in Norway. The pace of trade grew so rapidly that a string of German towns was founded on the Baltic coast in the early thirteenth century. The leagues led by Lübeck, Hamburg, and Cologne combined into a single 'German Hanse' that is first mentioned in London in 1281; in 1282 the German merchants received a charter of privileges at Bruges, where they joined Italians and Castilians in maintaining resident colonies. The Hanse became the conduit for the raw materials of the East toward overpopulated Western Europe, handling the distribution of furs, fish, honey, and wax, and eventually grain from the East, and importing mainly English wool and Flemish cloth.

Further evidence that princes fostered only the trade that could benefit them financially is shown by their treatment of foreign merchants. In England King John (1199–1216) and particularly Henry III (1216–72) used economic warfare, taking reprisals against French and other merchants from unfriendly powers and trying to strike at the French by hitting their potential trading partners. Native merchandising was severely hindered in England by the reliance of the kings on foreign moneylenders, whose collateral on their loans (see p. 84) was commercial privileges that were not enjoyed by denizens. Wherever German or Italian extraterritorial colonies existed, they controlled the export trades and much of public finance of the areas where they resided. Foreign merchants were able to export wool from England at a lower customs rate than natives, probably because they paid so dearly for the privilege and were a vulnerable group. For most of the thirteenth century Italian merchants were not restricted to the ports and thus controlled much of the distributive trade in the English interior, at the fairs. In 1303 alien merchants were given the right to live in their own hostels and trade with other foreigners, rather than going through native brokers, and were permitted to sell spices and other merchandise retail.

The situation of Italy

Geography made Italy the commercial outpost of Europe, linking it with the luxury-producing Byzantine and Islamic economies. The commercial links of Venice and Amalfi to Byzantium long predate the great economic changes of the twelfth century. Venice virtually controlled Constantinople's western trade after 1080. On the west coast, Pisa dominated Tuscany in banking, finance, and overseas trade until its harbour silted up in the late thirteenth century and Florence surpassed it. Pisa's main interests were in the central Mediterranean and southern Italy and Sicily, colliding with the Genoese over interests in the Tyrrhenian Sea (see Map 2). The Genoese merchants, who like the Venetians were always supported by their city government, concentrated on the Ligurian coast and contested Sardinia and Sicily with the Pisans until 1284, when the Genoese navy crushed its rival. With the north Italian coast thus secured, Genoa then tried to prevent merchants from the south French cities of Narbonne, Montpellier, and Marseilles from trading directly with the kingdom of Sicily, insisting that their boats should dock at Genoa instead.

The crusades had some impact on Italian economic fortunes. There can be no doubt that commercial contacts quickened in the twelfth and thirteenth centuries. The Genoese and Pisans, then the Venetians and other Italian cities, established merchant colonies (*fondachi*) in the crusader cities and along the north African coast, as well as in the East. These quarters were considered overseas extensions of the home city and were governed by its law. Thus, while before 1000 most recorded contacts between western and eastern merchants were on an individual basis, regular commercial contacts involving large groups of persons, and substantial cargoes with large values, developed during the central Middle Ages. The later crusades were financed by using banks to transfer funds to the Holy Land, thus accelerating the drain of bullion from West to East. It is most unlikely that bullion seized on even the First Crusade compensated for these losses.

Even before Pisa's decline, Venice and Genoa were the great rivals for control of Constantinople, which involved both control of the oriental goods coming through Constantinople and provisioning the city itself with grain and Western-manufactured goods. The capture of the city during the Fourth Crusade (1202–4) inspired and financed by the Venetians, forced Genoa to concentrate on trade with Egypt. But the re-establishment of the native Greek Palaeologus dynasty at Constantinople in 1261 was an anti-Venetian reaction, and Genoa, with Palaeologus support, was able to found colonies at Pera, across the Golden Horn from Constantinople, then at Caffa on the Black Sea itself. Yet increasingly from the late thirteenth century Genoa was oriented towards the Atlantic and the Mediterranean islands. Genoese capital financed much of the economic expansion of Castile, particularly Seville, its leading port.

The trade of Aragon–Catalonia is another aspect of the Christian Mediterranean economic expansion in the thirteenth century. Its expansion in the western Mediterranean came at the expense of the Muslims of northern Africa and created the base for Barcelona's growth. The Catalans also established important outposts in Greece and seized Malta in 1284. Their trade was in alum, Mediterranean dried fruits, oil, and leather; the Barcelonese exported their own and Flemish cloth to the eastern Mediterranean and northern Africa in exchange. After Sicily fell to Aragon in 1282, the island became Barcelona's granary. Aragon then seized Sardinia from Genoa in the second quarter of the fourteenth century.

Most Mediterranean trade was in 'spices'. This term includes not only the edible flavouring spices, most of which came from the Far East (pepper, the most prized, was also grown in Africa, but of an inferior quality to Asian), but also dried fruits, drugs, cotton, silk, and other luxury fabrics, alum, and dyes. Western Europe produced only madder and pastel. The Italian network of colonies is critical. Each spice was brought overland to a particular export depot on the coast or on an island, where western maritime powers vied for influence, but it was thus a very diffuse trade. The Zaccaria family of Genoa got an alum mine monopoly at Phocaea in Asia Minor from the Byzantines in 1275. This gave Genoa a new commodity and helps to explain the start of the voyages to Flanders and the increased tonnage of Genoese ships; for alum, a mordant for fixing dyes, was critically important for the luxury cloths of the north. Cotton was much more important for western textiles than was once thought, but the best grades were grown in the Middle East: Venice sent a 'cotton fleet' to northern Syria, the plain of Antioch, and Asia Minor,[20] and northern Europeans had to obtain their supplies through Italians.

While the Italian coastal ports did a thriving trade with the East even in the early Middle Ages, the cities of interior Italy remained farm markets, with a considerable trade in provisioning the households of nobles and bishops and transmitting the goods imported through the coastal emporia to the interior. Their economic growth in the thirteenth century is associated with banking, and the great population upsurge that accompanied the expansion of urban industry, as Florence, for example, developed a thriving textile industry within the city and consequently tried to hinder weaving in its *contado*.

Credit and banking

The greater complexity of the goods and services exchanged in Europe during the thirteenth century naturally evoked major changes in commercial techniques and credit mechanisms. Until the eleventh century most borrowing was by the rural nobility and kings. 'There were practically no financial mechanisms to facilitate the transformation of saving into investment.'[21] But the need for credit was much broader in the urban economy, given the need for orders in advance for goods and the costs of ships to transport them. Deferred credit thus became normal, furthering both expansion of consumption and pooling resources through investment.

Church doctrine hindered investment. The term 'usury'* was applied in the Deuteronomic sense of any guaranteed interest on a loan, whatever the circumstances, but it was applied before the late twelfth century only to loans between Christians. The Jews were still a major source of commercial credit in the twelfth century, but persecutions of them during the early crusades were accelerated by royal policies in France and England, and they gradually lost their importance.

---

[20] R. H. Bautier, *The Economic Development of Medieval Europe*, trans. H. Karolyi (New York, 1971), 135–6; Hunt and Murray, *History of Business*, 100.
[21] Cipolla, *Before the Industrial Revolution*, 194.

The Jews were replaced by the growth of moneylending among Christians. Various south Europeans extended casual credit, notably the 'Cahorsins' (named after Cahors in southern France) and 'Lombards', who were involved mainly in small-scale operations, often through pawnbroking. As they were joined by natives of the cities in which they operated, 'Lombard' and 'Cahorsin' came to mean anyone who openly charged interest on loans. Some princes began establishing legal rates of interest that they might charge: 2 pence per pound per week uncompounded, or 43.5 per cent annually, was common in the north. North Italian bankers in the early thirteenth century were charging 20 per cent per year and up, on both commercial and personal loans. At that time there were perhaps 150–200 Lombards at the fairs of Champagne and a comparable number at Paris, probably the same persons. Philip IV in 1294 confined the Cahorsins and Lombards to four cities and the Champagne fairs, then levied taxes and forced loans from them and confiscated their property, using usury as the pretext. Many of them thus emigrated to Bruges and Avignon, which were more receptive to them and lay beyond French royal control.[22]

The *commenda* contract appeared in the tenth century, and somewhat later the *colleganzia*, the version of it used at Venice. In its pure form it involved two partners investing unequal amounts of money in an enterprise but sharing profits and losses equally, since the lesser investor was the 'working partner' who accompanied the goods and did the actual work. These arrangements were not considered usurious; for, although guaranteed interest was forbidden, the Church was satisfied when there was a chance of loss as well as gain—for example, through loss of a cargo.

There were hundreds of such partnerships. They were initially made for short terms, usually for a single voyage, and involved a few persons. The more investing partners who could be found, however, the greater were the potential profits and the more diffused the risks. Thus in the thirteenth century some businessmen who had international connections developed partnerships that amounted to joint-stock companies. They were made for a long term, usually several years, after which time the arrangement could be liquidated or

---

[22] A. Derville, *L'Économie française au Moyen âge* (Paris, 1995), 201.

renewed. These 'super-companies'[23] are associated with the Italian interior cities, whose business linked the Mediterranean towns with north-western Europe through participation in the Champagne fairs; then, after the beginning of direct voyages from the Mediterranean to the North Sea ports in the late thirteenth century, they maintained resident colonies in the major cities. Since the greatest banks were based on merchant companies, a strong basis in exchange of goods was a prologue to banking. Much of the impulse for banking came from papal business, especially at Siena and Florence.

Most of the companies had investments mainly from powerful families and their clients (the *corpo* or 'body') during the twelfth century, but in the thirteenth they were transformed by taking deposits (the *sopracorpo*) from outsiders. When the Peruzzi Company was reorganized in 1300, 60 per cent of its capital was held by seven members of the Peruzzi family, the rest by other wealthy Florentines. The 'super-companies' bought wool, grain, oil, wine, and other necessities, sometimes paying the growers years in advance and thus getting an advantage over the competition. The Florentine companies controlled a huge grain trade from southern Italy, involving much more than was needed to feed Florence, and accordingly re-exported to other grain-poor regions of the Mediterranean. Southern Italy became a major market for cloth manufactured in Florence. The three greatest Florentine companies, the Bardi, Peruzzi, and Acciaiuoli, invested in overseas trade and merchandising at the fairs, but all except the Acciaiuoli also made loans to north European princes. Their security for the loan consisted of commercial concessions, such as the right to collect taxes and tolls and operate mints, export licences and monopolies. Before the fourteenth century most merchants accompanied their goods in transit or sent trusted agents, but the changes in commercial techniques made it possible for businessmen to become more sedentary.

The exchange of goods also made movement between coinages very important. Before the fourteenth century money-changing was more often done as a sideline by the great companies than by independent operators, but by the twelfth century in Genoa and other Italian cities money-changers were accepting deposits repayable

[23] E. S. Hunt, *The Medieval Super-Companies: A Study of the Peruzzi Company of Florence* (Cambridge, 1994).

on demand. Obligations were often handled simply by making book transfers between the accounts that debtor and creditor had at the same money-changing firm without transferring coin. The exchange banks usually kept about one-third of their deposits on hand to satisfy demand, investing the other two-thirds.

Piacenza, Genoa, Siena, and Florence were the earliest cities to use the contract of exchange, which was the dominant instrument of their transactions until around 1300. Exchange contracts were necessary for northerners at the fairs to buy spices from Italians and for Italians to buy northern wool and cloth. They could also disguise loans by concealing the interest in the exchange rate, which satisfied the Church's criterion of risk, since it could move up or down. Occasionally interest was stated openly. A Genoese letter of exchange of 1252 was payable at Troyes in Champagne, then two months later repayable at Genoa, in both cases at a stated rate; the total interest in three months was 47.06 per cent.[24]

The successor of the exchange contract was the bill of exchange. The earliest surviving example is a Genoese notarial contract of the late twelfth century. Most users were Italians, although merchants from all regions except Germany and Scandinavia were drawn into the network through the Champagne fairs. The borrower could buy a bill that was repayable in another coin at a stated interval in the future, most often six months, and in another place, most often where the coin in which the bill would be paid was legal tender. The bill was addressed to a business partner or creditor of the buyer, and payment was made through a bank. Interest was concealed in the exchange rate, which could change unpredictably and thus involved risk. The bill was a very flexible instrument, for it could be used to lend money, to pay for goods, and also simply to speculate on the exchange rate.

In the late thirteenth century the companies at the Champagne fairs were permitting overdrafts on accounts, another means of extending credit and an important foundation of banking. By 1330 merchants doing business in the leading centres of international exchange, such as Florence, Barcelona, Avignon, and Bruges, had what we would call bank accounts at the local exchange. Such credit instruments, as fiduciary money, extended the available supply of

[24] Case cited by Derville, *L'Économie française*, 203.

money even when, as happened in the fourteenth century, there was a dearth of coin.

The Italians pioneered other innovations in the thirteenth century that were in common use by 1330, including cheques and insurance contracts. Double-entry bookkeeping originated in Italy in the late thirteenth century: parallel columns, one each for assets and debits, were used instead of separate lists or ledgers for the two.

The fairs

The great international fairs began in the second half of the twelfth century. There were six mature fair systems in the thirteenth century: in northern Italy, England, Flanders, Champagne, and the lower and middle Rhine. Further east and south, fair systems were developing that would assume many of the same functions for the economic development of those areas in the fourteenth century that the older ones provided for the West in the thirteenth. The fairs received privileges from princes, which specified times of the year and duration of the fairs, the 'infrastructure' such as inns, security arrangements for transient traders, and a 'clear hierarchy of market opportunities' in the region of the fair, where merchants visiting them could also trade without being required to go through the intermediary of local brokers. Most fairs were in or on the edge of areas producing exportable crafts or raw materials. They were thus an intermediate stage between the diffused commercial networks of the early Middle Ages and the situation after the early fourteenth century, when most exchange took place in centrally located cities that served as successors to the fairs.[25]

The Flemish fairs are mentioned early, and by 1200 a cycle of five fairs, each lasting thirty days, was held every two months between the end of February and the beginning of November; wool and cloth were the main products sold. Intervals of two to four weeks between the fairs permitted merchants visiting them to return home or visit

[25] F. Irsigler, 'Jahrmärkte und Messesysteme im westlichen Reichsgebiet bis ca. 1250', in P. Johanek and H. Stoob (eds.), *Europäische Messen und Märktesysteme in Mittelalter und Neuzeit* (Cologne, 1996), 12–13, including quotation.

other fairs. Obligations incurred at the Flemish fairs could be paid at a later fair in the cycle or at one of the Champagne fairs. The Flemish fairs declined only when Bruges became a year-round market at the end of the thirteenth century. Similarly the English fairs were creations of the twelfth and thirteenth centuries. The regional fairs handled mainly agricultural goods, but six (Winchester, Boston, Bury St Edmunds, St Ives, Northampton, and Stamford) were held for several weeks at a time and served as places where foreign merchants could deal with local producers without having to visit the countless village markets. The English fairs, too, developed credit mechanisms with deferred payments in the cycle that were similar to what the Champagne fairs provided on an international scale. The foreigners generally bought wool and sold luxuries.[26]

The famous Champagne fairs originated as local agrarian marts, then were transformed around 1175 when the count of Champagne gave privileges to foreigners. At precisely this time, when the supply of money was increasing rapidly, Italians began visiting the fairs, and Flemish and northern French cloth began its conquest of the luxury market. Six fairs were held, lasting six weeks each, in four places (two each at Provins and Troyes, each of which produced cloth for export, and one each in Lagny and Bar-sur-Aube, which did not). During intervals between the fairs merchants could return home with their acquisitions or visit a regional fair before returning for one of the later fairs of the trading season.

Although most merchants who visited the fairs were transients, the Italian cities established consulates for their resident colonies in the fair cities, which from 1278 chose a single captain to handle their relations with outsiders; the Provençal and Languedoc merchants quickly followed suit. Italian merchant banking houses had offices in the fair cities, and contracts that were engaged elsewhere were often paid at one of these branches. The Flemish merchants had an interurban Hanse of the Seventeen Towns, but it lacked the firm organization of the Italians. Some Italians remained permanently in Champagne and intermarried with the local urban elites. Terricus Teutonicus, a Cologner who settled at Stamford, was there primarily for the cloth trade, but he was also involved in beer brewing and in

[26] Britnell, *Commercialisation of English Society*, 89–90.

the wool, spice, and horse trades, and he owned a London wine cellar and considerable property at Stamford.[27]

Since the Italians at the fairs were buying mainly English wool and Flemish cloth but were selling spices, cotton, and other eastern luxuries, northern Europe in the thirteenth century had an adverse balance of payments with Italy. Until the development of negotiable instruments in the thirteenth century, northern merchants had to take silver in addition to their goods to the fairs, since they were buying a greater value of goods than they sold. This was obviously dangerous and inconvenient. Thus the fairs had a pioneering role in the development of new commercial techniques. Money-changing was an important part of their business. Notarial instruments, promissory notes payable at a later fair, and book transfers were used to facilitate exchange transactions. The 'fair letter' amounted to a negotiable promissory note that acknowledged one merchant's debt to another, payable at a later fair in the annual cycle. The last fair of the year, at Troyes, became a clearing house, but obligations could be carried across years. A 'court of the fairs' adjudicated debt litigation and developed a generally applicable merchant law. If a debtor refused to accept its jurisdiction or refused to pay and his home town or state protected him, the officials of the court could interdict not only the offender but also his fellow citizens from selling and buying at the fairs. Their goods could be seized for up to the value of his debt.

The 'commercial revolution' of the late thirteenth century?

Important changes become apparent in the late thirteenth century that signal the late medieval economic crisis. Population had grown beyond the capacity of existing agricultural technology to feed it. The climate also began worsening at the turn of the fourteenth century, affecting food production. Population was declining in parts of Italy in the late thirteenth century, in the north shortly after 1300, particularly after the devastating famine of 1315 and the subsequent plagues. By

---

[27] N. Fryde, *Ein mittelalterlicher deutscher Grossunternehmer: Terricus Teutonicus de Colonia in England, 1217–1247* (Stuttgart, 1997).

1330 all parts of western Europe had substantially lower populations than in 1270.[28]

Signs of an overheated economy mounted. Interest rates at the Champagne fairs declined sharply after 1245. The large cities of Europe almost without exception experienced food shortages, which led in Italy to even stricter repression of the *contado* in order to extract more grain from the countryside. Violent conflicts after 1280 led to some broadening of the membership on town councils. By 1320 most city councils in the economically developed parts of Europe were chosen on the basis of guild affiliation; but, given that most nominally artisan guilds were dominated by merchants who furnished the raw materials of the trade to those who actually practised the craft, the result was something less than artisan control.

Some have seen yet another 'commercial revolution' in the late thirteenth century succeeding that of the late twelfth. There are two obvious signs. First, the mines whose opening had provided the liquidity for the great changes of the thirteenth century were becoming exhausted, and before 1320 a serious shortage of bullion was being felt in an economy that had become accustomed to a limitless supply of coin. Yet the trading structure that had developed in the thirteenth century was so strong, in the use of fiduciary money and negotiable instruments, that patterns of interregional trade were modified but not altered fundamentally. Trade became more reciprocal, particularly in the case of the Italians in England: prior to 1300 the English merchants had amounted to middlemen for the Italians, conveying their goods from the ports to and from the fairs in the interior, but by the middle of the fourteenth century most of the crucial wool export was in native English hands.

Secondly, regular voyages between the Mediterranean and the north began when the Genoese alum galleys began visiting the northern ports in 1277, returning with English wool. The ships used for Atlantic voyages could carry larger cargoes and move goods more cheaply than was possible in the overland trade leading to Champagne. The fairs accordingly declined, although not sharply, and they maintained their importance as banking centres until the 1320s. Granted that it required some years before this meant large-scale movement of

[28] W. C. Jordan, *The Great Famine: Northern Europe in the Early Fourteenth Century* (Princeton, 1996).

goods, since only a few boats came per year, the Genoese were coming to Bruges and London almost annually by 1300. Over the long term goods that previously had been largely in inter-Mediterranean commerce now came to the north in profusion, leading to an elevation of the standard of living for those in the declining population who survived, particularly after the onset of the great plagues.

The Italians became more conspicuous at Southampton, but they docked by preference at Sluis, the outport of Bruges. Cloth production in both Ghent and Ypres declined sharply around 1320; evidently the major problem was the loss of the market of cheaper grades to Italians, who now had easier access to English wool. This led to the Flemings concentrating on luxury cloth thereafter. Furthermore, just when the Italians began visiting the north directly rather than dealing with Flemish merchants at the fairs, the merchants of the German Hanse set up resident offices at Bruges, which thus became the proverbial 'marketplace of the medieval world'.[29] With the nearly simultaneous establishment of Italian, German, and Castilian colonies at Bruges, the northern and southern economies were linked more commodiously than through the fairs.

In summary, during the central Middle Ages the production of agricultural surpluses, the expansion and intensification of settlement, the movement of Europeans outside the Roman and Germanic heartland, and a growing demand for luxuries by the ruling elites led to a hierarchically ordered market economy and the integration of Europe as an economic region. Western Europe produced far more food in 1330 than in 980, and the relative increase in commercial activity and industrial production was even greater. Fuelled by a quantum increase in the volume of coin in circulation, the development of new credit mechanisms and by increasing sophistication of transportation technology, an 'infrastructure' was born that gave birth to commercial capitalism, fixed the essential contours of the urban map of Europe and established the service or tertiary sector as a significant component of the production and exchange of goods.

---

[29] R. Häpke, *Brügges Entwicklung zum mittelalterlichen Weltmarkt* (Berlin, 1908).

3

Politics

Björn Weiler

The central Middle Ages witnessed dramatic political change. Within a few centuries, Latin Europe was transformed from a society deeply rooted in the Carolingian revival of classical Roman values and institutions into one that, despite its many fundamental differences, foreshadowed the concerns, the organizational mechanisms, and the ideologies of the early modern period. At the same time, underneath this rapid change, continuities remained. The aim of this chapter is to highlight this complexity, and it will do so by sketching out some common norms of political life in Latin Christendom during this period.

The political geography of Europe

Let us begin by contemplating the political map of the medieval West (see Introduction). In 900, few of the political entities with which we are familiar from the later medieval or the modern period existed. There was no kingdom of France as such (although there was, of course, a *Gallia* and a *Francia*), and no Holy Roman Empire, but rather an ill-defined *imperium*, divided among the descendants of Charlemagne, but still ruled by them. In Iberia, the Christian polities were largely confined to an inhospitable stretch of land north of the River Ebro, while in Italy Franks, Lombards, Muslims, and Byzantines

This chapter owes much to the outline that Timothy Reuter devised for it before his death. (B.W.)

vied for political control. In England, the hegemony recently established by the house of Wessex under Alfred the Great (871–99) came under threat by internal dynastic squabbles, and Danish and Viking invasions. As for Scotland, Wales, or Ireland, Scandinavia or central Europe, the evidence remains too fragmentary to reach any clear understanding of what their political organization may have been like.

Four hundred years later, this map had changed beyond recognition. Charlemagne's empire had disappeared. New polities emerged: the kingdom of Portugal was established in 1139, and that of Sicily in 1130. Stephen, on converting to Christianity, also assumed the title of a king of Hungary in 1000 (see Chapter 6), and in 1318 the duke of Poland was made a king by Pope John XXII. In other regions of medieval Europe kings had been able to stabilize their power and drive out princely rivals—as perhaps best exemplified by the case of the Canmore dynasty in Scotland, which between the eleventh and the thirteenth century subdued not only its western neighbours in Galloway, but also expanded into the distant north and the formerly Norse regions of the Orkneys and the Western Isles. A similar process of consolidation occurred in Scandinavia from the tenth century onwards (see Chapter 6). The core of the Carolingian *imperium* experienced a similar transformation. By 1225 much of West Francia came under the control of the Capetian monarchy, established in 987, which, from the late twelfth century onwards, entered a period of unprecedented territorial expansion, both within the borders of its kingdom, and against its neighbours, and which had become the dominant political force in western Europe by the end of our period. The rulers of East Francia, on the other hand, had taken over the mantle of imperial lordship and presided over a loosely structured 'Holy Roman Empire', which encompassed the modern countries of Germany, the Netherlands, Austria, the Czech Republic, Switzerland, parts of eastern France, and most of northern Italy, and which stretched from Hamburg to Pisa, from Lyon to Prague.

These kingdoms clearly were not 'nation states' in any modern sense. There were polities such as Sicily, with Norman French, German, Byzantine, North African, and Italian elites and subjects, or England after the Norman Conquest of 1066, which combined a Norman royal dynasty with Flemish, Breton, Manceau, and Angevin nobles, ruling over an Anglo-Saxon subject population. In others, ethnicity was less of a defining issue than religious affiliation, as, for instance, in the kingdoms of Iberia with their large Muslim population, or in Hungary, where the Árpád dynasty ruled over Christians, Jews, Muslims, and pagans. This also applied to the core of western Europe, and the Capetian kings of France, for instance, faced a situation in which their subjects in the south viewed those in the north as aliens, where they spoke different languages and followed different legal and political customs. Similarly, in the German heartlands of the Holy Roman Empire, regional aristocracies viewed each other suspiciously. In 1073, for instance, the decision of Emperor Henry IV to man his castles in Saxony with knights from Swabia was one of the factors contributing to the Saxon uprising that nearly cost him his throne. People frequently defined their communal identity in terms of regional rather than regnal or national affiliation.

Moreover, individual Europeans could belong to a variety of networks that superseded such modern constructs as the nation. These could include trading links, like those that in the twelfth and thirteenth centuries brought about permanent English colonies in Valencia or Cologne; and institutional affiliations—after all, many monastic houses had a variety of bonds with those in other kingdoms, with some religious orders, like the Cistercians, very much priding themselves on their transregnal nature—and ecclesiastical structures: Saint Anselm, archbishop of Canterbury (1093–1109), had previously been abbot of Bec in Normandy, but had been born and brought up in Aosta in Lombardy, while Bishop (Saint) Hugh of Lincoln (c.1140–1200) originated from Burgundy. Equally, members of the aristocracy could be active across the borders of several kingdoms. In the thirteenth century, the Montfort family (from Montfort-l'Amaury near Paris) was active in the kingdom of Jerusalem, in Cyprus, Italy, northern and southern France, and England, and the counts of Savoy held important positions in Burgundy, Italy, and Germany, while also being related to successive popes and emperors, as well as the kings of England, France, and Sicily. Kingdoms and regnal identities existed, as we will see, but they formed part of a complex web of affiliations and communities, and defy categorization along modern concepts of statehood or nationhood.

This gradually began to change near the end of our period, and perhaps most famously in the case of England, where, in 1258, the English barons rebelled against their king and demanded that he draw his advisers and officials from among the *homines naturales*, the natives of England. At the same time, the fact that this movement was led by Simon de Montfort (d. 1265), a Frenchman, should warn us against viewing these events from too modern a perspective. The English barons did not invoke a feeling of English ethnic identity, but sought to impose limits upon the degree to which the king could draw on those from outside the ruling elite in running the kingdom. The aliens in question were not foreigners *per se*, but the king's Poitevin and Savoyard relatives, and the *homines naturales* the descendants of French warriors who had shared in the process of conquest and colonization since 1066. We encounter a more familiar phenomenon in the case of Bohemia and parts of North Wales, where issues of language and cultural tradition led to a more clear-cut definition of ethnic identity. The princes of Gwynedd sought to subdue their Welsh rivals by claiming that they alone could maintain the independence of *Pura Wallia*, of Welsh Wales—defined by its language and legal traditions—against the king of England, while in Bohemia the respective roles of the king's German and Czech subjects became the subject of heated debate in the early fourteenth century.

Finally, kingdoms and principalities emerged and disappeared again. In 1016, for example, England had been absorbed into a Scandinavian empire straddling the North Sea, while, near the end of our period, Scotland nearly ceased to exist as an autonomous political entity when, in 1296, King Edward I (1272–1307) incorporated it into the realm of England. It was not until the 1320s that the realm of Scotland gained international recognition again when Pope John XXII recognized the kingship of Robert Bruce (1306–29). Similarly, territories could be divided among a ruler's relations, as in the late twelfth century, when Henry II (1154–89), contemplated dividing England (with Normandy and Anjou), Aquitaine, Brittany, and Ireland among his sons. In his testament of 1250, Emperor Frederick II planned to share his possessions in the empire, Sicily, Jerusalem, and Burgundy among his sons. In twelfth-century Iberia, kingdoms such as Aragon, León, and Castile merged and re-emerged following marriages, succession disputes, and rebellions, while few of the colonial polities established in the Eastern Mediterranean during the twelfth and thirteenth centuries—such as the kingdom of Jerusalem, or the duchy of Athens—lasted for more than a century.

Alongside all this, concepts of imperial lordship, as a secular institution standing alongside the papacy and with similar claims to universal authority, while experiencing a renaissance in political thought
by the end of our period, began to decline as an organizing model
in practice. While in the tenth and eleventh centuries emperors might
have exercised a sort of hegemony across the West, this rarely translated into a claim to exercising actual political power over other
kings—unless they shared a border with the Empire—and was often
a matter first and foremost of prestige and standing. Both King Cnut
and William the Conqueror sought imperial backing for their conquests of England (Cnut by attending an imperial coronation, and
William by dispatching an embassy), but neither viewed this as essential for the legitimacy of their conquest. It heightened the moral
authority of their action, but was neither a legal nor a political
requirement. This began to change from the late eleventh century
onwards, and one factor in this process was the increasingly awkward
relationship between Holy Roman emperors and the papacy. After all,
of eleven emperors and emperor-elects who ruled between 1056 and
1245 only two—Lothar III (1125–37) and Henry VI (1190–7)—were
not excommunicated at some stage of their reign, while popes even
declared Henry IV (1056–1106) and Frederick II (1194/7–1250)
deposed, in 1076 and 1245 respectively. From the mid-eleventh century onwards, successive popes began to define the liberty of the
Church ever more widely, and opposition against lay influence on
ecclesiastical matters began to extend from hostility towards local and
regional potentates to include that of kings and even emperors. One
of the key principles that had underpinned the rebirth of empire in
the ninth and tenth centuries—that of the emperor as protector and
guardian of the Holy See—was being called into question. Another
contributing element was the emergence of new political entities that
had never been part of the Carolingian *imperium*, such as Portugal,
Poland, Bohemia, or Scotland, as well as the arrival on the European
political scene of dynasties and peoples, such as the Normans in
France, Sicily, Syria, and England. It was in these regions, too, that
short-lived attempts were made to adopt an imperial title, as by the
kings of Wessex in the tenth century and the kings of Castile in the
twelfth. However, unlike under the Carolingians and their East
Frankish or German successors, this imperial lordship did not define
itself as succession to the Roman Empire of Augustus or Constantine,

but as lordship over several kings or kingdoms (the other Anglo-Saxon and Welsh kingdoms in the case of Wessex, and León and Aragon in the case of Castile). Although their titles did not catch on, the role that these 'emperors' performed did, and by the thirteenth century some of the functions of imperial overlordship were exercised either by the papal court or by those rulers who exercised political hegemony within a given part of the medieval West—such as the Capetians within the regions bordering France, or the kings of England in Britain and Ireland. Instead of one universal empire, high medieval Europe faced a multiplicity of regional ones.

Qualifications for kingship

An important fact has emerged from this: the idea of monarchical rule as the 'natural' form of government. This did not mean that royal authority was equally strong in all parts of Latin Christendom. In fact, powerful comital or ducal dynasties, like those of Barcelona, Normandy, Provence, or Austria, were formidable players on the international stage, many of them exercising quasi-regal powers within their territories. Nonetheless, they still derived their political legitimacy from their relationship to a dynasty or realm to which they were subservient in name, though not always in deed. Similarly, the peasant community of Frisia and the Italian city republics still accepted that they were subject to royal or imperial authority. Finally, even the Icelandic experiment, which for several centuries had existed without royal authority, came to an end in 1262 when the king of Norway was invited to take control of the island by its inhabitants. By 1320, in short, virtually all inhabitants of western Europe were—in one way or another—ruled by kings. What, however, did this monarchical rule entail in practice, and how did its form and function change between the tenth and the fourteenth centuries?

Let us begin by addressing the question of how one became king. First of all, it helped being related to a previous monarch. In the tenth century, succession within kingdoms was at best loosely defined: most commonly, one member of the royal dynasty followed another, but there was no guarantee that it would be a ruler's eldest son or closest male relative. Both Emperor Otto I (936–73) and his grandson

Otto III (983–1002), for instance, faced rival claimants in their brothers, cousins, and uncles. The history of twelfth-century Norway was one long list of murdered and expelled kings, of rival siblings, distant cousins, legitimate or illegitimate progeny seeking to claim the throne. In fact, with the exception of Capetian France, which had the unusual fortune of an unbroken male dynastic line from 987 to 1328, most European kingdoms experienced some political turmoil over how exactly rules of succession were to work in practice. Although there was an increasing tendency to postulate primo-geniture as a guiding principle, where an eldest son (or the closest surviving male relative) would succeed to all of a lord's or king's possessions, what this meant in practice was still open to debate. We should also keep in mind the role of dynastic accidents: kings died without male heirs or heirs in general, and then the question arose as to how a new ruler was to be chosen. In 1135, for instance, the English barons had to choose between Matilda, daughter of Henry I (1100–35), and his nephew Stephen of Blois, with Henry's illegitimate son Robert of Gloucester, Stephen's elder brother Theobald, and King David I of Scotland also mooted as potential successors. Similarly, in 1199, the succession to Richard the Lionheart in England brought up the question of who held the better claim to the throne: his younger, surviving brother, John, or Arthur, the son of John's deceased older brother Geoffrey? In both cases, the rules of succession were elabor-ated in a prolonged process of dynastic wars and civil unrest. Still it is worth remembering that normally claimants were members of the deceased ruler's family, ideally by descent, but sometimes also by marriage. Occasionally claimants went to great lengths to claim dyn-astic legitimacy: when Sverrir claimed the Norwegian throne in 1177, for instance, his supporters spread word of a vision in which both the prophet Samuel and Saint Olaf, the patron saint of Norway, appeared to him and revealed that Sverrir was not, as he himself had believed, of plebeian stock, but rather the illegitimate son of a king. Rules were debated and open to interpretation.

The two exceptions to this rule, on the surface at least, were the Holy Roman Empire and the papacy. Both had, by definition, an elective form of rulership. Popes were chosen in a complex process, which, in combination with the principle of celibacy, ruled out a dynastic succession. Nonetheless, in reality the succession to the see of Saint Peter reflected the changing predominance of one group or another among the leading aristocratic families of Rome as much as the composition of the College of Cardinals (see Chapter 4). In the tenth and eleventh centuries, for instance, the dynasties of the Crescentii and the Tusculani provided the majority of popes, while even in the thirteenth century clans like the Conti, Frangipani, or Orsini dominated the College of Cardinals. Similarly, emperors were usually elected by the German princes, but in practice between 919 and 1254 a ruler normally ensured the election of his eldest son during his lifetime. Election to the imperial throne mattered only when no heir was available, as in 1002, 1024, or 1125, or when, as in 1197, the chosen heir was himself under age. It was only after Richard of Cornwall (king of the Romans 1257–72) failed to secure the succession of his son Henry that electoral imperial lordship developed its full potential. Not once between 1273 and 1376 did son follow father.

Secondly, it helped to be a man. Outside Byzantium, where empresses such as Zoë (d. 1050) and Theodora (d. 1056) occasionally ruled in their own right, queens normally assumed a prominent position only once they lacked a husband, and when they either acted as regents for their sons, or when marriage to them conferred dynastic legitimacy upon whoever seized the throne. This is not to deny the fact that some queens were powerful and historically significant political players, as, for instance, Theophano, the Byzantine princess married to Otto II, who for ten years (983–93) exercised the regency for the young Otto III; Queen Urraca (1109–26), the heiress of Castile and León, who resisted the wars of a spurned husband (the king of Aragon) and the misgivings of an aristocracy who refused to submit to the authority of a woman; or Blanche of Castile, the mother of Louis IX of France, who not only steered the realm through the troubled times of her son's minority (1226–30), but continued to exercise such a dominant influence on Louis's governance that it may not be unfair to say that his personal rule started only with her death in 1252. At the same time, for every Theophano or Blanche there was a queen like Margaret of Provence (d. 1295), Saint Louis's wife, who was deliberately ignored by her husband, or Isabella of Angoulême (d. 1246), the wife of King John of England (1199–1216), who was mistreated by her husband and ignored by those who organized the regency of her son Henry. Even Theophano had come to act as regent because serious doubts existed as to the seriousness with which young Otto's male relatives would resist the temptation of claiming the throne for themselves, while Urraca's power originated in the dynastic legitimacy she could convey onto her successive spouses. In fact, men were generally unwilling to accept the succession of women, which was one of the key difficulties facing Matilda when she wanted to succeed her father to the English throne in 1135. Women, in short, were believed to be able to exercise power through and on behalf of their male relatives only.

Needless to say, the reality of medieval queenship was more complex, and we must draw a distinction between queens regnant, including some queen mothers (like Theophano, Urraca, or Blanche), who actually exercised political authority in the absence of a monarch, and queen consorts (such as Isabella of Angoulême or Margaret of Provence), who were much more immediately dependent on the degree of authority their husband was willing to grant them. As in so many other areas of medieval life, it was the personality of the individual king or queen that decided the real extent of female power. We know, for instance, that Ottonian queens other than Theophano exercised considerable influence over their spouses and sons, while Emperor Conrad II (1024–38) even insisted on describing his queen as sharing in his exercise of royal power, while, in the twelfth century, Constance (d. 1198), the heiress of the Norman kingdom of Sicily, governed her inheritance with a considerable degree of independence from her husband, Emperor Henry VI (1190–7). Most commonly, queens and queen mothers appear as intercessors, as those who were approached to soften the king's rigour; they took a prominent role in exerting religious patronage; and they frequently oversaw the education and training of the ruler's heirs. Although important, these functions were also much less clearly defined and much less frequently commented upon than those of kings and princes, and we all too often hear of the political role of royal women only when they surpassed or when they violated the limits of their authority. The reality of medieval queenship, we may assume, lay somewhere between Conrad II's wife being described as equal partner in kingship, and the miserable marriage of Isabella of Angoulême.

The theory and practice of kingship

What were kings expected to do? In theory, the role and function of kingship remained largely unchanged during our period: a ruler had to be pious, just, prudent, act with valour in arms, never succumb to greed, ambition, or anger, always take the advice of his nobles, and be generous to his foes. The one new element that emerged in the course of the twelfth century was *mansuetudo*—that is, ease of manners. In the early thirteenth century, this was elaborated upon by Gerald of Wales, a former clerk for the Angevin kings of England: *mansuetudo* made a ruler's other virtues shine ever more brightly; after all, a true monarch was to be loved rather than feared, as the best means of ensuring that firm rule would not lapse into tyranny.[1] Later on during the thirteenth century, the growing reception of Aristotle (see Chapter 5), increasing access to a much more abstract theory of political power, was also reflected in a greater variety of theoretical treatises on the proper exercise of kingship, such as Vincent of Beauvais's *De Morali Principis Instructione* (*c.*1250), the anonymous *Libro de la nobleza y lealtad* (*c.*1250–60), dedicated to Ferdinand III of Castile (d. 1252), the Norse *Konungsskuggsjá* (*c.*1260), or Giles of Rome's *De Regimine Principum* (*c.*1277–9). All these texts shared an increasing emphasis on the degree to which kingship constituted an office that had been granted by God, and that brought with it temptations as well as duties and opportunities. Kings ruled their realm not as their private property, but on behalf of their subjects and with the obligation to work for the common good.

At first sight, it may seem a contradiction that our period also witnessed an increasing emphasis on the sacrality of kingship. This emphasis on the transcendental legitimization of power and its origins is evident, for instance, in the increasing use of the *Dei gratia* ('by the grace of God') formula in the self-titulation of kings, and the frequency with which kings and their chancery emphasized the divinely ordained nature of the monarch's office. This was taken furthest by the Capetian kings of France, who, from the late eleventh century

---

[1] 'De Principis Instructione Liber', *Giraldi Cambrensis Opera*, ed. J. S. Brewer *et al.* (8 vols., Rolls Series; London, 1861–91), viii. 9–12.

onwards, were credited with the ability to heal scrofula. From the twelfth century, this was combined with a representation of royal lordship, which, in the writings of Abbot Suger of Saint-Denis (d. 1151), sanctified the kingdom of France and the position of its rulers by linking both to the cult of Saint Denis (d. *c.*250), the 'Apostle of Gaul', and which, in the late thirteenth century, derived further sacral legitimacy from the canonization of Louis IX (1226–70). No other European monarchy went to similar lengths, although all of them witnessed efforts to emphasize the sacral nature of a dynasty or office. We can thus, for instance, witness a growing number of royal saints, especially in Hungary and Bohemia, but also in Scandinavia. Equally, the Ottonian rulers of Germany produced a series of saintly princesses, as well as Saint (Emperor) Henry II (1002–24) and 'Saint' Charlemagne, canonized in the twelfth century, while in England both Henry II and Henry III sought to foster the cult of Edward the Confessor (1042–66).

None of these cases led, however, to claims of dynastic sanctity. Rather, this emphasis on sacral legitimacy was aimed at underlining the standing and prestige of a ruler and his relatives by emphasizing the number of virtuous relatives their dynasty had produced in the past, to exemplify the divine favour that had been shown to them before, and to underline the degree to which the success of a ruler, his legitimacy and authority, were ultimately derived not from men, but from God alone. This was thus not a licence for royal power to be exercised without constraint. Rather, it was an attempt to bind those who held power to a set of abstract rules and principles. Power used unwisely or without due consideration would endanger not only the welfare of the realm, but also the souls of rulers and ruled alike. Notions of divinely inspired kingship certainly served to raise the numinous status of a ruler, but they also reduced the ability of the individual monarch to override fundamental principles of good kingship. Exactly because the royal office had been divinely ordained, an individual king might be deemed to have failed his duties not only to men, but to God, and could thus be more justly rejected and replaced.

This emphasis on the sacral nature of power went hand in hand with an unprecedented expansion in the tools and the apparatus of governance. Most importantly perhaps, an explosion in the use of literacy from the eleventh century onwards provided monarchs (as well as many local or regional lords) with a whole new set of mechanisms to perform their duties. One indication of the increasing use of literacy in royal government is the exploding number of charters produced by royal chanceries. In the Holy Roman Empire, for example, we have about 500 surviving charters for the fifty-year reign of Henry IV (1056–1106), about 1,200 for the thirty-eight years of Frederick Barbarossa (1152–90), and an estimated 2,600 for the thirty-eight years of Frederick II (1212–50). This rise in the production of royal documents from the eleventh to the thirteenth century remains remarkable, especially when we take into account that these figures do not always include letters and other shorter texts. Even the output of Frederick II's chancery pales, however, in comparison with that of his contemporary, Henry III of England. A rough estimate of the various *acta* recorded in the Pipe, Liberate, Close, Charter, and Patent Rolls for the reign of Henry III (1216–72) would come to about 30,000 individual items being issued every year. From the twelfth century onwards, rulers also began to utilize the increasing refinement of legal training provided at both cathedral schools and the emerging universities (see Chapter 5). More and more, monarchs drew on a legally trained pool of clerics to staff their administration. We thus also witness an elaboration of the administrative apparatus available to kings. In France during the reign of Philip Augustus, the number of *prévôtés*—administrative sub-units designed to oversee parts of the royal domain—increased to about 40–50 by 1200, while from the 1180s onwards *baillis*, or groups of itinerant royal officials, were appointed to sit in judgment in legal cases, explore royal rights, and administer royal prerogatives. Although England and France are perhaps the best-documented examples for this development, they were not the only ones. We know, for instance, that the kings of Norman Sicily produced a similarly elaborate system of record keeping and administration, as did many Italian cities, and, from about 1260 onwards, the rulers of Aragon.

This increasing administrative sophistication also strengthened the significance of the court, where the majority of records were produced and kept. The increasing bulk of business dealt with by royal courts (and some ducal or comital ones, like those of Flanders, Normandy, and Barcelona) required their expansion in size and personnel, and that they remained fairly static. One of the key developments of this period was thus the development of preferred residences: Paris in the case of the kings of France, Burgos in the kingdom of Castile, Palermo and Naples in Sicily, Kraków in Poland, or Westminster in England. This did not apply everywhere, of course: the sheer size of the Holy Roman Empire, as well as the lack of a tradition of 'central locations', required its rulers to keep touring the realm. At best, as under the Ottonian and Salian emperors (919–1125), some royal palaces or towns—such as Speyer, Bamberg, or Magdeburg—were visited more frequently than others, but this often changed from ruler to ruler, and no permanent royal centre emerged. Furthermore, despite successive attempts in the thirteenth century, no firm system of centralized royal control developed in the empire, and administration remained largely devolved to regional lords: there were no central archives, for instance, and the imperial charters that are still extant survive largely as copies kept by their recipients. This did not mean that rulers themselves remained static. In November and December 1268, for example, Henry III of England stayed at Westminster (until 9 Nov.), before travelling via Windsor (11–12 Nov.) and Guildford (15 Nov.) to Winchester, where he stayed 17–25 Nov., and Clarendon (28 Nov.–10 Dec.). He then visited the Cistercian house at Beaulieu (14–15 Dec.), the town of Southampton (16 Dec.), and Bishop's Waltham (19 Dec.), before returning to Westminster.[2]

This increasing bureaucratic sophistication also meant that the functions of rulers were more and more devolved to their officials, and that the codification of legal procedures and principles became a common phenomenon. With the exception of England, where the Conquest of 1066 presented a special case, few official attempts were made to codify laws and legal customs until the thirteenth century. Many of those compiled were produced by lawyers or private individuals, such as the so-called Laws of Edward the Confessor, William I, or Henry I in twelfth-century England, the *Très ancien coutumier* (*c*.1200 and *c*.1220), and the *Grand coutumier* (*c*.1250) in Normandy, or the *Sachsenspiegel* ('Mirror of the Saxons') compiled by Eike of Regpow in Germany in *c*.1220. That is, they were often academic treatises, without legal force, and frequently describing local customs rather than those of the realm as a whole. The lead, as so often, was taken by churchmen (see Chapter 5). It was not until towards the end of our period, however, that rulers and princes attempted

---

[2] *Calendar of Liberate Rolls Preserved in the Public Record Office*, vi. 1267–72 (London, 1964), nos. 461–560.

anything comparable. In 1231, for example, Frederick II issued the *Liber Augustalis*, a compilation of his and his predecessors' legal pronouncements as kings of Sicily, followed, in 1235, by the *Reichslandfrieden* (imperial land peace) of Mainz, which sought to codify basic principles defining the relationship between princely and royal authority. In France during the 1240s Louis IX began to compile royal rights, privileges, and laws, as did Edward I in England during the 1270s. Similarly, Alfonso X of Castile (1252–84) commissioned a series of legal codes: the *Fuero real* of c.1255, the *Especulo* of c.1261, and the *Siete partidas* from c.1265.

This did not necessarily engender legal uniformity. New law codes often took several generations to be accepted—the *Siete partidas*, for instance, were not fully used until the mid-fourteenth century—and certain groups within the realm, depending on their political clout, could easily maintain special rights and privileges. Thus, across Europe, certain laws did not apply to members of the clergy, while in France in 1315 members of the aristocracy united in provincial leagues to maintain their privileges. Similarly, the subjects of the Crown of Aragon could cite different municipal laws, and could demand to be judged according to their religious status, with different procedures and norms applying to Christians, Jews, or Muslims. Nonetheless, that these variant customs were codified confirms the growing importance of having rights and privileges put into writing.

The codification of legal customs could serve both to strengthen royal power and to resist it. While monarchs or magnates sought to extend their power by defining more clearly the services they were owed, their subjects could equally use codification to document and defend what they deemed to be their rights. This in itself was by no means a new development: many monastic houses had used similar means to document (or claim) their freedom from episcopal or noble control. Nonetheless, the desire of laymen to have their privileges and customs codified was given an added sense of urgency, as noble prerogatives were increasingly challenged by the burgeoning bureaucratic apparatus at the disposal of kings and many of the more powerful territorial lords. To some extent, the rise of administrative kingship from the twelfth century onwards created its own countervailing forces. The thirteenth century was also a period when kings were increasingly forced to concede charters of liberties and to codify the exemptions customarily claimed by their nobles. This formed the background, for instance, to Magna Carta in England (1215), the *Statutum in Favorem Principum* ('Statute in Favour of the Princes') in Germany (1232), and the privileges granted by the duke of Poland in 1284.

Part of the reason why nobles began to insist on having their rights codified was because the maintaining of justice and the maximizing of royal revenue were not always kept clearly separate. After all, the favourite sanction for the violation of laws was a monetary fine, directly benefiting the royal treasury (or the coffers of whoever controlled justice). This was stated explicitly in some of the surviving law collections from the eleventh and twelfth centuries, which presented a carefully constructed catalogue of fines, a proportion of which was to be handed to the king or his agents. The kings of England developed the system to particular perfection: even the wrong choice of phrase in legal documents triggered a fine, normally at the king's discretion. There was thus a good reason why Magna Carta contained a clause that justice was not to be sold or bought. Similarly, when, in Aragon in 1320, the so-called Shepherds' Crusade resulted in attacks on Jewish communities—in theory under the king's protection—this resulted in half-hearted efforts to protect Jews, and in an impressive bureaucratic exercise to extract fines from those localities where massacres had occurred. In addition, royal officials were called upon to oversee the administration of royal estates, and to collect dues and taxes from local communities. Many of these payments were defined on an *ad hoc* basis, and for much of the central Middle Ages general taxation remained a rarity. One exception was the Danegeld due to the kings of England until the early twelfth century, which originated in payments to fund the defence of the realm against the Vikings. From the thirteenth century onwards, developing mechanisms for financing the crusades led to a more regular taxation of ecclesiastical income, initially overseen by the papacy, but increasingly utilized by rulers to pay for their own expenses as well. General taxation of the laity, by contrast, remained rare. Rather, a system of voluntary aids and contributions continued from the tenth until well into the fourteenth century. Instead, rulers took to taxing commerce, including the Castilian sales tax of *alcabala*, introduced by Alfonso X, or the *moneda ferera*, paid since 1202 to the king of Castile in exchange for the promise that he would not debase his kingdom's currency.

To some extent this increasing emphasis on the fiscal benefits of royal power reflected the changing nature of warfare in our period. We can witness a move away from armies levied from noble or free landholders who owed military services to their monarch, and towards the hiring of professional soldiers who lent their services in exchange for pay. This was, of course, no linear development that led straight from the Anglo-Saxon *fyrd* or the German *Heerbann*—that is, the levy of the freemen of the realm—to the mercenary companies of the early fourteenth century. Rather, we can observe a mixture of forms of recruitment and reward, and the balance was frequently conditioned by the specific circumstances of a particular campaign or region. While, in the eleventh century, the Anglo-Saxon kings of England still recruited their armies from across the free men of the realm, some of their counterparts on the mainland hired troops in exchange for the promise of land or pay, as had been the case in Sicily, when the island's Muslim rulers sought to recruit Norman knights to fight on their behalf. The Byzantine emperors from the late tenth century maintained the Varangian Guard, which consisted largely of Scandinavian and Norman mercenaries. Nonetheless, from the twelfth century onwards, advances in military technology made warfare a much more uncertain and expensive undertaking, with campaigns getting longer, and requiring a greater range of military expertise. Kings and rulers thus had to spend larger amounts on provisioning their armies or purchasing materials for siege weaponry (and on strengthening the defences of their own castles). Equally, the equipment an individual knight had to procure became more expensive. In England, to give but one example, we witness a steady decline in the number of men owing knight-service, from about 3,000 in *c.*1100 to about 1,200 in *c.*1300. This shortfall in manpower had to be made good by hiring knights for pay. Many of the campaigns of the thirteenth century, such as those of Emperor Frederick II against the Lombard League, and even a number of crusades, were thus fought by knights who did so in exchange for monetary rewards. In fact, a number of aristocrats made a career out of selling their military expertise. Don Enrique, for instance, the younger brother of King Alfonso X of Castile, fought in the armies of the Muslim ruler of Tunis, was invited by the king of England to lead an invasion of Sicily, before joining Charles of Anjou (d. 1285) on his Italian campaign of 1263, which led to his election as a senator of Rome.

The rising significance of royal bureaucrats also led to a new phenomenon in the legitimization of political conflicts: the revolt not against the king, but against his evil advisers, and with the aim to control the selection of those individuals who ran the king's administration. That kings were asked to expel unsuitable advisers was not a new development: it had played a major part during the Investiture Controversy, when Pope Gregory VII listed Emperor Henry IV's reliance on morally corrupt members of the clergy as a token of Henry's own depravity, and in England later chroniclers frequently illustrated the tyranny of William Rufus (1087–1100) by his appointment of unsuitable advisers. Nonetheless, ultimately it was still the ruler's responsibility to choose good advisers, and if he picked morally corrupt officials the fault for doing so rested largely with him. This began to change from c.1200, and most dramatically so in England. From the civil war of 1215 onwards, the question of who administered the realm on the king's behalf became as important an issue as the political limitations imposed upon royal governance in Magna Carta. Henry III faced two serious rebellions, in 1233–4 and 1258–65. In both cases, most contemporaries (including the rebels themselves) exempted the king from responsibility for the state of the realm, and instead focused their attack on his chief ministers: in 1233–4, for instance, the rebels decided to plunder only the lands belonging to royal advisers, not those of the king himself. Similarly, the demands they made, and how they were recorded by chroniclers and annalists, focused not on the king, but on those who ran his administration: the turbulent state of the realm was the fault not of the king, but of the bureaucrats who cheated him as much as they oppressed his subjects. Equally, when in 1258 the barons demanded a reform of the realm, the issue was not that the king acted like a tyrant, but that his officials did, and that their selection thus ought to be controlled jointly by king and barons. This was a remarkable shift in emphasis compared to the eleventh and twelfth centuries, and as such highlights the increasing political (as well as financial and judicial) importance of royal administration: the fact that every new means that strengthened royal control also brought with it heightened resistance, and a new means by which that resistance could be translated into political action.

The community of the realm

Throughout this period, political power was exercised by a small elite, comprising, at best, 3–5 per cent of the overall population. What, then, about the remaining 95 per cent? As far as the rural population was concerned, various writers in our period sought to emphasize the responsibility those in power held towards the peasantry. We thus witness the elaboration of origin myths that—modelled on David's elevation from shepherd to king in the Old Testament—emphasized the humble origins of powerful families, most famously perhaps in the case of the Přemyslads of Bohemia, who traced themselves back to the peasant Přemysl, the mythical first ruler of Bohemia. In some cases, the care for the peasantry was ritually enacted, as, for instance, when in 1024 Emperor Conrad II demonstratively interrupted the procession prior to his coronation to do justice to a peasant, and in fourteenth-century Carinthia, where peasants symbolically humiliated the new duke as part of the installation ceremony. As far as their actual involvement in the day-to-day conduct of politics is concerned, that could take a variety of forms, frequently on a local level (see pp. 41–2, 54–6). Moreover, peasants could leave the lands of particularly oppressive lords, and we can, in fact, trace major population movements across Latin Christendom throughout this period. There may have been little formal provision made for the majority of the population to take part in politics, but they still possessed the means to counteract, thwart, or delay the actions of their superiors.

Furthermore, from the eleventh century onwards, a new and formidable challenge to the power of kings and territorial lords alike emerged in the form of urban centres (see also Chapter 2). These towns mattered because of their economic power and their population resources. One contemporary observer, for instance, estimated that after 1158 the income Emperor Frederick Barbarossa received from the rights he claimed over the Italian cities reached £30,000 per year. Not surprisingly, therefore, towns began to play a greater part in politics, too. In 1167 Milan took the lead in forming an alliance of cities, the Lombard League, whose aim it was to resist Frederick Barbarossa's expansion of power in Italy, while in Castile, England, and Aragon representatives of urban communities became regular attendants at parliaments and consultative meetings. Some towns became major players in their own right, and the Italian maritime cities soon took a significant role across the Mediterranean. In fact, by the thirteenth century many of these towns came to rule over sizeable territorial empires themselves. Rulers did not always eye these developments favourably; Emperor Frederick II, for instance, not only banned towns from taking in new citizens without the permission of their princely neighbours, but also outlawed confederations of towns. Nonetheless, the sheer financial might towns could muster soon made them a much sought-after ally in politics, and we can see more and more frequently how a ruler's political power depended on the support he was able to muster from within the urban centres of his realm. During the dynastic wars in late-twelfth-century Poland, the civil war in England of 1215–17, the German Interregnum of 1257–72, or the Sicilian Vespers in 1282, success depended on controlling key cities, rather than the country at large. As always, there were, of course, exceptions to this rule: apart from Paris, few French towns managed to reach a position similar to those of the Rhineland in Germany or Lombardy in Italy. Equally, the twelfth-century kings of Sicily suppressed communal movements within their own realm, and went to great lengths to ensure that they and their officials oversaw the internal governance of urban centres, rather than the citizens themselves. Neither Palermo nor Naples was thus able to match the degree of influence and independence exercised by London, Cologne, or Milan.

What, however, about the traditional elites? How did the upper and middling ranks of the aristocracy engage in politics? To them, politics certainly mattered, but it was just as often politics on a local as on a regnal or international level. Much depended on status and influence—quite frequently, keeping one's peasants in order, checking the territorial ambitions of a neighbouring prince or town, or dealing with the variety of administrative tasks small lords faced was probably political engagement enough. These more localized concerns, as well as the manner in which the wider world of regnal or international politics could have an impact on small and middling aristocrats, is illustrated by the documents that Count Sigiboto IV of Falkenstein, active primarily in the archdiocese of Salzburg, assembled before setting out on Frederick Barbarossa's Italian campaign of 1166. These included a collection of conveyances, a manorial register, two texts confirming the free legal status of the count and his family, a letter ordering the assassination of a rival, and a family portrait.[3] The great princes and magnates of the central Middle Ages straddled the regional and the regnal. On the one hand, they had to engage with the affairs of the realm at large, while, on the other, they found that their position in dealing with their dependants and less powerful neighbours frequently resembled that of the king in relation to them, and they found themselves bound by similar expectations, restraints, and mechanisms of governance.

One of the constants of our period was the role attached to the process of consultation between kings and nobles, and this extended to almost every aspect of political and royal life, and included marriages of a ruler or his family as well as matters of war, justice, finance, or ecclesiastical administration. This had ideological as well as practical reasons. After all, as we have seen, kingship was perceived as an office, with the ruler expected to act for the welfare of the realm. The process of consultation was one means by which this communal aspect of royal power could be demonstrated. Kings made their decision only after taking the advice of those who were to be bound by their decision. This leads to our second point: taking the advice of one's leading subjects was above all a matter of public confirmation, and it created a greater number of witnesses for an agreement or a decision. In fact, one can often gauge the importance of a particular act by the occasion when it was made public. Quite frequently, this involved important religious feast days, such as Christmas or Easter, when a larger number of prelates and nobles attended a king's court. The more splendid the occasion, the larger and more prominent the list of those witnessing a decree. Furthermore, those participating in these assemblies not only witnessed a decision, but by their presence also volunteered themselves to be called upon in future to enforce or corroborate it. In moments of political crisis we thus find rulers taking particular care to ensure that their claims and actions were corroborated by as many people as possible, and, if required, by as many assemblies as needed. In eleventh-century Germany, this could mean that rulers were not fully accepted until they had toured all the regions of their realm, while in twelfth-century England King

---

[3] J. B. Freed, *The Counts of Falkenstein: Noble Self-Consciousness in Twelfth-Century Germany* (Philadelphia, 1976).

Stephen in 1135 and King John in 1199–1200 traversed the realm to demonstrate both their royal status, and to force a public recognition of their succession from as many nobles, towns, and prelates as they could. Assemblies provided a ruler with advice and counsel, they symbolized the political structure of the realm, and they demonstrated the necessary public backing for important political decisions.

The form these consultative bodies could take varied across Europe. In Iceland, for instance, regional assemblies, the quarter courts, existed to deal with matters pertaining to the judicial administration of parts of the 'free state' (commonwealth), while at the annual althing*, attended by the chieftains of the four quarters of the island and their entourage, those issues were dealt with that had not been settled previously, or where important decisions concerning the community at large were negotiated. In Castile–León, on the other hand, the *cortes**, as it began to emerge from about 1187/8 onwards, consisted of elected representatives of the towns and royal officials who had been appointed by the king. Members of the aristocracy participated as royal officials, not as members of a—however loosely defined—body of royal vassals. That, by contrast, was one of the defining characteristics of English parliaments. Their membership could vary greatly, depending on whom the king chose to summon, and from the 1250s onwards they normally included elected representatives of the shires and royal boroughs, as well as barons, who included both major aristocratic landholders as well as the prelates of the realm and the heads of religious houses. Last but not least, in the Holy Roman Empire, consultative meetings or 'diets'* were called irregularly by the monarch, and no formalized criteria existed until the fourteenth century as to who was to participate in them. Partly because the exact composition of these bodies was at best loosely defined, we need to keep in mind that a full parliament consisted not only of those who had been called upon to attend, but also their attendants, relatives, and friends. The Icelandic althing, for instance, was as much a prolonged feast, an opportunity to trade goods, make payments, or arrange marriages, as it was one for debating issues such as whether to adopt Christianity or how to reform the community's legal organization; imperial diets, like the one at Mainz in 1184, included tournaments, the knighting of the emperor's sons, and a feast of legendary proportions; while even English parliaments were as much a social as they were a political occasion. In 1270, for instance, King Henry III ordered the citizens of Southampton to provide 200 casks of wine for an imminent parliament, 'which cannot be celebrated without wine'.[4]

The range of business conducted by such assemblies changed throughout this period, as did the importance attached to them. To some extent, this reflected the increasing scope of royal power as well as the increasing need for funds on the part of kings. While in the tenth and eleventh centuries the chief business of such assemblies had been matters of law and political organization, by the thirteenth century issues of finances became more and more significant. The Castilian *cortes*, for example, was a forum where royal demands for money were granted in exchange for the confirmation of privileges, while in the Empire, from 1277 onwards, Rudolf of Habsburg called assemblies by towns and others directly subject to the king's authority to have their agreement in raising levies from them. Increasingly, such public assemblies became one of the chief means by which royal policy could be discussed, and throughout the thirteenth-century West a demand to hold such assemblies on a regular basis, and to define more clearly what their role and function were, became evident. The most notorious example for this was probably England, where in 1258 the king was forced by a group of rebellious barons to promise a regular holding of parliaments, and to cede control over his government to his barons and to parliament. Although the extent to which parliament was intended to take control in England was unusual, the greater significance attached to public assemblies in governing the realm or kingdom was not. Alfonso of Castile equally had to concede a greater role to the *cortes* in the 1260s, while in 1284 the duke of Poland had to issue a privilege in which he promised to call a consultative meeting at least once a year.

Similar mechanisms applied to the regional and local level. In Austria, for instance, the death of the last Babenberger duke in 1246 initiated a period during which a loosely structured assembly of knights, town representatives, heads of monastic houses, and bishops took over much of the running of the duchy; by the end of the thirteenth century, it had begun to have a decisive say in who could claim to act as duke of Austria. Equally, in England shire and manorial courts brought together the most important political officers

---

[4] *Calendar of Liberate Rolls, 1267–72*, no. 1341.

and landholders in a given region, and provided a forum to discuss regional and local concerns, as well as issues of significance to the kingdom as a whole, with similar mechanisms in place in most towns and cities across the medieval West.

The means and ends of political communication

Having considered the institutional and organizational framework of politics in the central Middle Ages, let us now turn to the means and ends of political action. What were the tools people had at their disposal to express their demands, beliefs, and concerns, and to what ends were they employed? Let us begin by looking at the process of communication. After all, people had to convey their aims, their demands, and complaints; they had to consult, advise, and sometimes even debate. All this normally involved an audience: of rulers, their courts, advisers, and attendants, but also the friends, lords, subjects, clients, and officials of the individual who had a complaint, request, or point to make. Politics, in short, were as much a public affair then as they are today. However, for this process of communication to work, certain mechanisms had to be elaborated to ensure that chaos was avoided and the right political order of the world maintained. Not everyone could easily approach everyone else, and certain rules of behaviour had to be obeyed. These rules, in turn, could be used to express messages: the way an individual acted, the number of attendants he had with him, how he approached others, the occasions he chose to do so, the rituals or ceremonies that were conducted in the process, all this (often called 'symbolic communication' by modern historians) informed bystanders of the status of the persons involved, of the business they had to conduct, of their aims and objectives. We will return to a number of these points as this section continues, but at this stage we ought to focus on two key aspects of symbolic communication: its public nature, and the ease with which it allowed complex legal, social, theological, and political messages to be condensed into one highly visible act. The act of knighting, performed with increasing regularity from the eleventh century

onwards, provides a good example. It demonstrated a clear hierarchical relationship, it denoted the new knight's legal status, his
coming of age and ability to exercise fully his functions and duties as
a lord, and it confirmed his membership of the military and social
elite of his community, while also reminding him of the moral obligations and duties this entailed. The public handing over of a belt or
ring, or of other insignia of knighthood, conveyed all these concepts
and messages much more poignantly and publicly than any written
document would have done. Finally, it also provided numerous witnesses who could be called upon in future to confirm the act and the
obligations it represented. Because of this public nature, and because
of the political and legal implications of such occasions, the exact
structure of rituals could be hotly debated. In 1162, for instance, negotiations about the terms of reconciliation between the citizens of
Milan and Emperor Frederick Barbarossa centred on the form in
which this submission was to be performed, and, in particular,
whether the Milanese were to encounter the emperor barefoot or
wearing sandals or shoes. The degree of humiliation expressed in
each version was directly related to the political consequences facing
those who performed them.

This increasing use of ritual and symbolic acts soon combined
with a familiar phenomenon: a desire to codify. Gestures and
encounters like the ones described posed particular problems: after
all, rituals were inherently ambivalent. When in 1013 Emperor
Henry II demanded that Duke Boleslaw Chobry of Poland carry the
emperor's sword, this was both an honour—someone was singled
out before others to perform a particular function—and a sign of
subservience by one ruler towards another. How could this balance
of meaning be defined? In the course of the twelfth and thirteenth
centuries we thus find increasingly elaborate ceremonials in communication between rulers—such as in the rituals surrounding the
homage that the kings of England had to perform to their French
counterparts for the lands they held in fief from their Capetian
neighbours, which aimed both to underline and to soften the hierarchical relationship thereby expressed. The act of homage might
thus not be performed by the king of England, but by his eldest son
(as in the cases of William, son of Henry I, in 1120, and Eustace, son of
King Stephen, in 1137). That way, the obligations they owed as dukes
of Normandy would be fulfilled, while, at the same time, their royal

status would not be undermined by having to perform an act that made them hierarchically inferior to the king of France. Even so, contemporaries realized that the dilemma at the heart of their relationship remained unresolved, and increasingly elaborate steps were taken to embed the act of homage in a public and ritual display of equality and friendship. In 1187, for instance, when Count Richard of Poitou (the future Richard the Lionheart) met King Philip Augustus, Richard's homage was surrounded by manifestations of his and Philip's amity and companionship, and included them sharing a bed and feeding each other. These acts were performed in public and before as many witnesses as possible, and should thus not be read as sexual encounters. Rather, they had been designed as public demonstrations of the friendship that tied Philip and Richard together, and that superseded their legal relationship as lord and man. On the other hand, and especially in thirteenth-century Germany, we find more and more written documentation that outlined exactly how public rituals were to be performed.

What was absent, however, was the attempt at systematization that we have encountered in the case of law codes and legal texts. The specific ritual to be performed in a given context may have been defined, but there was no equivalent of the Byzantine *Book of Ceremonies*, a treatise compiled in the late tenth century that claimed to give a detailed description of how ceremonies ought to be performed. That is, what exactly happened was a matter of negotiation and planning, rather than of following a clearly defined and unchangeable precedent, although such precedent was sometimes invoked, of course. We should thus not make the mistake of assuming that ritual and literacy excluded each other. Rather, the surviving evidence seems to indicate that the two frequently entered into a symbiotic relationship, with the one drawing and depending upon the other. Rituals enabled those who performed them to emphasize those elements in their relationship or position they wanted to be highlighted and made public. The same was true, for instance, of King Ladislas I of Hungary (1075–95), who was famously said to have refused to wear a crown. By doing so he demonstrated his humility and thus his moral suitability to occupy the throne. That, in turn, legitimized the act of usurpation that had made him king: unlike his brother Solomon, whom he had driven from the realm, he had the moral make of a proper ruler.

Like any tool of communication, however, ritual, ceremonial, and symbolism were inherently ambivalent. The meaning and performance of ritual were open to challenges, and could be rejected as well as accepted. In the case of dealings between the kings of France and their Norman vassals or between the Canmore kings of Scotland and their English neighbours, the exact meaning of the homage performed, and the power that this granted to those who received it, remained a point of conflict that was settled only when Philip Augustus of France seized most of the Angevins' French lands in 1204, and when Edward I set out to conquer Scotland after 1296. Moreover, rituals could be appropriated to mean something different from the context within which they had first been employed. In twelfth-century Sicily, for instance, Roger II sought to demonstrate his independence from Byzantine claims to overlordship by adopting some of the paraphernalia and ceremonial of Byzantine kingship. Rituals were not static, but developed in relation to the broader context within which they were performed. Equally, those who objected to the message or concept a ritual act was to convey could seek to disturb it. In 1268, for instance, the question of whether the men of London or those of Winchester were to provide the services of butler to the king resulted in a riot that forced Henry III to abandon a solemn ceremony of crown wearing. Finally, men could refuse to attend a meeting or assembly, and in 1073 Emperor Henry IV was forced to seek a compromise settlement with his opponents in Saxony when the German princes refused to attend a diet in which he had planned to have the Saxons condemned as traitors.

The ambiguity of ritual leads to a final point we need to consider— that is, the complex goals that politics were meant to achieve. Ultimately, it would be futile to try to distinguish clearly between material objectives (a desire for lands, castles, offices, or money) and a desire to meet abstract moral and ethical norms. More often than not it was impossible to separate the one from the other. If a lord attacked his neighbours, he never claimed that he did so for economic gain alone, but usually justified his action by arguing that he simply did what was necessary to defend his honour or his right, to protect his subjects or the Church. Equally, however, he would be unable to defend his honour or his dependants if he did not have the economic, military, or political resources to do so. This complex relationship is illustrated by the exercise of patronage, one of the chief means available to any lord for rewarding his followers, for recruiting new ones, and for assuring himself of their loyalty. Patronage certainly included palpably material benefits, such as grants of land and castles, of privileges, of positions of power. In fact, as for most of our period land and its proceeds were the chief sources of wealth, considerable pressure existed on monarchs and princes to make new properties available to their dependants. An inability to do so, or to reward them for losses they might have experienced, could cause considerable political difficulties, and was, for instance, a contributing factor to the problems facing King John of England after he had lost most of his possessions on the Continent in 1204. This was not, however, the only means at a monarch's or lord's disposal. Equally significant was one of the age-old tools of rulership: distributing the spoils of war. In fact, when first approached about claiming the Norwegian throne in 1177, Sverrir was said to have turned down the offer as he was too poor to reward his supporters, and too inexperienced to become a successful leader at war. In this context it is worth remembering that much of medieval warfare consisted of raiding parties, aimed primarily at weakening an opponent's economic basis of power. Consequently, the distribution of plunder and tribute assumed considerable political significance, especially in those regions like the Welsh Marches, the eastern regions of Germany or Bohemia, the crusader states or Iberia, where small-scale border warfare was a fact of everyday life. Material rewards mattered, and being able to provide or receive them was often a motivating factor in political actions. Moreover, they were one means by which abstract lordly virtues—generosity, justice, protecting one's inferiors—could be defined in practice.

Issues of status and prestige played, however, an equally prominent part in patronage relations. To some extent this was the case because the standing of one noble in relation to another was publicly demonstrated and expressed through their role in acts of representation. Prestige was visualized, for instance, through proximity to a lord or king, the functions with which he entrusted his followers in the performance of public rituals, the manner in which he asked for the counsel and advice of a particular person, or the tokens and gestures of friendship he displayed. Being invited to sit next to a lord, a king attending a feast given by a noble or bishop, the value and frequency with which presents were made or honours conveyed and confirmed mattered. Rank was demonstrated publicly, and it depended on being demonstrated frequently and lavishly. Equally, keeping someone waiting for several days before receiving him, as Pope Gregory VII did with Emperor Henry IV in 1077, for example, expressed dissatisfaction with and a loss in status for the latter, while, on the other hand, the willingness with which, in the 1230s, Henry III of England invited the bishop of Winchester, whose appointment he had bitterly fought and whom he had sought to prevent from entering his cathedral, to share his meal with and sit by him, symbolized the latter's restoration to favour.

Because of the public nature of its demonstration, a loss or increase in status could have palpable political consequences. Someone regarded as close to his superiors and on good standing with them would be more capable of rewarding his own followers; he was expected to be more successful in gaining grants and privileges, and to plead the case of his supporters. This should alert us to the fact that abstract concepts such as honour, for instance, could play as important a part in the conduct of medieval politics as economic or legal issues. After all, one's honour was the public expression of one's legal, political, social, and economic status. Furthermore, medieval men, too, could go to war for their beliefs. They went on crusade, they fought for the reform of the realm, and they took up arms to defend their king and kingdom against foreign invaders or their ancient liberties against royal encroachment. Abstract moral good was something by which actions and undertakings could be justified, and by which resistance could be legitimized. No rebel ever admitted resisting his king out of greed, a lust for power, or as a result of regional or dynastic rivalries, but always justified his actions by arguing that a king was unjust, impious, sought to oppress his people, or was unable to defend the realm. Success in medieval politics all too often depended on the ability to force one's position upon one's neighbours, peers, or subjects, but at the same time a system of values existed that was intended to channel the use of power, and to direct it towards accomplishing a greater good.

Last but not least, those engaged in politics were bound by a variety of personal bonds. These could include dynastic links (whether by blood or marriage), ties of friendship or dependence, bonds of rank or institution. Nobles and kings were expected to reward their friends, family, and followers, while at the same time balancing this against the need of their dependants as a whole. If they were too mean in their patronage, they would alienate the former, and if they were too generous, they violated their duty to protect and safeguard the latter. This problem was perhaps most pronounced in the case of rulers, and rebellions were frequently justified by the undue favour kings were accused of having shown to one group within the realm over another. This happened, for instance, in Saxony in 1073, in England in 1258, or in Bohemia in the early fourteenth century. Equally, personal ties might lead to conflicts of interest. Nobles normally formed part of a complex web of friendships, alliances, and family relationships, and frequently found themselves forced to choose between their friends and their lords. Monastic houses could face a not dissimilar problem, especially in the eleventh and twelfth centuries, when many were forced to choose between their ecclesiastical superiors and their secular patrons and relatives. The forming, strengthening, restoring, or destruction of such ties was a key element in the day-to-day conduct of politics. Kings, magnates, and nobles constantly sought to make new friends and keep their old ones, while trying to win over those who might have resisted them in the past and to isolate or terrorize those who might oppose them in future.

All this should warn us against too simplistic a view of the political structure of the central Middle Ages. Those involved in the conduct of politics, whether on an international, regnal, regional, local, institutional, or dynastic level, had to operate within a complex web of ideas, precepts, power relations, and harsh economic and social realities. More importantly, there was an inherent dialectic at the heart of medieval politics. Every means, every innovation or tool that provided a new way by which a lord or prince might increase his power at the expense of his peers and subjects, also gave the latter a new set of ideals against which to judge the performance of their rivals and lords, by which to legitimize resistance or through which to practise it. A greater emphasis on legal and administrative procedures strengthened the ability of those who could afford them to increase their economic and political power at the expense of their peers and neighbours, but the latter also gained a means by which to challenge them. More elaborate theoretical concepts of power certainly raised the standing of a particular group within society, but at the same time also imposed new obligations upon them, and gave their dependants the means to thwart and resist their ambitions. Negotiating the balance between privileges and obligations and defining what abstract values and concepts meant in practice was rarely a smooth or peaceful process. It was, however, what gave European society in the central Middle Ages its political dynamic.

4

Religion

Julia Barrow

Religion was one of the principal means of identification in this period. It provided many of the rituals that articulated social and political activity, and supplied a store of learning, transmitted orally, in writing, and pictorially. It was central to everyone's experience. Since in western Europe in this period the dominant religion was Christianity, this will receive most attention in what follows, but with discussion of other religions at the end of the chapter.

Sources

In terms of religious history the timespan covered in this book can be viewed as forming the end of the earlier Middle Ages, a period characterized by ritual, then a phase of transition lasting from the mid-eleventh to the mid-twelfth centuries, and finally the opening of a more bureaucratic and legalistic period beginning in the later twelfth century. This periodization is helpful provided that one remembers that it is conditioned by the pattern of source survival, and some remarks on sources are necessary at the outset.

The main changes observable in sources for this period are, first, an increase in the numbers of texts, and, secondly, a growing variety of types of text. These developments are especially marked from *c*.1100 onwards. For the study of the Church in the tenth and eleventh centuries, the principal sources are hagiographical and liturgical. Bishops and their activities, for example, are studied through 'lives' (biographies) of bishops and histories of dioceses made up of sequences of lives of bishops. Liturgical sources essentially consist of prayers, but can contain other information, for example, lists of benefactors and inmates in books known as *libri vitae* or 'books of life' (alluding to the great Book of Life in the Book of Revelation in which the names of the souls to be saved were recorded), allowing the historian to recreate the network of patronage of particular major churches. More purely administrative sources such as charters and law codes, though not lacking, are few by contrast with the period after *c.*1100, and tend to preserve tradition. The past recorded in charters and legal compilations might often be fictive—Bishop Burchard of Worms (1000–25), for example, in writing his *Decretum*, a compilation of rulings in ecclesiastical law, invented numerous sources—but the authority of tradition mattered, and perceived gaps in documentation were sometimes filled with forgeries in the belief that this was what earlier generations would have approved.

The most obvious difference between sources for the post- and pre-1100 periods is that far more exist for the latter: whereas, for Pope Gregory VII (1073–85), only about forty-five letters are preserved for each year of his pontificate, nearly 200 a year survive for Pope Alexander III (1159–81), and 730 for Innocent IV (1243–54). Quantity of documentation is not simply a question of survival. Mandates from popes and bishops to their subordinates became ever more numerous; the holding of synods (meetings) at every level in the Church hierarchy became more frequent, and so did the issuing of legislation, in the form of decrees of papal councils and the synodal statutes of thirteenth-century bishops. At the same time, those in authority began to make official copies of outgoing correspondence. More informal copies might also be made: papal mandates were often preserved for their legal content in collections, known as decretal collections, compiled by teachers of ecclesiastical law in the later twelfth century.

The temptation is to see the shift towards legal matters in the surviving sources as a movement away from ritual towards documentation. It was not quite so simple. Ritual continued to matter even while society became more eager to make use of the written word: indeed, the issuing of charters could be marked by ceremonial, and symbolism was built into documentation itself in the designs of the seals used for validation. A significant development was the emergence of professional lawyers in the twelfth century, while a less obvious, but more important, underlying change was the growth in population, which made the closer and more informal contacts of earlier medieval politics harder to maintain.

The Church's *ancien régime*: bishops and ritual *c.*1000

The principal figures of authority in the medieval Church were bishops, a word deriving from the Greek for 'overseer', each in charge of a territory called a diocese. Popes were themselves bishops, being bishops of Rome (the term 'pope' is a nickname meaning 'father'). One of the most significant ecclesiastical developments in the period was a change in the role and status of the pope, from being a figure respected because he was the successor of the chief apostle, Saint Peter, and the guardian of the latter's shrine, to being the fountainhead of authority within the Latin Church, and head of the final ecclesiastical court of appeal, to whom all the Church turned for rulings on disputed points of law or dogma. He became the symbolic head of western Christianity itself, necessary for those moments, such as the organization of a crusade, when western Christendom, politically divided and happy to remain so, required a focus of unity. This process had been effectively achieved before Pope Innocent III (1198–1216) declared himself to be the vicar of Christ rather than of Saint Peter, but Innocent's pontificate set the seal on the new order of things. A parallel result of the process was a decline in the independence of the pope's fellow bishops. By the thirteenth century popes might still refer to a bishop when writing to him as 'venerable brother', but the distance in the hierarchy between the two was considerably wider than it had been in the tenth century.

Bishops in the tenth century were mostly great lords. The dioceses over which they presided were often ancient institutions, in many cases (especially in France, Italy, and Germany west of the Rhine) dating back to the third century or even earlier. During the course of their existence these institutions had acquired landed endowments, which made bishops lords over many tenants, with the superior tenants organized into small armies. These forces, though under the bishop's command, were not his own to use exactly as he liked: bishops were usually under royal authority, or, if this happened to be weak in a particular area (for example, Brittany, Catalonia, and, for much of the period down to the mid-eleventh century, Rome itself), under the influence of powerful local noble families. The ability to summon episcopal armies was not the only or even the main motive that kings had for controlling bishops: kings principally valued bishops for their role in performing rituals. Above all, bishops alone were able to inaugurate kings through anointing and coronation. Bishops also, until the papacy took over the process in the late twelfth century, presided over the canonization of saints, a procedure effected by removing a saint's body from its original place of burial to a more honourable one near an altar (the 'elevation' of a saint). Bishops could also supply appropriate backdrops for royal or imperial ceremony, since each one, following a tradition established in the later Roman Empire, was the leading figure in a city. The bishop's main symbol of status, his throne, stood in his principal church ('cathedral' church from Latin *cathedra* or chair), and this ideally was supposed to be situated in a city. Like other great landowners, bishops moved around their estates for much of the year, but they had a close relationship with cities and incorporated them into ecclesiastical and royal rituals.

The relationship between bishops and rulers was two-sided. In areas where kings were powerful, bishops generally owed their appointment to kings, for, whereas much office holding in the Middle Ages was hereditary, it was unusual, though not unknown, for son to succeed father in the episcopal office. Bishops-to-be often won royal attention through service as a cleric at the royal court, and the German rulers from the later tenth century onwards turned their royal chapel into a nursery of potential future bishops, by requesting selected cathedral chapters to send young canons* to court for short periods of royal service. Kings also sought to underline their control over episcopal appointments, and, since ritual was necessary to effect change in status, rulers would themselves hand over the staff, which symbolized the bishop's role as pastor, or shepherd, of his flock. In return, bishops could seek royal protection against powerful neighbours, or at least wish for it: the letters of Fulbert, bishop of Chartres (1006–28), show that he longed for Robert the Pious's powers as king of France (996–1031) to be more effective. Or bishops might require royal support for a course of action that might arouse opposition, as when the strongly pro-monastic Bishop Æthelwold of Winchester (963–84) sought military help from King Edgar in 964 to expel clergy from Winchester Cathedral and replace them with monks (valued by Æthelwold because they were more ascetic than clergy), drawn from his abbey of Abingdon.

Around 1000, bishops exercised authority within their sees in quite informal ways. They were usually so close to their cathedral clergy, living near them and sharing the same sources of income, that they could supervise them directly. The *Life* of Bishop Burchard of Worms, written by a member of the chapter of Worms Cathedral, stresses this aspect of Burchard's activity above his work as a compiler of a major canon (ecclesiastical) law* collection, or his political role in the German *Reich*. Where, occasionally, monk-bishops were in charge of monastic chapters, as in the case of Æthelwold at Winchester, the relationship might be even closer and the bishop's role as teacher more clearly defined. Together, bishops and cathedral clergy preserved the traditions and rights of the see, the former by defending these rights against aggressors, the latter by preserving charters and writing histories of the diocese.

As far as the relationship between bishops and parish clergy was concerned, this too could be informal, but varied considerably from diocese to diocese. Some had, as yet, relatively few parish churches, and here bishops could maintain contact with their clergy easily. In many other dioceses, however, the number of parishes was already rising steeply in the eleventh century. In north-eastern France and western Germany bishops found new subordinates to assist them in diocesan administration by developing the role of the archdeacon, originally one of the senior clerics in the cathedral chapter, into that of an episcopal deputy who could preside over ecclesiastical law courts in place of the bishop. Nonetheless the bishop was expected to play a fatherly role in the diocese himself. Gerhard's *Life of Bishop Udalrich of Augsburg*, written between 983 and 993 to set a good example to the next bishop but one after Udalrich (923–73), can be read as a manual of episcopal duties: visitation of the diocese every fourth year (in Germany the archdeacon carried out visitations in the other years), readiness to dedicate churches in remote areas, and the ability to teach parish clergy the rudiments of Christian theology so that they could instruct their flocks. Very similar guidelines, but in the form of letters, were written by the English monk Ælfric of Eynsham at the request of Bishop Wulfsige of Sherborne (d. 1002) and Archbishop Wulfstan of York (1002–23) in the early eleventh century.

The process of transition

This traditional world, with its mixture of ritual and informality, underwent a profound change in the eleventh and early twelfth centuries. We will return to the bishops shortly to see how they were affected, but we now need to look at the mechanism of the change itself. It was a process normally known, after one of the popes involved, as the Gregorian Reform, though it began before the pontificate of Gregory VII, and the term 'reform' was hardly ever used by Gregory himself. The movement led to the increased bureaucratization of the Church, though this was not the result that its leaders had desired. They had wished to see a church in which the sacred was more clearly differentiated from the worldly. Clergy, monks, and nuns, already differentiated from the lay population of the Church through clothing and (at least theoretically) behaviour, were to be more sharply defined still; by contrast, there was a tendency to treat the laity, although members of the Church through baptism, as profane. The roots of the movement lay outside Rome itself, in tenth-century Italian monastic movements inspired by Greek hermits, and among some leading Italian, Burgundian, and Lotharingian ecclesiastics in the eleventh century. The views put forward—hostility to clerical marriage and the inheritance of churches (which the reformers termed 'Nicolaitism'*), and to the purchase of sacred office (known as simony*, after the attempt by Simon Magus to buy the ability to work miracles recorded in the Acts of the Apostles)—had been standard features of canon-law collections from the late Roman period onwards. In practice, however, the ban on marriage had not been strictly enforced at sub-episcopal level. Simony, in the sense of purchase of sacraments such as the consecration of bishops, was probably relatively unusual, but in the sense of making gifts to patrons in return for the landed endowments of churches, a tactic that the reformers disliked, it was perfectly normal. Possibly an increasing use of money in transactions in the eleventh century led to inflation in the size of such gifts, and aroused anxiety as to their appropriateness, an anxiety felt most acutely in northern Italy and southern France.

Members of the reforming circles made their entry into the Roman Church through the Emperor Henry III (1039–56), who approved strongly of their ideas and who wished to see them reflected in the papacy itself, since a papacy with enhanced moral authority would confer more prestige on the role of the emperor, who was crowned by the pope. Henry was responsible for nominating a series of reforming popes of non-Roman origin. One of these, Leo IX (1049–54), made the firmest statement yet against simony at the synod of Rheims in 1049 by ordering those bishops present to state whether they had bought their office, and removing the staffs of those who admitted that they had. Leo also transformed the senior clerics in Rome, the cardinals, from a body of clergy of Roman origin and Roman horizons into a much more international group, some of whom could be sent as legates (envoys) to hear disputes outside Rome, thus building up a range of contacts for the pope in France, Germany, Spain, and elsewhere. Slightly later, Pope Nicholas II (1059–61) gave the cardinals the exclusive right to elect his successors. This would have been a step too far for Henry III, who approved of imperial involvement in papal elections, but he had died three years earlier, and his heir, Henry IV, was a child. The papacy continued to consolidate its links with places outside Rome in the last four decades of the eleventh century. Contacts with northern Spain led to strong papal support for campaigns by the northern kingdoms against al-Andalus (Muslim Spain), including the capture of Toledo in 1085; contacts with France led to papal involvement in ecclesiastical disputes, which in the case of Archbishop Manasses of Rheims (1060–80), one of the most prominent members of the French episcopate, led to his deposition by the legate Hugh of Die (d. 1106). This was confirmed by Gregory VII, illustrating the increase in papal authority north of the Alps. The papacy also began to intervene in disputes in the imperial Church, above all in the disputed election of the archbishop of Milan, in which Gregory VII supported a populist reforming movement, the Pataria, against the candidate desired by Henry IV.

It was this dispute over Milan that began what was to be a lengthy breakdown in relations between the papacy and the empire, which continued under Henry IV's and Gregory VII's successors until as late as 1122, even though both sides were actively seeking a solution to the impasse from 1111 onwards. During the course of the dispute the point at issue became the question of whether laymen, including kings, should have the power to invest churchmen with office, centring particularly on the ritual by which kings invested bishops with their staffs. Henry IV obtained the support of the imperial bishops in 1076 for Gregory VII's deposition, to which Gregory speedily retaliated by excommunicating Henry. Peace between the two sides was briefly achieved through a penitential ritual performed by Henry at Canossa in 1077, but in 1080, having once more deposed Gregory, he created a rival pope (or antipope* in the eyes of his opponents), Clement (III) (Archbishop Guibert of Ravenna), while the official line of popes, finding it hard to maintain their position in Rome, spent more time elsewhere—sometimes in southern Italy with the support of the Norman rulers there, and sometimes in France. Their widening political contacts made it easy for Urban II to ask a 'second tier' of European leaders (including the count of Toulouse, the duke of Normandy, and the south Italian leaders) for help in protecting Christians in the East at the Council of Clermont in November 1095. Increasingly frequent papal intervention in ecclesiastical affairs far from Rome, and the authority assumed by the pope in declaring what became the First Crusade (see Chapter 6), now began to encourage parties involved in ecclesiastical disputes to appeal to the pope. A steadily growing papal involvement in litigation led to a steady rise in appeals to the pope and thus in the documentation of legal proceedings. What had begun as an anxiety about ritual and the purity of the sacred was turning into a need for notaries and lawyers.

Law and the Church hierarchy in the twelfth and thirteenth centuries

As we have seen, this period saw a huge expansion in the use of the written word. The education of those members of the clergy aiming at high positions in the Church became more prolonged and thorough. The concentration of higher studies in a relatively small number of centres in the twelfth century (see Chapter 5) encouraged mobility and brought together clerics from across Europe. The study of

theology was often an opening to a distinguished career in ecclesiastical administration, as, for example, in the cases of the early
thirteenth-century bishops Stephen Langton (archbishop of Canterbury 1207–28) and Robert Grosseteste (bishop of Lincoln 1235–53),
but the most profitable subject for young clerks was law, in any of its
branches: civil (Roman) law, common or customary law, and canon
law. Canon law not only had direct application in the field of ecclesiastical administration but was also useful to those entering royal
administration.

The personnel of the papal Curia* saw steady expansion in these
two centuries, to cope with the volume of litigation arising out of
appeals and the rising quantity of documentation. We learn something of the obstacles that could present themselves to unwary
petitioners from accounts written by Thomas of Marlborough and
Gerald of Wales about their experiences in the early thirteenth century. Wiser litigants often delegated the task of making such requests
to proctors who, in exchange for fees, could devote time to making
the journeys to Rome and to building up the contacts that would
bring success. Usually, the popes would hear petitions and then dele-
gate the hearing of the cases to papal judges-delegate, who would
be selected from bishops and other prominent clerics living in the
country from which the plea originated, and who would hear the
cases there. Already by the time of Eugenius III (1145–53) the pope's
day was filled with administrative duties, chiefly hearing lawsuits.
Eugenius, a Cistercian, complained about this to his friend and
fellow-Cistercian Saint Bernard (abbot of Clairvaux, 1115–53). In
response, Bernard wrote De Consideratione, a treatise urging Eugenius
to devote more time to contemplation. Papal withdrawal from the
world, however, became less and less possible. In the eyes of the
college of cardinals, the best-qualified candidates for the office of
pope were, usually, canon lawyers. Alexander III, Innocent III, and
Innocent IV, to take a few examples, were all trained canonists. This
did not preclude them from displaying spiritual qualities, but meant
that they approached their duties from a lawyer's standpoint. The
stand taken by Lucius III (1181–5) in 1184 against heresy, for example,
was a legal one. Although sometimes military means might be used
against heretics, as in the Albigensian Crusade (see p. 145), the normal approach was through law, hence the development of the Inquisition, a system of judicial inquests, in the thirteenth century. The

growing involvement of the popes in the canonization of saints in the twelfth century became a legally enforced papal monopoly over the process under Innocent III, and the method of establishing sanctity involved the preparation of a dossier of evidence, which had to be checked. The range of topics covered by papal legislation at the great councils of the Church—for example, the Third Lateran of 1179, the Fourth Lateran of 1215, or the two Councils of Lyon in 1245 and 1274—was wide: the structure of religious orders, the organization and funding of crusades, and the control of heresy, as well as the discipline of the clergy, monks, and nuns, and the insistence (from 1215) that marriages should receive an ecclesiastical blessing.

Surprisingly, it was only relatively late that the papacy developed an interest in the compilation of canon law. Compilations of canon law were a private matter until at least the end of the twelfth century. The great compilations of the eleventh century—by Bishops Burchard of Worms, Anselm of Lucca (1074/5–86), and Ivo of Chartres (1090–1115/16)—were made by bishops, selecting legal decisions for educational purposes. Burchard's compilation was, indeed, rather anti-papal (he preferred to record decisions made by episcopal synods); Anselm's, however, strongly supported papal authority. The great compilation of the twelfth century, Gratian's *Decretum*, completed in the early 1140s, was written as an educational tool for lawyers, and, although it was used by popes, it did not receive their formal approval. By the middle decades of the thirteenth century, however, the papacy was more involved in the process of codifying canon law: it was Gregory IX (1227–41) who commissioned a compilation of papal decretals of the period following Gratian from a canon lawyer called Raymond de Penyafort, the *Liber Extra*, completed in 1234. Many of the items contained in it, however, had originally been collected privately, since they were letters written by popes giving advice to papal judges-delegate, which the latter had saved in small collections for their own reference, copies of which were passed on to canonists in the schools for educational use. At this stage they were recopied into more carefully organized collections before being fully organized in Raymond's work.

The changes in the status and activity of the papacy between the late eleventh and the late thirteenth centuries led to changes in the functions and activities of bishops, whose role was simultaneously affected by the rise in population. The growing authority of the papacy aroused relatively little hostility among bishops, save in late-eleventh-century Germany. On the contrary, bishops sought papal advice on a wide variety of topics. Sometimes the issues might be of major political importance, as, for example, the disagreement between Thomas Becket (archbishop of Canterbury 1162–70) and Henry II of England (1154–89), which culminated in Becket's murder; mostly, however, they were routine matters, as when Roger, bishop of Worcester (1164–79), sought rulings from Alexander III on clerical marriage in 1164. Roger knew perfectly well that priests, deacons, and subdeacons should not marry, but desired a statement from the pope to strengthen his authority in disciplining his clergy.

Most of Roger's correspondence with Alexander dealt with aspects of the relations between bishops and clergy, an area that in the twelfth century was starting to be better documented. This was a sign of the need to regulate the position of the clergy, particularly parish clergy. Growth in population had led to an expansion in the number of parish churches in the eleventh and twelfth centuries. By the thirteenth century, when lists began to be kept, many dioceses had hundreds of parishes (363 in the diocese of Paris in 1268, 763 in the diocese of Amiens in 1301, 1349 in the diocese of Norwich in the mid-thirteenth century, for example), and it was impossible for bishops even in smaller dioceses to have close contact with parish clergy. Nor were all clergy beneficed (that is, holding a parish church or a cathedral prebend*): another result of the population increase, coupled with much wider availability of money, was the emergence, from about 1100, of unbeneficed, freelance clergy, who outnumbered the beneficed clergy by the thirteenth century. These clerics were able to make livings for themselves by assisting beneficed clergy or by saying masses for the dead; the luckier ones found permanent positions in cathedrals as chaplains and vicars choral, helping to chant the large number of daily services as well as to say private masses at the many side altars. To some extent they were replacing some of the cathedral clergy, who might be employed by kings or bishops as administrators or lawyers, but chiefly they allowed cathedrals to expand their liturgical activities in the twelfth and thirteenth centuries, with anniversary prayers for deceased benefactors and more elaborate music. Although most parts of church services were chanted in plainsong, polyphony was used for decorative effect increasingly in the thirteenth century, placing more demands on choirs. A core of resident canons ensured the proper direction of the course of daily services in cathedrals in all their complexity, regulating every aspect of the liturgy, such as the number of candles appropriate for a particular feast day or the correct clothing to wear in choir. They also had to supervise the cathedral school, though from the early twelfth century the teaching would be done by a hired schoolmaster, and they administered charities attached to the cathedral—for example, doles of bread for the poor.

For disciplining and advising the clergy the bishop was responsible, with the help of archdeacons, to whom the routine jurisdiction was delegated. In addition it was the bishop's duty to supervise the monastic houses in his diocese that had not won exemption from episcopal oversight—in practice this meant nearly all nunneries and many of the smaller male communities. The bishop's role was not simply to admonish nuns, monks, and clerics: he also had to protect their interests. Small monastic houses might find their financial resources threatened by bad management or greedy neighbours. Parish clergy needed to have their rights as incumbents protected where they were threatened by their patrons; bishops therefore had to record which clerics had been presented to them for which benefices and by which patrons, and details about the share of revenue due to the incumbent. At first it was up to the incumbents and patrons to preserve the documentation, but, in the thirteenth century, bishops had copies made of their outgoing correspondence in books known as registers, often with lists of the clergy they had ordained. Sometimes separate registers might be kept recording the bishop's visitations of his diocese, such as the minutely detailed one kept by Eudes Rigaud, archbishop of Rouen (1248–75), recounting the shortcomings of the clergy and of small monastic houses. These registers had to be maintained by the bishop's clerks. Bishops drew on their own resources to pay their household clergy, though they usually rewarded them with benefices or cathedral prebends in due course. On the whole, the wealthier the diocese the more effective its administration. It is no coincidence that heresies such as Catharism were more tenacious in poorly endowed dioceses such as Toulouse than in wealthy ones such as Cologne.

Disciplining and advising clergy involved much more than record keeping. From the late twelfth century onwards bishops encouraged priests to improve their skills as preachers and confessors; Bishop Maurice de Sully of Paris (1160–96) wrote a textbook on preaching.

Under the influence of the series of Lateran councils, bishops issued detailed legislation for their parish clergy in the form of diocesan statutes, covering all aspects of the behaviour of parish clergy, their supervision of their parishioners, and the upkeep of their churches. One of the most influential sets of statutes was issued by Bishop Odo de Sully of Paris (1196–1208), but the principal inspiration was the Fourth Lateran Council in 1215, which prompted large numbers of bishops—for example, Robert Grosseteste of Lincoln—to legislate. Numerous sets of cathedral statutes were compiled in the thirteenth century also; here too the leading figure was often the bishop, and the interest in maintaining correct standards of clerical behaviour was again prominent.

The lay experience of religion

The most frequent and regular experience the laity (all the members of the Church who were not clerics) had of organized Christianity was through their parish. In the earlier Middle Ages the network of local 'mother' churches with control over baptism and burial and the right to collect tithes within a particular area had often been sparse, though there might also be small chapels or 'field churches' built by lords for their estates, which would lack the rights of the mother churches. Now the local churches underwent a dynamic phase of change in the eleventh and twelfth centuries. Many new ones were founded, almost always by lords of estates, to serve new centres of population; very often they were sited next to the lord's own residence, a hall or castle. They acquired rights of baptism and burial from their origin or soon after: for example, the tiny church at Raunds Furnells in Northamptonshire, originally built in the early tenth century, acquired a graveyard about fifty years later. Gradually the old mother churches lost their monopolies over baptism and burial, and, even though they might still be distinctive by having richer endowments or bigger buildings, there were, by the start of the twelfth century, no real differences between them and the newer churches in most areas: by then a fairly dense network of parish churches covered much of western Europe.

The creation of new parishes also affected towns, which were split up into multiple parishes. New parishes might exist to serve suburbs growing up round abbeys on the fringes of towns; in England and in Scandinavia the creation of urban parishes might be more extensive—London, for example, had well over 100 parishes by the twelfth century, some of them containing only a couple of streets. The new churches, rural and urban, were often tiny when first constructed, simple two-celled structures with only a nave and a chancel, but most were progressively enlarged, and by the thirteenth century the richer ones had side aisles, allowing space for the saying of private masses or even to run a small school.

Local churches were usually founded by the lords of the manors on which they were situated, though manorial tenants made their own contribution through donations or building work. However, the lord of the manor, by providing the land on which the church stood and the house and land needed to support the priest, enjoyed the rights of patronage over the church: that is, the right to choose the priest. During the eleventh and twelfth centuries, as a result of the Gregorian reform, which discouraged ownership of churches by the laity, lay patrons were encouraged to bestow their rights of patronage on monastic houses: over a quarter of parish churches passed into monastic ownership. The impact of this development on the recruitment of parish clergy was mixed. There was a tendency for lay patrons to present their relatives to benefices; equally, any patron, lay or ecclesiastical, might feel like maintaining the status quo by allowing a relative of the previous incumbent to succeed. Bishops and kings, not content with the patronage they enjoyed on their own estates, often applied pressure on other patrons to provide well-endowed livings for their own protégés; so too did thirteenth-century popes. As a result, the range of clergy serving parish churches was quite varied, although they were normally men of some social standing, with local connections. The belief that parish incumbents generally came from peasant families is misplaced: benefices were usually too valuable to be given to low-born clerics, and the latter usually found subordinate positions as chaplains. The educational standards of beneficed clergy varied from those with only very limited knowledge of Latin, who might have difficulties coping with the simple oral examinations set them by thirteenth-century bishops such as Eudes Rigaud, to those with a university education. A twelfth-century example of an episcopal protégé as an active parish priest is Gilbert of

Sempringham (d. 1189), who gave up a promising administrative career in the household of Bishop Alexander of Lincoln to concentrate on his duties as parson of Sempringham (Lincs.), and who eventually founded a monastery for young women in his parish, which grew into a small monastic order.

Relations between the parishioners and their parson were not entirely harmonious: the duty on the former to pay tithe, an ecclesiastical tax of one-tenth of all produce, led to numerous disputes. Nonetheless the role of the parish church as a focal point in the life of the local community was accepted. Babies of the parish would be brought for baptism to the font to mark their entry into the community, and the deceased of the parish would normally be buried in the churchyard. Groups of parishioners, often split up according to age and sex, would band together in confraternities to provide money for repairs to the church, or to pray, like the group of twelve matrons venerating the apostles in a Rhineland parish described by Caesarius of Heisterbach in his *Dialogue of Miracles* of the early thirteenth century. Parishioners were expected to attend mass once a week, though they took communion much more rarely, usually only at Easter. The Fourth Lateran Council (1215) fixed the minimum requirement for communion as once a year. Before this they would confess to the priest.

Although the parish church provided the main framework of religious experience for the laity, it was not the only source of spiritual advice and consolation. The instruction provided by parish clergy, often limited, was sometimes supplemented by preaching and counsel from members of monastic communities, such as the monks of Worcester Cathedral in the eleventh century, or from hermits. Wandering preachers, a common phenomenon in France in the late eleventh and the twelfth centuries—for example, Robert of Arbrissel (d. 1116), active in Anjou—might introduce the faithful to a much wider range of ideas, not necessarily orthodox: bishops kept a wary eye on wandering preachers, and tried to ensure that they operated only under licence. In the thirteenth century this role was taken up by Dominican and Franciscan friars, who were carefully trained in both doctrine and preaching skills, and who carried with them handbooks of suitable sermons for different social groups (known as sermons *ad status*) and collections of stories with which to illustrate their preaching.

For moments of great need—illness or famine—potent mediators between God and mankind were required, and in these extremities people prayed to saints for help. This was not a new development: saints had been a focal point for prayer from early in the history of Christianity. Nonetheless the cult of saints, even the most ancient ones such as the Virgin Mary, was not an unchanging phenomenon. At the end of the tenth century, for example, saints' cults acquired a new significance at the heart of the Peace of God movement, an attempt by bishops in parts of France to quell private warfare. The assemblies where the faithful swore to abstain from violence were dominated by reliquaries (boxes, usually shaped like small houses, containing saints' relics), brought by monasteries of the region in a display of solidarity with the movement. Oaths made while touching reliquaries had great force. We can see how the ceremony was conducted from the famous scene in the Bayeux Tapestry in which Duke William of Normandy forced Earl Harold to swear obedience. The use of reliquaries in the Peace of God movement relied on the long-popular view of saints as harsh taskmasters, but a shift in this perception is visible in the twelfth century as the more human and even fallible qualities of saints come to be stressed in saints' lives. Walter Daniel's *Life* of the Cistercian abbot Aelred of Rievaulx (1147–67), for example, mentions how Aelred had prayed in homely English rather than in Latin or French on his deathbed. This trend did not completely dispel the image of saints as severe: in the early twelfth century, against historical evidence, Saint Cuthbert (d. 687) was reinterpreted as a harsh opponent of women by the monks of Durham, who wanted to exclude women from most of Durham Cathedral. However, the new stress on the humanity of saints proved popular, especially if it was combined with a reputation for performing healing miracles. With these incentives the guardians of shrines, usually monks, nuns, or cathedral canons, could attract a larger, more socially diverse range of pilgrims and benefactors. Miracle stories were recorded and then disseminated in sermons or vernacular verse. Pilgrims would flock to shrines in search of cures, and the shrines benefited from their donations.

Although many pilgrimages were undertaken in search of healing, these journeys were principally intended to be penitential: they were serious events, sometimes involving long distances. Rome, Jerusalem, and Compostela (the shrine of Saint James in north-west Spain) all attracted pilgrims from afar. Wealthy pilgrims might use the journeys as opportunities to show off or to carry out political negotiations (for example, Cnut, king of Denmark and England, who in 1027 visited Rome, dispensed alms lavishly to display his wealth, and negotiated with the king of Burgundy about the tolls paid by English merchants crossing the Alps), but even for them the journeys presented dangers. The more vulnerable poor looked on pilgrimage as a journey from which there was no certainty of a return. Rodulf Glaber in the mid-eleventh century recounts how some gladly accepted this in the hope that they might, by dying at their destination, achieve salvation.

Penance did not have to be performed by the penitent in person: it could be delegated to others, preferably those better equipped for it through a greater reputation for holiness: monks and nuns. As a result, links between members of religious communities and the better-off laity, who could afford to pay for prayer, were close. Patronage of monastic houses by laymen and laywomen began to expand over a wider social range. At the start of the eleventh century only royal or aristocratic families could afford to be patrons of monastic houses, but in the twelfth century the growing numbers of small monastic houses made it possible for knightly families to be patrons, too, while in the thirteenth century the mendicant orders attracted benefactions from almost all social classes. Gifts of money or land to monasteries provided anniversary prayers or masses for benefactors after their deaths, and favoured benefactors might be buried in the monastery church. Some major churches became family mausolea: Speyer Cathedral for the Salian emperors in the eleventh century, Fontevraud Abbey for the Angevins (Plantagenets) at the end of the twelfth century. By these means the benefactors hoped not only to secure salvation but also to have their memory preserved.

Prayer was the key. It was a vital part of penance; it helped to articulate all sorts of ceremonies; and it was resorted to by those suffering from illness or threatened by disaster. Prayer was expected from all, but believers felt that the most efficacious prayers were said by the holiest people. The people regarded as most holy were the contemplatives who had withdrawn from worldly affairs (though retaining enough contact with the world to be in touch with their benefactors). The role of contemplatives within the Church was a very ancient one: monks, nuns, and hermits were long-established features of the religious scene by the start of our period. Although they were technically a side shoot rather than part of the main hierarchical framework of the Church, the respect that they could obtain for their asceticism and discipline gave them moral authority, and they often acted as opinion-formers. Moreover, monks could become priests (by the tenth century in the West they normally did), and some of them became bishops. Many popes in the eleventh and early twelfth centuries were monks.

Monks, nuns, regular canons, and friars

In the tenth century monastic houses were relatively few in number, though numbers increased considerably from the 990s onwards, especially in northern and western France and southern Germany. Houses of nuns were relatively rare, since nuns could not celebrate mass and therefore could not perform private masses, the form of prayer most highly valued by the laity. The pattern of monastic life was not very varied, for, even though each abbey was autonomous and had its own, jealously preserved, liturgical peculiarities, almost all abbeys in the West observed the Benedictine Rule (named after Saint Benedict of Nursia, d. c.550) by the tenth century. The principal duty of the inmates was to chant the Office, a sequence of services running through the day from Matins, well before daybreak, to Vespers in the evening. To make the liturgy more impressive, the time spent in choir was prolonged by increasing the number of prayers and psalms forming the Office: this, and the decorous, formal behaviour that well-run monasteries enforced, attracted the support of benefactors, especially kings, noblemen, and noblewomen. In the middle decades of the tenth century the Ottonian rulers of Germany, the counts of Flanders, and the English kings all encouraged the imposition of the Benedictine Rule in many churches previously served by secular clergy rather than monks. Individual houses regarded as having particularly effective liturgy and discipline sent small groups of monks to train other communities in their observances. Most influential were Cluny, a Burgundian house that exported its practices to many French monasteries, and Gorze, near Metz, which was influential in Germany. Fleury, which itself had received Cluniac customs, influenced several English monasteries. Supplying training in liturgical practices did not, as yet, in the tenth century, imply any hierarchical superiority amongst monasteries, but, in the early eleventh century, Cluny, under Abbot Odilo (994–1049), established a numerous family of dependent priories throughout France and beyond, establishing a precedent for religious orders.

Throughout the tenth and eleventh centuries, monasteries were essentially aristocratic. Only rich families could afford the necessary entrance gift of land to accompany the oblation ('offering') of their children as young monks or nuns in monasteries. The ties between abbeys and noble families were strengthened not only by the existence of relatives in the cloister, but also through the grants of land themselves, which were often granted back to the donors to hold for their lifetimes. Tenth-century monastic sources sometimes dwell on the hostility of aristocrats towards monasteries, but this hostility (for example, the attacks of Ælfhere, ealdorman* of the Mercians, on monasteries in the English midlands in 975) was displayed by nobles towards abbeys patronized by their rivals. Houses that they themselves patronized (Abingdon in Ælfhere's case) were safe. The guiding principles of Benedictine monasticism—discipline and respectability —won the favour of the ruling elite.

It would be a mistake to see tenth- and eleventh-century monasticism as monolithic. A variant version existed in southern Italy, where communities of hermits grew up, influenced by Byzantine monasticism. Their asceticism aroused the interest of many from outside Italy, for example, John of Gorze (d. 976), who visited them; the emperor Otto III (983–1002) also took a keen interest in hermits. Within Italy itself, monastic communities inspired by hermits were set up not far from Rome at Grottaferrata and in Tuscany at Camaldoli and Vallombrosa. The latter two followed the Benedictine Rule but laid particular stress on solitude and private prayer. Another eleventh-century development was interest in the concept of *vita apostolica*, the communal life with shared possessions practised by the Apostles in the earliest days of the Church. This movement, especially active in Italy and southern France, led to the remodelling of many communities of clergy along quasi-monastic lines. A letter of Saint Augustine outlining a way of life for nuns was considerably expanded to form a rule (the Rule of Saint Augustine) that these communities could follow. Both models of religious life, the hermit life and the apostolic life, were to be very influential in the period that followed.

In striking contrast to the fairly uniform picture presented by monastic life in the tenth and for most of the eleventh centuries was the huge variety of different patterns of monastic existence which sprang up in western Europe between the last quarter of the eleventh century and the middle of the thirteenth. No longer was there simply one monastic *ordo** or 'order' in the singular, but many new orders, each with its own identity. The traditional form of Benedictine monasticism was joined by orders that could specialize, some in asceticism, and some, by contrast, in tasks that brought them into contact with the world, such as care for the sick or preaching.

One important consequence was that the number of religious houses in western Europe soared in the twelfth century, with foundations still continuing in many areas in the thirteenth century and beyond. The diocese of Worcester (to take one example) had had twelve religious houses in the late eleventh century, all Benedictine; by c.1200 there were thirty-one, including Augustinian and Cistercian foundations. Parts of Europe that had had no, or very few, traditional Benedictine houses experienced a wave of monastic foundation: these were essentially the peripheral areas of Europe, namely Scotland, northern England, most of Scandinavia, Germany east of the Elbe, Poland, Bohemia, Hungary, and the parts of the Iberian peninsula conquered by the northern Christian kingdoms from al-Andalus. Landowners in these areas were able to grant huge swathes of territory to monastic houses. However, it is a mistake to see growth as exclusively a feature of Europe's borderlands: it was just as strong in the 'heartlands' of Europe—for example, Burgundy, the Rhineland, and the Loire valley.

The large numbers of new religious houses created opportunities for a much wider cross-section of society to enter the religious life. Many of the new religious orders deliberately set out to appeal to social groups previously less involved in the monastic life, or even actively ignored. Several of the late-eleventh- and early-twelfth-century monastic founders, Robert of Arbrissel and Norbert of Xanten (d. 1134), for example, attracted large numbers of female as well as male followers, and then set up double houses of men and women, carefully segregated to appease the nervous ecclesiastical authorities. Eventually Robert's foundation of Fontevraud in Anjou became, essentially, a nunnery with communities of male clerics and servants in support. Norbert's community of regular canons at

Prémontré became an order with numerous (male) daughter-houses*, and established separate nunneries for the female inmates, downgrading their significance within the order as a whole. The twelfth-century English order of Sempringham, which largely consisted of double-houses, was more successful in preserving a balance. Although opportunities were widening for women to become nuns, nunneries remained only a small proportion of the total number of monastic houses, and few were wealthy or large. Fontevraud, which attracted the support of the counts of Anjou, was a notable exception; also, rather unusually for a nunnery, it acquired a family of daughter-houses. More frequently, nunneries, even where they claimed to belong to an order, lacked much contact with other houses and were supervised by their local bishop.

Monastic life became possible for members of a widening range of social classes in the twelfth century. Knights, many of whom had been too poor in the eleventh century to patronize Benedictine houses, save on a small scale, or to think of entering their children in them, could now found monasteries. A small house of Augustinian canons or of nuns did not represent a large outlay: often a minor landowner could establish one by giving away a few parish churches (from which, as a member of the laity, he or she was no longer supposed to extract wealth). A Cistercian house in a remote area might be endowed with unpopulated land unprofitable to a lay landowner. The new orders dispensed with child recruitment, preferring to attract adolescents or young adults, and were less demanding about entry grants. A formative moment in Cistercian history came when the adolescent Bernard, later abbot of Clairvaux, arrived at the abbey of Cîteaux in 1113 with a band of youthful kinsmen, all from knightly families, to become monks. Bernard's family background helps to explain his enthusiasm for the military order of the Templars, for which he wrote a rule in 1128, and his preaching for the Second Crusade.

Members of the peasant class were also recruited into some of the new orders in large numbers, though social distinctions were carefully preserved. Peasant recruits, almost always illiterate, were not expected to learn to read (indeed, they were often prevented from doing so), and so could not learn Latin liturgical texts and chant the Office in choir. Separate choirs were created for them in the naves of abbey churches where they could recite the few prayers they were taught. Vallombrosa in the mid-eleventh century was the first house to alter the use of the word *conversi**, hitherto a term used to describe adult recruits to the monastic life, to mean lay brothers, a group whose main duty was to carry out manual labour to support the rest of the community. Fontevraud likewise had separate groups of lay brothers, for farm work, and lay sisters, as domestic servants for the nuns. However, the economic possibilities of *conversi* were exploited most fully by the Cistercians in the twelfth and thirteenth centuries. In the twelfth century steep population growth brought a flood of peasant recruits who were prepared to accept an ascetic life in return for a secure existence and an enhanced possibility of salvation. The *conversi* supplied the workforce for the empty stretches of land given to the Cistercians (sometimes, where unsettled land was not available, the Cistercians cleared away whole villages to obtain it). Surplus crops and the by-products of animal husbandry, above all wool, made the Cistercians rich.

The new orders were all moved by one or more of the following aims: withdrawal from the world and leading the life of a hermit; sharing things in common like the early apostles; and adhering more strictly to the Rule of Saint Benedict. Interest in the apostolic life led, as we have seen, to communities of clergy living under the Augustinian Rule, known as 'regular canons' because they lived by a rule, *regula* in Latin. Augustinian communities were often founded in or near towns, making it easy for them to engage in teaching (like the canons of Saint-Victor in Paris) or care for the sick: many of the numerous hospitals that were set up in twelfth- and thirteenth-century Europe to care for the elderly and bedridden poor adopted a form of the Augustinian Rule to live by. Norbert of Xanten's Premonstratensian canons also followed the Augustinian Rule, but their houses were linked together in a more organized form influenced by the framework of the Cistercian Order. Groups of hermits in remote forested areas of France in the late eleventh century were the points of origin for the Carthusians, the Grandmontines, the Savignacs, Tironensians, and, indirectly, the Cistercians. The Carthusians combined the solitary life of the hermit with community living by making each monk live in his own small house, and bringing the community together only on Sundays. The principal driving force for the Savignacs, Tironensians, and Cistercians was the desire to lead the Benedictine Rule 'more strictly', by which they meant stripping away some of the liturgical accretions of the ninth and tenth centuries that had lengthened the time spent in choir, and also avoiding some practices that brought monasteries into close contact with the laity, such as providing food and accommodation for the sick and elderly. The most successful of all these groups were the Cistercians, who had founded over 300 abbeys by the middle of the twelfth century and over 600 by the middle of the thirteenth. The success was partly the result of aggressive campaigning by the most prominent figure in the order, Bernard, abbot of Clairvaux, who engaged in a polemical debate with the abbot of Cluny, Peter the Venerable (1122–56), about how best to observe the Benedictine Rule. Bernard's argument with Cluny originated in the decision by one of his relatives to leave the Cistercians and become a Cluniac, which Bernard regarded as backsliding. Moreover, he felt that he had to go on the offensive to justify his order: questions were sometimes raised about its origins, for Cîteaux had been founded in 1098 by an abbot and monks who had abandoned another community. Cistercians wrote sanitized versions of their past for internal as well as external consumption. Factions within the order had axes to grind: supporters of Bernard put the date of his entry into Cîteaux a year too early (1112), to suggest that the foundation of Cîteaux's earliest daughter-house had been made possible only because he and his relatives had boosted the number of monks at a crucial moment.

Traditional Benedictine houses, such as Cluny, sometimes felt that their noses had been put out of joint by the new orders, but by the middle of the twelfth century it was clear that their position was not threatened. Their wealth gave them stability and a political influence often lacked by the newer foundations, and their traditions, their sense of the past, and, above all, their collections of books and documents, encouraged them to write history. Many members of new orders did this too, but for command of detail and range of coverage Benedictine historians such as Orderic Vitalis and William of Malmesbury in the twelfth century and Matthew Paris in the thirteenth were outstanding (see Chapter 5).

There was also room on the stage for forms of religious life more appropriate to the laity, or directed towards the laity. In particular those laywomen who were not rich enough to become nuns might become anchoresses, walled into cells next to churches, or (especially in the Low Countries) might become Beguines, a less strictly regulated way of life than being a nun, allowing inmates to earn a living making cloth or nursing the sick. Ecclesiastical authorities were uneasy about many lay religious movements, however, and tried to suppress some of them, for example, the Waldensians (see below), for preaching without theological training. Only in the thirteenth century did Pope Innocent III try to win acceptance for some of the Waldensians, and for a similar group called the Humiliati. He also gave approval to two semi-monastic groups of a new type that were to be enormously influential in European towns, the supporters of Francis of Assisi (known as Friars Minor or Franciscans) and those of Dominic of Osma (the Preaching Friars or Dominicans). Francis attracted lay-men, but increasingly also clerics, in search of the apostolic life; Dominic, at the head of a small group of clergy, had spent several years preaching against Catharism in south-western France. In 1217 both the Franciscans and the Dominicans sent out groups to carry their mission across Europe, setting up houses (known as convents) in towns. To perfect their preaching skills, both orders began to lay stress on education, sending members of their order to study at universities; friars also, as we have seen, developed a variety of preaching aids.

Heretics

Heretical movements, though relatively rare in the medieval Christian West, occurred sporadically in the eleventh century and then more noticeably in the twelfth and thirteenth. Some were local-ized and ephemeral, like the quasi-Gnostic movement among the cathedral clergy of Orléans in 1022. Longer lasting were Catharism, a dualistic form of Christianity, which viewed all created matter as evil and which probably spread from the Byzantine Empire into Italy and south-west France, perhaps as early as the early eleventh century, and Waldensianism, an anticlerical form of Christianity originating as a movement of lay piety led by a merchant of Lyon called Waldes. Catharism and Waldensianism, even at their peak, attracted relatively few supporters across Europe as a whole. In the mid-twelfth century Catharism won support among weavers in towns in north-eastern France and the Rhineland, but faded in these areas after the 1160s.

It lasted much longer around Toulouse, and in some northern Italian towns, particularly where it managed to win over some of the upper classes. Strictly observant Cathars ('perfects') were heavily outnumbered by the rest of the population. Nonetheless, they were influential among their neighbours. Their existence caused anxiety in the ecclesiastical hierarchy, which feared that its authority was being undermined. Several of the south-western French bishops were too ineffectual to offer opposition, however, and action at first came from the Cistercians, who sent members of their order on preaching missions. These had little effect; more successful was the preaching of Dominic of Osma and his early followers in the early thirteenth century. The Albigensian Crusade (1209–29) did not kill off Catharism and in the 1230s the Dominicans, with the support of the Church hierarchy, set up the Inquisition. Among the Catholic laity, Cathars aroused a wide range of reactions: hostility, sometimes strengthened by a desire to profit from their misadventures (as in the case of the northern French nobility on the Albigensian Crusade), neutrality, and passive approval. Several noble families in south-western France contained both Cathars and Catholics, the latter often shielding the former. Cathars had to behave with extreme circumspection, since their behaviour—for example, reluctance to eat meat—might mark them out. This was especially true of those who had committed themselves fully to the religion and become 'perfects'. These were venerated by ordinary Cathar believers and were sought after as preachers and as the only people who could offer the *consolamentum**, a form of deathbed sacrament. Male perfects travelled to preach, while female perfects tended to live in small households together or with female believers, rather like small communities of nuns. The Inquisition steadily made it harder for perfects to operate in southern France, and in the 1250s they fled to Italy, but here too Cathar communities, even in small towns like Desenzano on Lake Garda, were persecuted into extinction in the late thirteenth century.

Jewish communities

Jewish communities, whether in Christian areas of Europe or in Islamic Spain, were rather larger, and far more influential, than communities of heretics, because they could have a more public presence. Jews tended to live in towns, usually on major trade routes such as the valley of the Rhine. It has been estimated that Rouen, one of the largest communities, had about 3,000 Jewish inhabitants by c.1200, although this figure may well be too high. Links between towns throughout Europe and far beyond were maintained through marriage, through the travel of rabbinical students to study with famous scholars, and through trade. Wherever Jewish communities existed, however, they were subordinated to polities that upheld alien religions, and, although Muslim and Christian rulers most of the time afforded protection to Jewish subjects, they were not always able, nor always motivated, to ensure the safety of the latter against hostile mobs. In 1148 the Almohads, taking power in al-Andalus, reversed a long tradition of Muslim tolerance, and many Jews left southern Spain for the Christian north. In Christendom, periods of crusading preaching were especially dangerous for Jews: at the start of the First Crusade the Jews of Mainz, Worms, and Cologne were massacred by followers of the unauthorized popular wave of the First Crusade in 1096. At the start of the Third Crusade, a group of Yorkshire landowners, embittered by debts, massacred the Jews of York in 1190. In 1290 Edward I expelled all Jews from England, and in 1294 and 1306 ordinances of Philip IV restricted the rights of Jews in France. Commemoration of victims of persecution was one of the main responsibilities of Jewish communities, and has preserved some detailed accounts of family life. Increasingly, archaeological excavations are providing evidence of the physical presence of Jewish communities in towns. Each had to have a synagogue (some towns had more than one), a ritual bath, and a slaughterhouse; Rouen in addition had a sizeable school, built of stone. These buildings were usually grouped close together, and members of the community often lived nearby, though this was not invariably the case. Leadership within the community was shared between the scholarly elite of rabbis, who might be quite numerous (nearly half the male heads of households among the Jews of Mainz in 1096 were rabbis), and the wealthier members of the community; in negotiations with Christian authorities, the richest and most prominent figure acted as leader, and was termed 'bishop' of the Jews by the Christians. Very occasionally this leader might represent Jews within a whole region, as in late-thirteenth-century Franconia, where Meir ben Baruch of

Rothenburg was a spokesman for Jewish communities in dealings with the emperor.

Muslims in Spain

By the late tenth century Islam was well established in Spain. Conversions to Islam probably peaked in the tenth century, and it is likely that Muslims formed the great majority of the population of al-Andalus by the year 1000, at which point it extended from the River Duero southwards across the peninsula. At this time al-Andalus found its political expression in the powerful caliphate of Córdoba, but in just over a decade this political unity disintegrated into numerous independent states, the *taifa** kingdoms (see Chapter 6). Islam in Spain drew its strength from cities. Each town had its great mosque, the responsibility of the ruler, and numerous smaller local mosques, funded by donations made by the faithful. The fakirs or holy men and the judges who had the duty of preventing blasphemy and heresy were mostly drawn from the urban middle class. Spanish Muslims were staunchly Sunni*: a flowering of Shi'ism* in the early tenth century in Tunisia found no echo in Spain, and Sunni orthodoxy was also insisted on by the fundamentalist Almoravids and Almohads who arrived from north-western Africa in the late eleventh and the twelfth centuries respectively. Within al-Andalus the three monotheistic faiths of Islam, Judaism, and Christianity coexisted, mostly in cultural isolation from each other, though the fact that c.1100 the legal expert Ibn 'Abdun thought it necessary to recommend that Muslim women should not enter Christian churches suggests a certain degree of syncretism. Coexistence of faiths in isolation was also a feature of the areas conquered by the Christian kingdoms from the late eleventh century onwards, especially in Valencia and the Balearic Islands, taken over by the kingdom of Aragon in the thirteenth century, which retained significant numbers of Muslim inhabitants (Mudejars), who were allowed to practise their religion and laws, usually in segregated communities.

Religion gave expression to communities, topographically and socially. Each Christian parish would be distinguished by its church, often prominently placed; much more discreetly, each Jewish community would have its synagogue and ritual bath. The rituals that articulated many actions in public life often had a religious basis. By these means religion maintained tradition. At the same time, however, the great population expansion experienced by western Europe in this period necessitated changes in the institutional hierarchies of religion, and in particular the Church acquired a much more legalistic structure than it had had hitherto.

5

Intellectual and Cultural Creativity

Anna Sapir Abulafia

One of the features of the central Middle Ages was a sense people had that they were living in times that were distinct from the past. The many changes they were experiencing were often interpreted as signs that the end of the world was approaching. Different thinkers held different views about the nature of those changes. Some thought all was going from bad to worse; others were far more optimistic about the perfectibility of society in readiness for what might be the final stage of its history. The awareness that there was a difference between past and present led more and more people to think about the role of human beings in the course of history and their own particular role in the new present. But excitement about present opportunities was commonly tempered by deference to the past. The statement of Bernard of Chartres (d. *c.*1130) that he and his contemporaries could see further than the ancients because they were dwarves standing on the shoulders of giants expresses well the ambivalence between reverence for the riches of the past and recognition of the real achievements of the present. Also, concentration on the human condition should not be confused with twenty-first-century ideas about people's unique individuality. In the central medieval period there was a strong concept of a normative form of nature that sets out what human beings should be. For Christian thinkers the concept of being human was intrinsically wrapped up with theological values and the institutional norms that were being promulgated by a rapidly developing hierarchical Church. The human being that people set out to discover within themselves was their true, unique self, which would bring them closer to God. In historical terms this was the personality of each individual in his or her relationship to God, operating within explicit constraints of communal civic and religious ties, rather than the relatively unrestrained individual free agent of our own century. The creative tension between individual personalities and their intimate identification with their communities is, in fact, one of the particularly interesting aspects of this period. On the intellectual front it moulded the range and the nature of academic achievement; culturally, it influenced what was produced for people's amusement and erudition.

Education and learning: the schools

The expansion and institutionalization of education in the twelfth and thirteenth centuries was the most important stimulus for the sustained output of learning in this period. Scholars followed in the footsteps of those who had gone before them in more haphazard circumstances. Gerbert of Aurillac (940–1003), who went on to be Pope Sylvester II (999–1003), benefited from wealthy patronage to acquire for himself the best currently available scientific education in Muslim Spain. As archbishop of Rheims, he steered the city's cathedral school in the direction of science. He showed his empirical bent in his own scientific writings and is known for his use of Arabic numbers, an abacus, and an astrolabe. The admiring students of Fulbert of Chartres (c.960–1028) compared Fulbert to Socrates and Pythagoras. But he warned them to rely more on faith than on their erudition to fathom the mysteries of God. The continuing interest in the eleventh century in speculative thought is marked by innovative close reading of texts that had previously been copied in monasteries engaged in the cultural revival of the Carolingian Renaissance. The reflections of scholars such as Berengar of Tours (c.1000–80), Lanfranc of Canterbury (c.1010–89), Roscelin of Compiègne (c.1050–c.1125), and Anselm of Canterbury (1033–1109) were inspired by their mastery of grammar, rhetoric, and dialectic (logic), the three subjects of the trivium* (the first tier of the classical seven liberal arts that had also lain at the heart of early medieval education). The translation of Aristotle's *On Meaning* and *Categories* by Boethius (c.480–524) and

Porphyry's third-century Neoplatonic introduction to Aristotelian logic, the *Isagoge*, together with some of Boethius' own writings and Cicero's *Topics* constituted the syllabus used to teach dialectic. This is known as the Old Logic (*Logica Vetus*) to distinguish it from the New Logic (*Logica Nova*), which comprised the logical works of Aristotle, which became known to the West after the first half of the twelfth century. Cicero was also used to teach rhetoric; Donatus (fourth-century *Ars Maior*) and Priscian (sixth-century *Institutiones*) to teach grammar. The nature of these texts prompted scholars to think hard about the meaning and status of words and the relationship between words and the subjects they named. The semantics of language coloured much of the philosophical work of this period. A major challenge these thinkers faced as a result of their reading of these non-Christian texts was to work out how much they should rely on reason (that is, human faculties not governed by faith) in their exploration of theological problems. The most important problems they confronted were the Eucharist, the Trinity, and the Incarnation.

Berengar's study of logic and grammar caused him to challenge the Eucharistic teaching on which the Church was beginning to insist, namely that the Eucharist did not just represent the body and blood of Christ but that it really (that is, substantially or materially) was the body and blood of Christ. Lanfranc accused Berengar of relying too much on reason. Nonetheless, he himself marshalled Aristotelian arguments in support of the doctrine of Eucharistic change. Berengar was forced to recant his views definitively in 1079. Roscelin's work on the Trinity was strongly influenced by his nominalist* convictions. As a nominalist, he did not believe that universals (for example, common nouns, that are notions that can be applied to more than one particular) were real; they were nothing more than the puff of air brought about by their utterance. This prompted him to ask how God could be one and three at the same time, if only the second person of the Trinity became incarnate. Did this not mean that certain particulars applied to the Son that did not apply to the Father and Holy Spirit? Did this mean all three persons had to become incarnate? Or was the implication that the Trinity was not as unified as Christians believed? Anselm had no patience for this kind of use of dialectic, and he admonished Roscelin to be silent if he was incapable of understanding what he, as a Christian, ought to believe. Anselm's own work was governed by his maxim *credo ut intelligam* (I believe in order to understand). Much of his scholarly work reads like a prayer; seeking understanding of faith was a contemplative tool in his hands. Anselm was confident that human reason could understand a very great deal in the presence of faith.

Anselm's ontological* proof of the existence of God, whom he defined as 'something-than-which-a-greater-cannot-be-thought', is found in the *Proslogion*. But his most interesting work is the *Cur Deus Homo?* ('Why God-Man?'), in which he sets out to prove by reason alone (*sola ratione*) that the Incarnation of the Son of God was both possible and *necessary*. It is here that he offers the satisfaction theory, a new explanation for the need for the Incarnation. Anselm did not utilize the traditional idea that Christ became man in order to snatch man from the jurisdiction of the devil, which he had rightfully held since the fall of man. To Anselm's mind the devil had no rights over man; man's problem was the debt he owed to God on account of the fall, which he could not pay because everything man had already belonged to God. Anselm argued that the only man who could pay this debt was 'God-man'. In exchange for his voluntary death, Jesus Christ (that is, God-man) could thus solicit redemption from God for his human brothers.

Lanfranc of Canterbury taught at the monastic school of Bec in Normandy before going on to Caen, where he became abbot of William the Conqueror's new abbey of St Stephen's, and then to England, as the first 'Norman' archbishop of Canterbury. His pupil Anselm also taught at Bec before his removal to Canterbury. Their connection with Bec gives us an excellent insight into both the opportunities and the restrictions of a monastic school. In the presence of luminaries such as Lanfranc and Anselm the school of Bec developed into a veritable centre of learning. But once these great scholars had departed, it returned to its real calling: a school catering primarily for monastic purposes—namely, prayer and prayerful study. For learning to be institutionalized, continuity and an academic sense of purpose needed to be fostered. Fertile ground for both were found in the cathedral schools of the late eleventh and early twelfth centuries. This is not to say that monasteries produced no scholars. The Benedictine monk Rupert of Deutz (*c.*1075/80–1129), the latter-day Benedictine, Honorius *Augustodunensis* (*c.*1070–*c.*1140), the nuns Hildegard of Bingen (1098–1179) and Elizabeth of Schönau (d. 1155), and the Cistercian Bernard of Clairvaux (*c.*1090–1153) are only a few examples that prove the opposite. Rupert, Honorius, and Bernard produced a wide range of original theological, exegetical*, and homiletical* material. Elizabeth and Hildegard are known for their fascinating mystical work. Hildegard's interests included medicine, science, poetry, and music. But, on the whole, monastic scholars did not study the liberal arts out of academic interest alone. Their studies were part of the monastic activity of *lectio divina* (holy reading), and, generally, their works of theology had a devotional flavour, mirroring their own spiritual interests and experience in contrast to the more specifically rationalistic enterprise being aimed at in the schools.

The traditional purpose of cathedral schools was to train the choir and the diocesan clergy for their tasks. Diocesan education was much encouraged by Church reformers, who needed effective and well-trained clergy. But good teaching also attracted extraneous pupils who were more interested in their own education than any parochial needs and concerns. The presence of a moving population of students and masters presented opportunities for steady availability of good-quality teaching personnel and a variety of interests and methods. Those schools and cities that could teach and offer accommodation to large numbers of extraneous pupils were able by the end of the twelfth century to emancipate themselves into universities: institutionalized communities of masters and students engaged in professional study. In northern Europe Paris possessed the right combination of resources to develop into the theological centre of Europe, outflanking neighbouring schools such as Chartres and Laon, which had contributed much to the development of twelfth-century scholarship. In southern Europe Bologna held pride of place for law; Salerno and Montpellier were centres for medicine.

The contribution of the schoolmen of the latter part of the eleventh and the first half of the twelfth centuries was their passion to examine creatively what they had inherited from the past and to reorganize it. They used the tools of the trivium to analyse all available authorities and to work out which were now the most useful. They set out to learn all there was to learn and by asking new and exciting questions to harness all the knowledge they acquired to their Christian view of the world. They sought out any possible contradictions they could find in their material in order to solve these through a careful textual analysis of their disparate sources. At Laon, Anselm of Laon (teaching between 1080 and 1117) and his brother Ralph (d. 1131/3) lectured on books of the Bible. Anselm's commentaries on the Psalms and the Pauline Epistles together with the commentaries of others like Gilbert of Auxerre (Gilbert the Universal, d. 1134) culminated in the *Glossa Ordinaria*, the interlinear and marginal gloss of the whole Bible, which came into being between *c.*1080 and *c.*1130. It seems that at Laon formal lectures were given in the morning; these were followed by informal meetings in the evening at which earlier points, based on close readings of especially patristic* sources, were summed up and expounded. These summings-up were called sentences and covered all kinds of questions dealing with aspects of God and creation. Before long the sentences of Anselm of Laon and other masters were gathered together by students and systematized according to subject matter. These sentence collections served as handbooks for those concerned with pastoral affairs. Their order and structure were intimately connected with the development of systematic theology: a professional discipline covering the full gamut of Christian dogma, discipline, and ethics.

Early twelfth-century scholars were also interested in the natural world. This work is usually associated with the cathedral school at Chartres, but some have claimed that it too originated in Paris. William of Conches (*c.*1080–*c.*1154) and Thierry of Chartres (*c.*1110–*c.*1155/6) both used Calcidius' fourth-century truncated translation of Plato's cosmological work, the *Timaeus*, for their studies; William nurtured his medical interests with ancient Greek medical material translated from Arabic by Constantine the African, a monk from Monte Cassino (d. 1087). He and Thierry wrote extensively about the origins of the world. Thierry also produced texts on all seven of the liberal arts: the trivium together with mathematics, astronomy, music, and geometry, which constituted the quadrivium*. In his scientific work *Philosophia Mundi* ('Philosophy of the World') William struggled to come to a Christian understanding of Plato's world soul, the universal spirit that acts as an organizing principle for the world. William looked for similarities between world soul and the workings of the Holy Spirit. But he had to abandon his ideas because they were considered to be unorthodox. Another scholar of the natural sciences was the Englishman Adelard of Bath (*c.*1070–after 1146), who travelled to Sicily and Antioch to collect Arabic translations of Greek science and transmit them to the West. In his *Questiones Natu-*

rales ('Questions on Nature') he defends man's power to use his reason to discover the laws of nature.

The Jewish convert to Christianity Peter Alfonsi (fl. 1106–26) brought Greek and Arabic knowledge of astronomy with him when he travelled from Aragon to England and France in 1106. He promoted the study of medicine and advocated the importance of personal observation. His *Disciplina Clericalis*, a didactic collection of stories, introduced the West to the fables and tales of the Orient. In his Christian–Jewish disputation, *Dialogues between Moses the Jew and Peter the Christian*, he offered north-western Latin Christendom an introduction to Islam and rabbinic writings. More positive than Peter Alfonsi's starkly negative portrayal of Jewish thought was the use made by biblical exegetes like Andrew of Saint-Victor (d. 1175) of the school of Saint-Victor near Paris of rabbinical explanations of the meaning of the Hebrew words of the Old Testament. Important centres of Jewish exegesis of the Bible and the Talmud developed in France in the wake of the illuminating work of Rabbi Solomon ben Isaac (Rashi, d. 1104) in Troyes.

Another Englishman, John of Salisbury (c.1115–1180), was renowned for his breadth of learning. John's many works display his concern to apply what he studied in Paris (and perhaps Chartres) to the practicalities of communal life and government and administration. John served Archbishops Theobald and Thomas Becket of Canterbury and was closely involved in the controversy between Becket and Henry II. John later became bishop of Chartres (1176–80). His *Metalogicon* is an impassioned defence of the importance of the skills engendered by the study of the trivium for enabling communities to function harmoniously. The *Policraticus* (the so-called Statesman's Handbook) perceives political communities as organic bodies, whose health depends on constructive interaction of all its members. A later example of someone who used his scholastic training for public life is Peter of Blois (d. 1211/12). Peter, like John, served in the households of successive archbishops of Canterbury and likewise had connections with the Angevin court, and left an enormous collection of letters that touched on every imaginable topic. The collection became the letter-writing textbook *par excellence* for many centuries to come.

One of most colourful figures of the Parisian schools that John frequented was Peter Abelard (c.1079–c.1142). During the course of a tumultuous career he did his most important teaching at

Mont-Sainte-Geneviève in Paris. Abelard's *forte* was dialectic in which he did interesting work on universals. He applied logic to theology in his search for a rational explanation of the Trinity. He discussed the Persons of the Trinity as the triunity of Power, Wisdom, and Benignity. His views were thought to conflict with the concept of the equality of the three persons of the Trinity, and they met condemnation in 1121 at Soissons. Abelard had the highest regard for the classical past, arguing that close reading of Plato's *Timaeus* revealed the truth of the Trinity, just as did an allegorical reading of the Hebrew Bible. In 1140 at Sens, Abelard was roundly condemned by Bernard of Clairvaux, who blamed him for relying far too heavily on reason. Abelard's most innovative work probably lies in the area of ethics, where he studied intention, virtue, and love. He taught that acts in themselves were morally neutral; their underlying intention defined how they should be judged. Moving beyond Anselm of Canterbury's satisfaction theory, he argued that the redemption of Christ had made man better than he had been before the Fall, because Christ's sacrifice unleashed in man unprecedented love for God. In addition, in Jesus, humanity had the perfect example for right living and loving. His *Sic et Non* ('Yes and No'), a collection of contradictory authorities (mostly patristic), reveals his interest in discerning rationally between them. In its prologue he wrote: 'by doubting we come to inquiry and by inquiry we perceive the truth.' His correspondence with his one-time pupil, lover, and wife, Heloise, contains a rule for her nuns at the Paraclete, which displays a genuine interest in the special needs of female monastics. Heloise was a remarkable woman. She was already very learned when Abelard became her tutor. It is very likely that Heloise's own erudition influenced Abelard's development as a scholar.

Abelard's contemporary Gilbert of Poitiers (*c.*1080–1154) also attempted to use Aristotelian logic to explicate the Trinity. Like Abelard he was accused of heresy by Bernard of Clairvaux and others; unlike Abelard he could command enough support from fellow masters to escape condemnation. Far less controversial than Abelard or Gilbert was Peter Lombard (1095/1100–1160), who produced the first really successful overview of systematic theology. Peter's *Sentences* consist of four books; they are the product of many years of teaching and display his deep knowledge of not only Abelard's and Gilbert's work but also of two works of Hugh of Saint-Victor (*c.*1096–1141), the highly influential theological overview *Liber de Sacramentis* ('Book on the Sacraments') and the *Summa Sententiarum*, a sentence collection that encapsulated Victorine responses to the school of Abelard. Peter managed to organize his material without the repetitions and inconsistencies of his predecessors. Using the skills of the trivium, he carefully assembled and made sense of a vast array of source material. He also made plain what man could know about God using reason. Extrapolating from sensible evidence, man could use his reason to know that God exists and that his nature is three and one. But, although philosophy could prove the existence of God and illuminate some of the most basic attributes of God (for example, eternity, omnipotence, and goodness), it could not do more than provide analogies for the Trinity. Peter stressed the transcendence of God but also maintained that God gave his creatures their own sphere in which to function naturally. This means that the workings of the natural world were open to philosophical enquiry. Peter too was passionately interested in Jesus' humanity. He stressed Jesus' humility, citing the crucifixion as particularly important on account of the response it elicited from the faithful. Peter's *Sentences* became the theology textbook at Paris *par excellence*, but it was used much further afield. In Alsace, Abbess Herrad of Hohenbourg (d. after 1196) quoted extensively from the *Sentences* in her *Hortus Deliciarum* ('Garden of Delights'), the encyclopaedic work she put together for the erudition of her nuns at the end of the twelfth century. The other authors Herrad used most heavily were Rupert of Deutz, Honorius *Augustodunensis*, and also Peter Comestor (d. 1187), who was a pupil of Peter Lombard and who compiled the widely read *Historia Scholastica* ('Scholastic History'), a summary of the history of the Old Testament.

Pupils of Peter Lombard who had assimilated newly available works on logic by Aristotle (the so-called New Logic) applied logic to theological conundrums like the union of the human and divine natures in Christ. Very interesting is the work on socio-ethical questions such as the morally right price (the so-called just price) of commodities and the issue of usury by the circle of Peter the Chanter (d. 1197). This demonstrates how keen Peter the Chanter's circle was to apply their scholarship in a practical way to contemporary social issues. Preaching was a major component of their programme. Preaching was also a concern of Alan of Lille (*c*.1120–1202/3), who studied in Chartres, Paris, and Montpellier. Alan was a prolific writer and an outstanding poet. One of his poems is *The Plaint of Nature,* which dwells on the authority of Nature within her own realm of activity and berates humanity for breaking her laws by acts of sexual impropriety. In another, *The Anticlaudianus,* Nature seeks God's help and together they create the perfect man. Another outstanding Latin poet of the second half of the twelfth century was Walter of Châtillon (1130s–1180 or 1202/3), who studied at Paris and Rheims. He is the author of the hugely popular *Alexandreis,* a grand epic in ten books recounting the history of Alexander the Great.

Education and learning: the universities

From the second half of the twelfth-century until the middle of the thirteenth century the Parisian schools gradually fashioned themselves into a *universitas* (university) of masters and scholars. Its teaching was organized into four different faculties: theology, canon law, medicine, and the arts, which included philosophy, that is, physics, metaphysics, and ethics. The arts faculty was deemed to provide the necessary study skills to progress to the other faculties. A structure of examinations was developed that took a student from studying the liberal arts to his bachelor of arts degree. This degree entitled him to teach these subjects. If he wished to progress to a master's or a doctorate, he had to join one of the other three faculties. Ultimately the university was under papal control, but in practice ecclesiastical control was mostly enforced by the faculties through the masters. Importantly, all masters and students fell under canon law, enjoying 'benefit of clergy'*.

Bologna was the university that from its inception was geared to the study of law. It was there that Roman law began to be studied again at the end of the eleventh century. The renewed interest in Roman law inspired scholars at Bologna to systematize all available ecclesiastical legal material into an overview of canon law*. Anders Winroth's ground-breaking work has demonstrated that this text was completed in two stages, the first in 1139 or 1140, the second by 1158. This was Gratian's *Decretum.* Gratian's *Decretum* drew on the work of Burchard of Worms (*c.*925–1025) and Ivo of Chartres (*c.*1040–1115) and many others. It was to canon law what Peter Lombard's *Sentences* were to theology. It gave canon law the structure that was required to put into practice the ruminations of the theologians in Paris. As the *Decretum* was used in the classroom, it accumulated layers and layers of commentaries and additional material. From 1210 onwards popes began to promulgate officially what additional material had to be taught (and used by ecclesiastical courts). Thus Gregory IX decreed in 1234 that his *Decretals*, an enormous collection of canonical materials, should supplement Gratian's work.

Medicine was already being taught in Salerno at the end of the eleventh century through practical demonstrations. But in the course of the twelfth and early thirteenth centuries scholars in Salerno collected a number of Hippocratic and Galenic medical treatises, which had been translated from the Arabic or Greek into Latin. They taught their students by commenting on these texts. In addition to this material they began to display an interest in Aristotle's works on natural philosophy, which were becoming available from the second half of the twelfth century in translations from the Greek into Latin by among others James of Venice (fl. 1130s and 1140s). New and further translations of the Aristotelian corpus from the Greek were executed in the thirteenth century by for example Robert Grosseteste (*c.*1175–1253) and William of Moerbeke (*c.*1215–1286). Aristotelian texts that were translated from the Arabic were soon replaced by Latin translations from the original. Only Aristotle's *De Animalibus* ('On Animals') remained in a translation from the Arabic (by Michael Scot, d. *c.*1236). As medicine declined in Salerno in the early thirteenth century, it gained a foothold in Bologna. The University of Padua followed. Montpellier had become a centre for medicine by *c.*1150. By 1220 Montpellier was a university and in 1289 it gained papal recognition for its teaching in law, the arts, and medicine. Medicine was also a major faculty in Paris. And it was here that medical scholars from the second half of the thirteenth century greatly enhanced the Aristotelian aspects of the subject by mining Aristotle's scientific works for information on anatomy, psychology, physiology, physics, biology, and the effects of drugs. Peter of Abano was one of these men. He taught in Paris from before 1295 to 1306 before returning to Padua to teach medicine, philosophy, and astrology there. His book *Conciliator of the Differences of the Philosophers and, Especially, the Physicians* was widely used in Italy.

The University of Oxford was well known for its endeavours in the field of theology, but it was in the area of natural philosophy that it proved particularly strong. Grosseteste, who was chancellor of Oxford before becoming bishop of Lincoln in 1235, was an accomplished scientist who wrote on magnification through the use of lenses. Moving beyond Aristotle, he insisted on the importance of experiments to the study of science, relying heavily on mathematics. To his mind science buttressed by sound mathematics should be studied as part of the whole corpus of knowledge, which included theology and ethics. Roger Bacon (c.1219–92), who spent many years in Oxford and Paris, continued this kind of experimental work, contributing much to the development of optical studies. His *Opus Maius* ('Greater Work') outlines a complete programme for research in and teaching of the natural sciences. But it also includes a section on moral philosophy. As far as biblical studies were concerned, Bacon insisted on the importance of the correct translation of the original Hebrew and Greek, and to this end he composed grammars of those languages.

The availability of Latin versions of Aristotelian natural philosophy and metaphysics and Latin translations of Arabic commentaries on these works was causing problems by the early thirteenth century in Paris. It seems that theologians feared that the works could form a threat to the Christian faith in the hands of their colleagues in the arts faculty. In 1210 and in 1215 and again in 1231 the books were banned from the syllabus. But renewal of the ban must have meant the books continued to be read. In any case by 1255 almost all Aristotle's works were made compulsory in the faculty of arts. We have already seen how they were used by medical scholars. We now need to see what theologians made of the comprehensive theory of the universe that Aristotle presented to them in contrast to their Christian outlook.

Almost as important as the works of Aristotle were the commentaries by Muslim scholars that were translated along with them. Especially important were the ideas of the Spanish Muslim philosopher Averroes (ibn Rushd, 1126–98), who commented on all Aristotle's works. Averroes taught that there were three routes to the single truth. Revelation conveyed the uneducated to truth. Theology directed the educated, while philosophy helped highly trained minds reach truth. Philosophy was seen as the best medium for solving any contradictions that might seem to arise from travelling these different routes. In an attempt to clarify what Aristotle meant in his *De Anima* ('On the Soul'), Averroes posited that what is personal to man is his passive intellect. This is man's potential disposition for knowing things and constitutes his individual make-up. The active intellect, which is a separate heavenly intelligence, enables our minds to activate our intellectual potential. This is material or potential intellect. Man's passive intellect dies with man; there is no personal immortality. The only immortality man has is a kind of common intellectual immortality through the material intellect that is one for all men. Obviously, these views were as at odds with Islam as with Christianity and, for that matter, Judaism. It is not surprising that Parisian Latin Averroists like Siger of Brabant (1240–84) were heavily censured for propounding that philosophy should be studied on its own terms without taking account of theology and for denying personal immortality of the soul. They also followed Averroes in claiming that matter was eternal and had not, therefore, been created out of nothing (*ex nihilo*). The approach of the Franciscan friar Bonaventure (1217 [1221?]–74) was strongly Augustinian*, subordinating all knowledge to faith. Bonaventure discussed God in terms of light. Using Neoplatonic concepts, he posited that God as light exists in order for human beings to know him and through the operation of his divine light to know other things. With Augustine (d. 430), he deemed the original models of all creatures to be ideas in the mind of God. God creates individuals by stamping these models onto created matter. Christ, the supreme model, functions as the rational principle of creation. Bonaventure considered God, the light, to be the Good, heading the Chain of Being* made up of goodnesses in descending order according to their status of being. In this way, the whole of creation could be seen as a set of steps leading back to God, the ultimate good.

The approach of the Dominican Thomas Aquinas (1224/5–74) was much less contemplative. Aquinas received his earliest education in the arts at the new University of Naples, founded in 1224 by the Emperor Frederick II. After becoming a Dominican he learnt his Aristotle from Albert the Great (1206/7–80) in his order's school at Cologne. He also studied in Paris and taught there in the latter half of the 1250s and again between 1269 and 1272. He composed his massive *Summa Theologica* ('The Summary of Theology') as a new theological textbook to show young students of the arts how Aristotle's ideas could be safely absorbed into Christian (Augustinian) thinking. At the same time, he was responding to the ideas of Averroes and the work of the Aristotelian Jewish philosopher, Maimonides (1135–1204), who had fled from Muslim persecution in Spain to Egypt and whose *Guide for the Perplexed* had been translated into Latin by the mid-1220s. Unlike Aristotle's unmoved first mover or first cause, Aquinas' God is a God who is actively engaged with his creation, which he has created *ex nihilo*. Using Aristotelian principles as well as Neoplatonic and stoic concepts of reason, Aquinas argued that Natural Law, which human beings know through reason, teaches them how to strive for good (that is, wholeness) and avoid evil (that is, disintegration). As such they can know that God exists, and they can discover a great deal about God as a grand organizer of creation and also know much about the kind of society they need to fashion in order to fulfil their natural potential. Aquinas' man is both social and polit-ical. Politics belong to the natural order of things. But there is, of course, a lot more to knowing God than what humans know through reason alone. Through faith Christians know that God is triune (three-in-one), became incarnate, and so on. But none of this obvi-ates what reason teaches about nature. Man is sinful and is in desper-ate need of grace to fulfil the dictates of reason. But grace perfects nature; it does not destroy it. And, once matters of Christian truth, like the Eucharistic change from bread and wine to the body and blood of Christ, are known through faith, they can be most usefully explored by using the tools of reason. In short, Aquinas presented a remarkable synthesis of the full Aristotelian world view with traditional Christian teaching.

Not everyone was enamoured of Aquinas' innovative work. There were many who were profoundly uneasy about the way Aristotelian thought was being absorbed into Christian thinking. In 1277 a group of scholars submitted a list of 219 propositions to the bishop of Paris for condemnation. The propositions included the 13 Averroist ones that had already been condemned in 1270; a number of others were ascribed to Aquinas. Aquinas' Dominican followers managed to get the statements that were attributed to their teacher removed from the list of banned propositions in 1325 after their beloved doctor had been canonized in 1323. But it would take many more generations before Thomist* teaching started to gain the prominence it now enjoys within the Catholic Church.

In the closing years of the thirteenth century scholars like Henry of Ghent (c.1217–93) adopted a more metaphysical approach to learning and displayed greater interest in knowledge that was not empirical. The Franciscan John Duns Scotus (c.1265–1308), who taught at Oxford, Cambridge, and Paris before retiring to Cologne, emphasized God's absolute freedom while stressing the limitations of reason. He felt that Aquinas had subjected God to the natural laws he had formulated for the natural world. Duns Scotus did not think that studying God's creation could teach man more about God than that He had desired to create things as He did.

The Oxford Franciscan William of Ockham (c.1285–1347) ended his life in Germany under the protection of the Holy Roman Emperor, Louis of Bavaria, after his papal condemnation in 1328 over the issue of apostolic poverty. He posited that, as far as theological matters were concerned, human beings were completely reliant on faith. God has absolute power; his essence surpasses human analysis. The authority of revelation and the gift of grace allow humans to know what they believe is true. Reason plays a role only in facilitating logical inferences from the data of faith. As a radical empiricist, Ockham taught that certain scientific knowledge does not extend beyond individuals; it does not cover the relationship between individuals or the laws of nature. Scientific knowledge of these abstracts can only be probable. 'Ockham's razor', the maxim that account should be taken of only what is strictly relevant to what is under investigation, refers to the fact that, when Ockham explained how phenomena worked, he rejected the need to discuss their being, essence, or purpose. Scholars have pointed to the fact that Ockham bequeathed starkly different positions to his successors. Some interpreted him as expounding a strict form of fideism that cut out reason altogether. Others concluded from his teaching that there was no discernible order in the natural world. Still others felt he had given them the licence to study natural phenomena without any interference from theology. As such Ockham is a suitable person with which to end this account of education and learning in the central Middle Ages!

Historians and (auto)biographers at work

Many important annals, chronicles, and histories pre-date the historical output of the eleventh, twelfth, and thirteenth centuries. What marks the central medieval period is the sheer volume of the works that were produced. In part this can be explained by the events unleashed by the Crusades, by the vicissitudes that took place in Normandy and England after the Norman Conquest of 1066, the acquisition of the kings of Germany of the imperial title, and the development of urban communes in Italy and elsewhere. In addition to these external factors, men and women in this period seemed genuinely interested in recording and exploring their individual and collective experiences. Although medieval historians were not attempting to be objective in any modern sense of the word, they were on the whole committed to gathering as much material as they could from available written and oral sources, carefully distinguishing between what they considered to be reliable and what they did not. William of Malmesbury wrote, for example, in his *Deeds of the Kings of the English*: 'Incited by different motives both Normans and English have written of William [the Conqueror]. The former have praised him to excess, alike extolling to the utmost his good and his bad actions, while the latter out of national hatred have laden their conqueror with undeserved reproach. For my part as the blood of each people flows in my veins I shall steer a middle course . . .'.[1] What separates them from their modern counterparts was their conviction that it was their duty to assess their material not just within their immediate context but also within the much wider framework of their view of unfolding salvific* history, from the Creation to their own age, which they placed before the second coming of Christ and the Last Judgment. Closely linked to these considerations, which were replete with theological overtones, was the fundamental belief that one of the purposes of recording events of the past was to impart lessons in morality to their readers.

Early in our period, Sigebert of Gembloux in present-day Belgium (d. 1112) produced a chronicle that reached 1111. An important model

---

[1] *The Normans in Europe*, ed. and trans. E. Van Houts (Manchester, 2000), 164–5.

for this kind of writing was the world chronicle by Eusebius (d. 340). Sigebert started his own chronicle in 381, the year after the ending of the Latin translation by Jerome (d. 420) of Eusebius' Greek *Chronicle and Canons*. For the period before his own day he abbreviated the texts of a great many sources, including the *Ecclesiastical History of the English People* by Bede (d. 735). Sigebert was very widely read and taken as the starting point by numerous later chroniclers. On a more local level, William of Jumièges produced the *Gesta Normannorum Ducum* ('History of the Dukes of Normandy') between 1060 and 1070. His work absorbed earlier work, notably the eulogistic *History of the Dukes of the Normans* by Dudo of Saint-Quentin (completed by *c*.1015); his own work was continued by Orderic Vitalis (1075–*c*.1142) and Robert of Torigni (writing 1139–1154). As a whole, the *Gesta* are an important source for the history of Normandy and after 1066 of England until the death of King Henry I in 1135.

Orderic Vitalis was chief among the historians of Normandy, one of the most productive regions for the writing of history. His history of his own monastery, Saint-Evroult, quickly turned into a history of the Normans in general before ending up as a universal ecclesiastical history. His *Ecclesiastical History* contains much valuable information for the history of Normandy, England, and France, which Orderic had gathered from many different sources between *c*.1110 and *c*.1142. He informed his readers what he had recorded on the basis of first-hand knowledge. The lengthy work closes with an epilogue in which Orderic put the details of his own life within the context of his faith: 'And so, a boy of ten, I crossed the English Channel and came into Normandy as an exile, unknown to all, knowing no one. Like Joseph in Egypt, I heard a language which I did not understand.'[2] The well-researched *Deeds of the Kings of the English* and the *Historia Novella* ('Modern History') by William of Malmesbury (*c*.1090–*c*.1142) were meant to start where Bede had left off. They give an account of the kings of England from the immigration of the Anglo-Saxons to 1142. William's explicit purpose was to edify his readers by the examples he gave in his text; he was widely read. Of the defeated English, William, for example, says: 'Drinking in parties was a universal practice in which occupation they passed entire nights as well as days. They

---

[2] *The Ecclesiastical History of Orderic Vitalis*, ed. and trans. M. Chibnall (6 vols., Oxford, 1968–80), vi. 554–5.

consumed their whole substance in mean and despicable houses unlike the Normans and the French who in noble and splendid mansions live in frugality. The vices attendant on drunkenness which enervate the human mind followed.'[3] Other important Anglo-Norman historians were Henry of Huntingdon (1109–1155), William of Newburgh (d. 1198), and Roger of Howden (d. 1201/2). Geoffrey of Monmouth's (c.1100–1155) very successful, and very fanciful, *History of the Kings of Britain* advanced the idea of a Christian Arthurian Britain that boasted Trojan origins (see below, p. 170). In Norman Sicily the *Liber de Regno Siciliae* ('Book about the Kingdom of Sicily') provides intriguing information about court life from the death of Roger II in 1154 until 1168/9. The author must have been a courtier; much later he was assigned the fictitious name of Hugo Falcandus. The work of another kind of courtier came from the pen of Galbert of Bruges. Galbert was a notary of the count of Flanders at Bruges and gives an eyewitness account of the tumultuous happenings following the murder of Charles the Good in 1127 in the shape of a diary (see pp. 42–3). *The Murder of Charles the Good, Count of Flanders* provides a remarkable insight into the political and social changes that took place in twelfth-century Flanders. Whether or not it was a true diary, it is the only such work we have of this period.

In the thirteenth century the monastery of Saint Albans was a centre for English historical writing. Roger of Wendover (d. 1236) composed his *Flowers of History*, which are especially informative for the period 1214–36, for which Roger gathered his own evidence, including a text of Magna Carta. Matthew Paris (c.1200–59) took over from Roger at his death. Matthew quoted documents at length and collected some 350 of them in an appendix. He also provided illustrations to his text. This approach did not, however, save the work from Matthew's many careless errors, deliberate inaccuracies, and embellishments. He betrayed his Benedictine bias in his frequent attacks on Dominican and Franciscan friars. In France the Abbey of Saint-Denis collected documentation and produced historical writing in support of the Capetian kings, many of whom were buried there. The *Life of Louis VI* by Suger (1081–1151) is an early example. Others such as Rigord (c.1145/50–1207) and Primat (fl. 1244–77) continued the tradition. Primat set in train the adaptation of these individual Latin

---

[3] *The Normans in Europe*, ed. Van Houts, 169.

histories and others into a multilayered vernacular compilation of French history known as the *Grandes chroniques*, which in its final redaction would go up to 1461.

In the German Empire we encounter Otto of Freising (*c.*1112–1158), who was in a prime position to gather material as the grandson of Emperor Henry IV and the half-brother of Conrad III with whom he went on the Second Crusade. Otto joined the Cistercian Order after having enjoyed a Parisian education. He became bishop of Freising in 1138. Otto's greatest work is *The Two Cities*. Writing in the vein of Augustine's *City of God* he aimed to write universal history from a theoretical point of view. To his mind, Augustine's two cities, the earthly city and the City of God, had become one city at the time of Constantine or Theodosius. This was the city of Christ, which he calls *ecclesia* (church); a mixed city, based on collaboration between empire and priesthood, a collaborative enterprise, which the struggle between King Henry IV and Pope Gregory VII threatened to undermine (see Chapter 4). In a biblical vein, Otto saw the end of the world as the culmination of earthly history, which would span four universal empires and which was marked by transfers from one empire to the next, from Babylon in the East to start off with to Rome in the West at the end. Latterly the Roman Empire had moved from the Franks (with Charlemagne) to the Lombards (with the tenth-century kings of Italy) and, finally, to the Germans (with the Ottonians, Salians, and, most recently, the Hohenstaufen). Otto drew a stark contrast between human sinfulness and the hope of Heaven. His intimate knowledge of the conflict between the empire and the papacy and the problems within the German Empire seem to have fed his gloom. The final book of *The Two Cities* set out Otto's vision of heavenly Jerusalem. His *Deeds of Frederick I* were more positive, in which he set off the accession to the throne of Frederick Barbarossa (1152) against the problematic years of Henry IV in the previous century.

William of Tyre was born in Jerusalem around 1130 and studied liberal arts and theology in Paris and Orléans and law in Bologna before returning to the kingdom of Jerusalem, where he became archbishop of Tyre in 1175. He died in 1186. His history of the crusades (*History of Deeds Done beyond the Sea*) gives invaluable information about that kingdom. He blamed Christian spiritual laxity and sin for the downturn in the fortunes of the Crusader Kingdom. Good examples of histories of the crusades that glorify the deeds of the Franks are *The History of the Crusades* by Fulcher of Chartres (d. 1127), *The Deeds of God through the French* by Guibert of Nogent (d. *c*.1125), and *The History of the Crusade of Louis VII* by Odo of Deuil (d. *c*.1162). Nor were accounts of the crusades written by Latin Christians alone. Byzantine reactions can be found in Anna Comnena's *Alexiad* (1140s) and Niketas Choniates' *O City of Byzantium* (written after 1204; see above, pp. 16–17); there were also a number of important Muslim sources. Three fascinating Hebrew Chronicles of the First Crusade were composed before 1150. They relate the persecutions of the Jews by the armies of the so-called popular crusade in the Rhineland in the spring and summer of 1096 and contain vivid, hair-raising accounts of Jewish self-martyrdom to preserve their own Jewish identity and that of their communities. Blending history with liturgy, the chronicles beg many questions concerning their historical accuracy. Did so many Jews martyr themselves? Do the chronicles accurately portray the martyrdoms as they occurred? Whatever the case may be, the chronicles forcefully portray human beings acting in the way they believe God intended them to, in order positively to affect the course of history.

Town chronicles reflected the burgeoning civic pride of developing communes of the period. An excellent example of this is Caffaro's history of Genoa. Caffaro (1080/1–1166) was involved in the formation of the Genoese commune and frequently served as consul. He started his history as a private enterprise, but it became official when he handed it over to the consuls of Genoa in 1152. A copy was made and placed in the archives of the town. With the help of Caffaro, material was added until 1163. The work was carried on after Caffaro's death until 1293. Town histories were also produced in Milan and Pisa from the middle of the twelfth century. Arnold fitzThedmar, alderman of Bridgeward, is probably the author of *The Chronicle of the Mayors and Sheriffs of London*, which was written between 1258 and 1272. This work does not just provide information on the City of London and its neighbouring abbey. It also touches on German affairs on account of the fact that Richard of Cornwall was elected king of Germany in 1257 (see Chapter 3).

Finally two thirteenth-century world chronicles need to be mentioned because of their enormous popularity. The first is the *Speculum Historiale* ('Historical Mirror') of Vincent of Beauvais (d. 1264), a vast historical encyclopaedia of the world until around 1250, consisting of extracts of a myriad of works. The second is *The Chronicle of Popes and Emperors* of Martin the Pole of Silesia (d. 1279), which was hugely popular in Germany.

The biography of Louis IX (St Louis, d. 1270) by Jean de Joinville (1224(?)–1317), which was written in French, should be added to the various royal biographies mentioned earlier. It mixed hagiography with analysis of the king's politics and exciting descriptions of his foreign adventures. Joinville made much use of the personal knowledge he had of the king, with whom he had been on crusade. His work also tells us a fair amount about himself. Autobiographies were a particularly important innovation of our period. The late-classical model for this was Augustine's *Confessions.* They reflect the period's genuine interest in the development of human beings, albeit within specific frameworks, established by communal and religious expectations. A good example is *On Temptations,* the work of Othlo of Saint Emmeran (*c.*1010–*c.*1079), work in which he movingly wrote about his struggles with religious doubt. Guibert of Nogent's autobiography reveals a very troubled old-fashioned monk's prejudices against the remarkable economic and social changes he was witnessing in northern France. Peter Abelard recorded his version of the controversial events shaping his career in his long letter *Historia Calamitatum* ('The Story of [Abelard's] Adversities'). The letters Heloise wrote in response reveal the burning love she had for her former husband. The *Opusculum de Conversione Sua* ('Short Account of his own Conversion') by Herman the Jew, which was composed around 1150, describes the tortuous path of the Jew David of Cologne to the baptismal font. Although some scholars have questioned its authenticity, most accept it as a *post factum* account of a real conversion. An exceptional, and exceptionally important, work of autobiography is the chronicle of King James I of Aragon–Catalonia (1213–76), which was written in Catalan, not Latin, and which describes from the king's viewpoint the Catalan conquest of Majorca (1229) and of Valencia (1238).

Obviously the previous examples can only give a glimpse of the historical output between 1000 and 1300. But they reveal a keen interest in human affairs that is such an important hallmark of the period. The increased use of the vernacular by historians prompts us to look more closely at processes by which a *literate* vernacular culture came into its own in this period.

Vernacular culture

Geoffrey of Monmouth's *History of the Kings of Britain* was really more fiction than history. To the history of Britain it harnessed Celtic vernacular oral traditions about King Arthur and his Round Table and the powers of Merlin. Geoffrey's Latin work was disseminated widely throughout Europe and was almost immediately translated into French, Middle English, and Welsh, and other vernacular languages in due course. Scholars have shown that a remarkable feature of the twelfth century is that Latin could be instrumental in boosting the development of literate vernacular culture by facilitating the textual transmission of one vernacular tradition into many others. Latin also helped transmit some of the old French epic poems known as the *chansons de geste*. The *chansons* concerned heroic deeds of saints or of military heroes. Ninth- and late tenth/early eleventh-century Latin versions existed of material concerning the exploits of William 'of Orange' (Count William of Gellone). French redactions stem from the beginning of the twelfth century. Wolfram von Eschenbach (fl. *c.*1200–20) used the *Bataille d'Aliscans*, one of the *chansons* about William of Orange, when he wrote his remarkable *Willehalm* in the 1220s. The best known *chansons de geste* concern Charlemagne and his vassals. The first redactions of the greatest of these, *The Song of Roland*, date from the late eleventh century. By this time the story had already been recounted in Latin and Old French versions with many local variations. *The Song of Roland* narrates graphically the betrayal of Charlemagne's loyal vassal Roland by the felon Ganelon and Ganelon's ultimate downfall. It is an action-packed story of heroes and villains rather than the stuff of keen human introspection, the story of Christian Franks overcoming Muslims in Spain on behalf of Charlemagne. Epics like *The Song of Roland* also show how historical themes were woven into works of fiction: Roland (d. 778) was Charlemagne's prefect of the Breton March who was killed by the Christian Basques, not Spanish Muslims.

In Germany, Old High German epic poems shared material with the Old Norse Eddas, episodic poetry that had been transmitted orally from the sixth century before the onset of written redactions in the tenth. The most important of these was the *Nibelungenlied*, which was redacted in Austria in the thirteenth century. The *Nibelungenlied* centres on the adventures of Siegfried, who had travelled to the Burgundian court to marry Kriemhild and relates the complicated events surrounding the vengeance that Kriemhild tried to exact from her kin for his murder. *Beowulf*, the most important Old English epic, is set in Scandinavia. It was probably composed in the eighth or early ninth century. Old English literature developed in Anglo-Saxon society, which had a long-standing tradition of using the vernacular alongside Latin for a wide variety of purposes, from religious texts to legal documents to chronicles like *The Anglo-Saxon Chronicle* from the ninth century until 1154. In Scandinavia, sagas and skaldic poetry were composed about leaders and kings of the Viking era. They were recited by skalds and committed to writing in the twelfth and thirteenth centuries. The most famous saga collection is the *Heimskringla* by Snorri Sturluson (1179–1241) of Iceland.

From the end of the eleventh century new literary forms took shape that fed off and reshaped older material into stories about young men striving to win the love of (usually) exalted ladies. The codes of behaviour were determined by chivalric norms. These works went far beyond the 'sabre rattling' of the *chansons de geste*. They dealt with courtly love and explored feelings of unrequited passion and situations that challenged individuals to search their conscience to make the right decision. This material would seem to epitomize the individualism so many scholars have 'discovered' in this period (see Further Reading). Although it is certainly possible to interpret this material in this way, one does have to be cautious. The composers of these tales and those who recited or performed them could not have been free agents in a society where patronage was a fact of life. The shape, durability, and indeed the very completion of long intricate compositions were directly reliant on the successful reception by those who had commissioned the work and had asked for it to be performed, or both. It is, therefore, equally valid to suggest that these explorations of courtly love say as much about the audiences for which they were written as about their composers. It would seem that we are encountering a similar kind of creative tension between individual artists and the multilayered social and religious conventions in which they worked, which we met in the case of authors of intellectual and historical texts who had to find their way within their own milieux (see above, p. 150). What must be true is that the mass of material produced on courtly love reveals the real interest and pleasure both men and women experienced in speculating about the psychological complexities governing human relations, especially between the sexes. Many patrons of these tales were lay noble women. This has prompted many scholars to wonder what this material actually reveals about the position of women in central medieval courtly society. For, next to the figure of noble ladies inspiring pure, and usually unfulfilled love, there are many scenes in which women are subjected to ridicule and violence. There is no simple explanation that would overwrite the contradictory messages it contains. Perhaps those contradictions accurately reflect the paradoxes women were faced with in their different functions in society.

Duke William IX of Aquitaine (1071–1125) adopted courtly love themes in his troubadour* poetry. By the first half of the twelfth century there was a proliferation of troubadour songs at the courts of southern France. Well-known troubadours were Marcabru (fl. 1150s), Bernart de Ventadorn (fl. 1147–70), and Peire Vidal (fl. late twelfth/early thirteenth centuries). Among female troubadours, Countess Beatrice of Die (fl. late twelfth/early thirteenth centuries) is particularly interesting, because in her poems women express their yearnings for love. In northern France trouvères* such as Chrétien de Troyes (c. 1140–90), Blondel de Nesle (b. c.1155), and Gace Brulé (c.1159–after 1212) carried on the work of their southern counterparts. The love lyrics of the 1170s and 1180s of Heinrich von Veldeke (Hendrik van Veldeken, d. c.1200) and Friedrich von Hausen (d. 1190) clearly show active Minnesänger* (poets of love) in Germany. Other notable Minnesänger were Hartmannn von Aue (fl. 1180–1220), Wolfram von Eschenbach, and, especially, Walther von der Vogelweide (fl. 1190–1230). South of the Alps, courtly love poetry in a form of Italian was introduced in the early thirteenth century under the patronage of the Emperor Frederick II (d. 1250). A particularly influential innovation of this 'Sicilian school' of poets was the fourteen-line love sonnet.

Courtly love themes were also introduced into epic poetry, softening the contours of their heroic protagonists. Scholars have illustrated this process by tracing the evolution of *The Poem of El Cid*, which was first redacted in Castilian around 1207. In reality the Cid was Rodrigo Díaz (d. 1099), one of the knights of King Alfonso VI of Léon-Castile (see Chapter 6). In *El Cid* Rodrigo falls out of favour with his king and has to leave court. He accrues great renown through his military exploits in the internecine battles between Christian and Muslim princes. The Cid dies saving Valencia from its attackers. Courtly love themes were added to the epic as it was recast time and again. Rodrigo is eventually transformed from a pragmatic fighter into a chivalric knight championing Christianity against Islam. In Germany Heinrich von Veldeke adapted the *Roman d'Eneas* (an Anglo-Norman adaptation of Virgil's story of Troy) to compose his *Eneit* between 1170 and 1185.

In France courtly love finally became the theme of romances. French romances took the shape of relatively short rhymed narratives; in Germany they were much longer. The concept of the quest for the Holy Grail, the dish or goblet used by Jesus at the Last Supper, was grafted onto Arthurian themes. Other Celtic traditions were used too, as were a variety of classical themes. Marie de France (*c.*1130–1200) produced twelve narrative poems (*Lais*) in which she explored themes of (usually adulterous) love by blending Arthurian and Breton material. Chrétien de Troyes wrote romances concerning the knights of the Round Table. His *Lancelot*, for example, explores Lancelot's adulterous love for Queen Guinevere. In *Perceval* Chrétien has his hero adopt celibate purity in his search for the Holy Grail. In Germany, Hartmann von Aue and Wolfram von Eschenbach adopted and adapted these themes, but, unlike Marie and Chrétien, they wrote in praise of married love rather than adulterous love. In addition their characters gained greater psychological depth. Hartmann translated Chrétien's *Erec et Enide* and *Yvain* to compose his own *Erec* and *Iswain*; Wolfram wrote *Parzival*, in which he developed Chrétien's *Perceval*. Central to Wolfram's work is the study of the evolution of a true Christian knight. Interestingly enough Chrétien's *Lancelot* was not translated into German, although an earlier *Lanzelet* was composed after 1195 by Ulrich von Zatzikhoven, who discarded the crucial theme of adultery. At the beginning of the thirteenth century Gottfried von Strassburg produced *Tristan and Isolde*; the adulterous lovers are destroyed by their own dishonourable behaviour.

Andreas Capellanus (fl. 1178–80) wrote a theoretical work in Latin about love for Countess Marie of Champagne (d. 1198), who was the daughter of Louis VII and Eleanor of Aquitaine. The work is full of contradictory statements about true love, advocating adulterous love in one part and condemning it in another. In the thirteenth century the *Romance of the Rose* was composed in French by Guillaume de Lorris (*c*.1213–*c*.1237) and continued by Jean de Meung (fl. 1275–1305). The work explores the meaning of love through the allegory of a lover dreaming about a walled garden containing a rose. The wall shuts out what the courtly lover must put aside, such as hatred, ill-will, greed, envy, old age, and poverty and allows access only to those engaged in, among other things, courtliness, delight, beauty, riches, generosity, and youth. The poem is full of contradictions, which are only compounded by its continuation. But perhaps Joachim Bumke is correct in pointing out how demanding courtly love was for its adherents by its unrealistic and contradictory requirements, which bore so little resemblance to real life (see Further Reading).

Many other forms of vernacular literature stem from our period. Old French *fabliaux* (short comic stories) were popular between the late twelfth century and 1250. Marie de France translated Aesop's *Fables* into French and wrote her own versions, in which she combined classical with Celtic material. In contrast to classical fables, medieval ones were less didactic, funnier, and usually rude. Besides religious poetry, a wide range of vernacular poetry was produced on all kinds of profane themes. Examples of this poetry are found among the so-called *Carmina Burana* ('Songs of Benediktbeuern'), some 300 Latin lyrics interspersed with lines in the vernacular including more than forty German verses. The material is in a thirteenth-century Austrian manuscript that once belonged to the Bavarian abbey of Benediktbeuern (*Benediktobura*). In Spain Jewish poets adapted Arabic forms of verse when writing in Hebrew. Their subject matter spanned everything from the highly spiritual to poetry about feasting, fighting, and making love. Prolific poets were Samuel Ha-Nagid (d. 1056), Solomon ibn Gabirol (d. 1053/8), Judah Ha-Levi (d. 1141), Joseph ibn Zabara (b. 1140), and Todros Abulafia (d. *c*.1298).

In the field of drama, mystery plays, which were liturgically based, had become so popular by the thirteenth century that they were translated into the vernacular and in due course laicized, joining all kinds of other dramatic forms. Excerpts from the Bible were put into vernacular verse, and Latin saints' lives were translated. Especially important were the vernacular translations of the widely popular collections of miracle stories of the Virgin Mary, which had circulated in Latin from the twelfth century. Good examples are the *Miracles de Nostre Dame* by Gauthier de Coinci (d. 1236) and the *Cantigas de Santa Maria* by Alfonso the Wise of Castile from between 1250 and 1284.

These final examples show how vernacular texts covered both the religious and the profane. Many texts combined both elements in innovative ways. Literate vernacular culture did not in any sense replace the products of Latin culture and learning that we discussed earlier. What it did do was offer large-scale possibilities for a wider spectrum of the population to participate in their culture through reading and listening to texts.

A twelfth-century Renaissance?

The years 1050–1250 have been dubbed the 'Twelfth-Century Renaissance' by many scholars. They have also been characterized as a period of humanism. How valid are these terms, and, even more importantly, how useful are they to convey the essential character of the central Middle Ages?

If 'Renaissance' is taken to mean the rebirth or reawakening of a period that seeks to bridge a gap of time in order to reconnect with classical antiquity, then it is clear that the term is far better suited to the Italian Renaissance (fourteenth–sixteenth centuries) than to the central Middle Ages. We have seen how important tradition was for the people of this period; they were not turning their backs on the centuries lying between them and the heyday of classical culture. Indeed, this survey has consciously reached back to c.1000 to give an account of the background from which new forms of intellectual or cultural activity arose. But, if the term is used to encapsulate the palpable excitement people experienced as they became aware of the treasures of antiquity, the term is apt. Classical ideas were not just revived; they were enthusiastically reinterpreted in the light of existing traditions and used to develop new areas of thought. Closing c.1300 has given us the opportunity to explore scholarly activity some fifty years beyond the time by which the full Aristotelian corpus had been uncovered. However, 'Renaissance' must not be used to convey the false impression that cultural aspects of the whole period can be typified by facile, chronologically defined classifications. As we have seen, there were many variations. This is especially true in the area of architecture. Romanesque and Gothic styles were adopted in special ways at various times in different regions. Having said that, the new Gothic forms, which Abbot Suger chose for Saint-Denis in order to manipulate light to make the church seem more like heaven, bring out a fundamental feature of this period's human creativity. A prelate like Suger might muse about how his church might 'brighten the minds [of people] so that they may travel through the true lights to the True Light where Christ is the true Door',[4] but others had to acquire advanced human skills to construct the required building.

This brings us to the term 'humanism'. We have already seen that the term 'humanism' in the sense of studying classical texts for their own sake would not appropriately characterize this period; nor would 'humanism' in the sense of concentration on human beings without regard to the divine. Severing the human from the divine was unthinkable. An essential aspect of this period is the interest people had in their own personal humanity and the human condition *within* the context of their understanding of God and the communities in which they lived. But, if 'humanism' is nuanced to take this into account, the term does become useful. For this kind of interest in humanity rather than stark individuality was definitely a phenomenon of 1000–1300. Although individualized pictorial representations exist, such as the mid-twelfth-century bronze likeness of Frederick Barbarossa and the thirteenth-century statues of the founders of Naumburg Cathedral, these do seem to be exceptions. More representative is one of the miniatures in Herrad of Hohenbourg's *Hortus Deliciarum*, picturing Herrad with her nuns. To be sure, all but two women are named, but the pictures of the nuns are remarkably similar. What Herrad was setting out to depict was not women who were free agents; she was displaying individual nuns within a vibrant monastic community. This period's interest in the self was wedded to a strong consciousness of the importance of the concept of community, whether in the widest sense of universal human fellowship or (as far as Christians were concerned) universal Christian fellowship,

---

[4] *Abbot Suger on the Abbey Church of St.-Denis and its Art Treasures*, ed. and trans. E. Panofsky, rev. G. Panofsky-Soergel (Princeton, 1979), 47–8.

or in narrower terms of collectivities such as the peoples of a specific kingdom, inhabitants of a town, members of an extended family, court, order, or scholarly community. 'Frameworked individuality' typifies the intellectual and cultural creativity of the period better than personal individualism.

6

The expansion of Latin Christendom

Nora Berend

Between *c.*950 and *c.*1300 Europe emerged through the incorporation of new territories (a process that had started before 950), the consolidation of political systems in the newly integrated areas, and transformations in western Europe itself. By the fourteenth century, Europe became the synonym of Christendom and the geographical area of the two roughly coincided. This chapter focuses on Latin Christendom, as the scope of the book allows only fleeting references to the Balkans, Rus´, and Byzantium. Expansion meant more than the simple addition of new territories and the enlargement of the previously existing western European political and religious system. It entailed the birth of a Latin Christendom characterized by new elements such as urbanization and the growth of commerce, claims of papal leadership, and the consolidation of several sovereign rulers. Latin Christendom, under the headship of the pope, developed its own sense of unity during this period. From the thirteenth century onwards, contemporary authors increasingly used *Europa* not simply as a geographical term, but as indicative of the community of (Latin) Christendom. Despite the rhetoric of unity, however, Latin Christendom was far from uniform. Christendom diversified as it expanded and came to incorporate a multiplicity of local religious practices and political systems.

This expansion took a number of different forms, including conquest and missions from the already Christianized areas as well as local initiatives from non-Christians. It led to the extension of already existing states and the creation of new ones. Rather than following one 'blueprint', these processes differed in the various areas. Most significant in terms of long-term consequences was the adhesion of new areas contiguous to western Europe: Scandinavia, northern and east-central Europe, and Iberia. Even this integration was not a uniform process. The Christianization of Scandinavia and east-central Europe meant conversions 'from above', initiated by chieftains, linked to the creation of new Christian polities. In contrast, Baltic Europe was conquered and converted mainly by force, whereas in Iberia already existing Christian kingdoms grew and were transformed at the expense of Muslim rulers. Another spectacular form of expansion, crusading, especially to Palestine, was at the time seen by many Christians as the most important, as well as the most expressive of Christianity. Yet these enterprises, although contributing to the consolidation of Christianity within Europe, especially in the north, brought only temporary successes outside Europe, and by 1300 the age of extra-European crusading tied to conquest was for all practical purposes over. Finally, travels, missions, and early geographical exploration—though not always leading to the acquisition of territories—contributed to the expansion of the mental map of Christians.

Christianization in Scandinavia and central Europe

In this period, Scandinavia and central Europe became a fully integrated part of Christendom. The Danish, Norwegian, Swedish, Czech, Hungarian, and Polish rulers opted for conversion to Christianity and its imposition on the people whom they ruled. Christianization 'from above' does not mean that no previous contacts existed with Christian areas; indeed, in most cases there is evidence of individual conversions and syncretism prior to the ruler's decision to convert. However, it was the official enforcement of a religious change to Christianity that marked the real turning point. Conversion was intertwined with political change as well: the rulers established dynasties, drawing ever larger territories under their control, and began to create structures through which they could exercise their authority more effectively.

The chronology and circumstances of conversions varied. The Bohemian case is controversial: one tradition holds that a number of Bohemian chieftains were baptized in Regensburg in 845; another, that Bořivoj (d. before 895), the first known ruler of the Přemyslid dynasty, accepted baptism in 883 from Great Moravia. Whatever the case, Christianization in Bohemia took off during the tenth century. In Poland, the baptism around 966 of Mieszko (d. 992) was linked to his marriage; through his Bohemian wife Dobrawa he relied on Bohemian missionaries to convert the Poles. Hungary's ruling family converted following the German defeat of Hungarian raiding armies (933, 955): the chieftain Géza (d. 997) invited Frankish missionaries and arranged the marriage of his son Vajk (baptized as Stephen) to Gisela, the daughter of Duke Henry of Bavaria. Missionaries in central Europe arrived mostly from Byzantine and German areas. Bohemia, once converted, also provided missionaries to neighbouring territories, most famously Adalbert (Vojtěch), killed by the Prussians while evangelizing them in 997, and claimed by all central European polities as their own saint.

After isolated missionary successes, Christianization took off in Scandinavia in the late tenth century. The Danish king Harald Bluetooth accepted baptism about 966; the Christianization of Denmark continued during the eleventh century. Christianity was introduced in Norway during the tenth century and imposed from 995–1000 onwards under King Olaf Tryggvason, who had been perhaps baptized and certainly confirmed in England. After 1016 King Olaf Haraldsson used force to Christianize the north-western parts of Norway. Missions to Swedish lands (Svealand), and even a royal conversion in the late tenth century, pre-dated widespread Christianization there, less tied to royal power and accomplished by the twelfth century. The pagan cult centre of Uppsala continued to exist until around 1080, and the evidence of burials and rune stones testifies to the coexistence of Christians and pagans throughout the eleventh century. An example of this coexistence is a mould for ironwork displaying side by side a cross and Thor's hammer.[1] Iceland, settled in the late ninth and early tenth centuries by Scandinavians (mostly Norwegians), adopted Christianity around 1000. Many parts of

[1] R. Boyer, *Le Christ des barbares: Le monde nordique (IXe–XIIIe siècle)* (Paris, 1987), 11, photo. 1.

Scandinavia were difficult to reach, and the Christianization of isolated communities took a long time.

Traditional beliefs and cults including the worship of forces of nature and sacrificial feasts did not disappear with the advent of Christianity. Indeed, the challenge to new rulers frequently came in the form of so-called pagan revolts, where political rivalry and religious contestation became intertwined (in 1046 and 1061 in Hungary, perhaps in 929 or 935 in Bohemia, some time between 1035 and 1038 in Poland, in 1060 and perhaps c.1080 in Sweden). In the Scandinavian case, contact with Christianity even triggered the elaboration of traditional beliefs and rituals: the systematization of the originally fluid pantheon of gods; and perhaps the building of a temple as the centre of the cult.

Nor was Christianization a uniform process. Various missionary centres vied for influence over the new territories. There was rivalry between Regensburg and Mainz for the subjection of Bohemia to their archdiocese. In Scandinavia until the mid-twelfth century most bishops were English or German, and drew on their own ecclesiastical traditions. Even church buildings show this duality: while Nidaros (Trondheim) Cathedral (Norway) shows English influences, especially in similarities with Lincoln Cathedral, the contemporary cathedral in Ribe (Denmark) was built of tufa from the Rhineland, and its structural elements and sculptures resemble those of German cathedrals.[2] Yet another player in this rivalry, the papacy, often tried to ensure that newly converted lands were directly dependent upon the Apostolic See, but in the end usually failed to achieve more than at most symbolic submission.

A variety of imported and local religious elements merged, creating distinct patterns in the new countries. Thus in Bohemia–Moravia and Hungary, strong Byzantine influences persisted, which originated in missions in the second half of the ninth century in Moravia and a century later in Hungary. Its most notable examples are Old Church Slavonic* hagiographic texts and liturgy until the end of the eleventh century in Bohemia, and the existence of Greek monasteries throughout the twelfth century in Hungary. In Scandinavia, rune inscriptions were used on church bells and baptismal fonts, and

---

[2] B. and P. Sawyer, *Medieval Scandinavia: From Conversion to Reformation circa 800–1500* (London and Minneapolis, 1993), 116, 118, figs. 5.4, 5.5.

rune stones served as Christian gravestones in pagan cemeteries. A rune stone at Jelling (Denmark) represented Christ surrounded by pre-Christian motifs.[3] In written culture and art, local and outside influences blended together. Latin writing was imported everywhere, but whereas in Hungary, for example, this also meant the introduction of writing itself and thus the beginnings of literacy, manifest in charters and chronicles, in Sweden runes that had already existed centuries prior to Christianization continued to be widely used after the introduction of Christianity, concurrently with the Latin alphabet. Vernacular religious literacy emerged locally. In Bohemia, a rich vernacular literature of saints' lives was already developed in the tenth century, whereas the first extant texts in Hungary, a prayer to the Virgin Mary and a burial speech, date from the late twelfth century, and Polish prose and poetry appeared in the thirteenth century. Religious texts in the vernacular began in Norway and Iceland in the twelfth century, in Denmark in the thirteenth, while Swedish vernacular literature developed only after 1300. In art, Byzantine, German, and Parisian models and often artists left their marks, but locals increasingly adapted rather than simply adopted art forms. For example, while in 1170–80 the metalwork of the portals of Gniezno Cathedral in Poland shows the influence of the art of the Meuse region,[4] in the thirteenth century Gothic architecture in northern Europe became distinct through the use of brick as a building material.

The newly emerging dynasties made use of Christian sanctity, propagating the cult of their ancestors. Thus Saint Václav (Wenceslas, d. 929 or 935) in Bohemia, Saint Stephen (d. 1038) in Hungary, Saint Olaf (d. 1030) in Norway, Saint Cnut (d. 1086) in Denmark, and Saint Eric (d. 1160) in Sweden were presented as Christian heroes fighting and (except for Stephen) dying for the faith against pagan adversaries. This image entailed the reinterpretation of the historical facts: for example, Václav was killed by his Christian brother in a fight for the throne; Cnut by magnates who opposed him. The role of these rulers in introducing or spreading Christianity in their respective countries became a part of national myth. Modern scholars have debated the relative role of native rulers, the German emperor, and the pope in

---

[3] Boyer, *Le Christ des barbares*, 90, photo 7.
[4] A. Gieysztor *et al.*, *History of Poland* (Warsaw, 1968), between 88 and 89.

these conversions. As contemporary evidence is scarce, interpretations have often hinged on assumptions and modern political agendas. What is certain is that a combination of the activity of missionaries arriving from established Christian centres, imperial participation in some cases (most famously Otto III's visit to Gniezno in 1000), and initiatives by local leaders led to the formation of new Christian polities. The Church remained under royal control in these countries: rulers presided over synods, and intervened in the election of prelates, except when magnates could press their own interests in episcopal elections, or when royal power was weakened through internal conflict, as was often the case in Sweden. Despite papal opposition, proprietary churches, whose lay owners had rights to the possessions of the church and controlled the election of priests (see Chapter 4), continued to be the norm. In most of Scandinavia lay ownership of tithes was prevalent at least until the thirteenth century, and in 1279 a council for Hungary and Poland decreed that the system of patronage must replace proprietary churches.

Christian structures were put in place at the highest level first. Missionary bishops were initially part of the itinerant royal retinues. Then new bishoprics were founded. That of Prague (976) and Olomouc (1060s) were suffragans of the archbishop of Mainz, so that Bohemia did not have ecclesiastical independence from the German empire. Bohemian bishops were invested by the emperor until 1212, when Frederick II granted the Bohemian king the right to invest his bishops. Polish bishoprics came under the archbishopric of Gniezno in 1000 (although the pagan revolt disrupted the ecclesiastical system and Casimir had to restore the church around 1040), and the Hungarian ones under that of Esztergom in 1001, creating independent ecclesiastical organizations in the latter two polities. In Danish areas dioceses were organized between the early eleventh century and 1060, in Norwegian ones at the end of the eleventh century, and in Sweden in the twelfth century, up to around 1170. Scandinavian rulers often tried but failed to shake off the authority of the archbishops of Hamburg–Bremen, until the pope created an independent Scandinavian province under the (Danish) archbishopric of Lund (1103 or 1104). Contested royal succession led some candidates to turn to Emperor Frederick Barbarossa, which in turn triggered a papal response of setting up a Norwegian archbishopric at Nidaros in 1153 and a Swedish one at Uppsala in 1164. Parish organization spread more slowly, over several centuries, with the building of small churches. Many of these in Scandinavia were first built with wood, then in the twelfth century rebuilt in stone. The Christianization of the population could be decreed by the first Christian rulers, as in Hungary, where strict laws were promulgated on duties such as attending church and not working on Sundays and on punishments for the infringements of these rules. 'If some persons, upon coming to church to hear the divine service mutter among themselves . . . if they are . . . common folk, they shall be bound in the narthex of the church . . . and punished by whipping and by the shearing off of their hair.'[5] Elsewhere—for example, in Denmark and northern Sweden—people gradually changed their beliefs and practices without such pressure from above. Monasteries were founded, initially with Benedictine monks from abroad. The full integration of these areas into Christendom is apparent in the speed with which newly founded orders appeared; local recruitment also became significant. For example, Cistercians arrived in these countries in the 1140s; in the following century Franciscans and Dominicans also established themselves rapidly, starting in the late 1220s in some cases.

Christianization was one element in the process of change; political development was the other. Kingdoms incorporating an area more or less securely under the power of one king ultimately replaced tribal organization under chieftains in central Europe, and shared power between many chieftains and lords in Scandinavia. Terms such as 'Denmark' or 'Hungary' serve the historian's convenience rather than portraying historical realities: no leader at the beginning of the period ruled over the entire area of what later became one kingdom; there were a number of rival local powers everywhere. Rulers, sometimes using the personnel and resources that Christianization brought from outside, consolidated their power through internal struggles and the physical elimination of rivals. For example, in Bohemia the Přemyslids had the Slavník family massacred in 995; in Hungary in 997 King Stephen distributed the severed limbs of his opponent Koppány to be displayed in some of the key centres. Tenth- and eleventh-century Scandinavian history also provides numerous cases of such contests: for example, in 999 the Danish

---

[5] J. M. Bak, G. Bónis, and J. R. Sweeney (eds. and trans.), *The Laws of the Medieval Kingdom of Hungary 1000–1301* (Bakersfield, CA, 1989), 5.

Sven (Swein) Forkbeard killed the Norwegian Olaf Tryggvason in battle, then Sven's son Cnut (also king of England, 1016–35) drove Olaf Haraldsson into exile, and Olaf was killed in battle in 1030.

The new polities of central Europe

In central Europe, three polities emerged, replacing earlier political organizations: the duchy of Bohemia, the kingdom of Hungary, and the kingdom of Poland. Politically, the three show important differences, though at least initially they faced similar challenges: the consolidation of power externally and internally. The three emerging polities at times became allies, often through marriage, and at other times fought against each other; exiled rival members of a ruling family from one country often found support in another to return and make their claim good by military force. Although rulers could enhance their power through Christianization, Latin Christianity did not necessarily determine political allegiances: rulers continued to form military alliances with pagans, and political ties to Byzantium served the interests of the Hungarian dynasty. At least during the early period of their development, all three countries were to some extent subordinated to and paid annual tribute to the German emperor, who at times waged war against them over territories, or to help a rival contender representing imperial interests to the throne, or to enforce subordinate status. Bohemia became part of the German Empire, although its rulers enjoyed full autonomy within their duchy and obtained the royal title in 1198. In contrast, Polish and Hungarian rulers, although often paying tribute or being subordinate to imperial interests, conserved their separate status. Political structures developed gradually over the course of the period. Borrowings from the West were manifest at the rulers' courts; courtly offices were generally modelled on Frankish ones and bore their Latin names. The *comes palatinus*, the highest official, supervised the court. Others fulfilled a number of functions at court (for example, in the treasury and chancery) or in the country as representatives of the ruler, administering estates, dispensing justice, collecting revenues, and serving as military leaders. However, there were local differences: for example, the Hungarian conquest entailed the incorporation of local

Slavic populations during the tenth century, which resulted in linguistic and institutional borrowing. The administrative system grew more complex over time. One example of this was the establishment of a separate chancery at the royal court, with a concurrent rise in the number of charters issued.

There was nothing predetermined about the shape of the three central European countries. The kingdom of Hungary emerged following the conquest of the area from the 890s onwards by the Hungarian (Magyar) tribal association and a period of raids in German, French, Italian, and Byzantine territories. Large territories changed hands even repeatedly—for example, Silesia belonged at times to Bohemia and at other times to Poland, and attempts continued well beyond the period radically to extend the area of sovereignty of the various rulers. The most important territorial acquisitions included the Bohemian conquest of Moravia by around 1021; subordinate rulers from the Přemyslid family were installed. Hungarian rulers attached the territory between the Rivers Drave and Save to their kingdom in the eleventh century; Croatia became part of Hungary in the late eleventh and early twelfth century, as did Dalmatian coastal towns for a period, which then led to conflict with Venice. In the mid-twelfth century competition erupted between Hungary and Byzantium for the possession of Bosnia and Serbia. Polish rulers tried to expand their territories towards the north and were involved in recurring hostilities with Rus´ and the German Empire. Poland and Hungary both tried to gain suzerainty over Galicia in the late twelfth century. In the second half of the thirteenth century, the Teutonic Order and the German margraves of Brandenburg, the Lithuanians, and Bohemian rulers all threatened various territories under Polish rule. In the 1240s the Mongol attack devastated all three central European countries. The Mongols killed many people, took captives, and destroyed crops and cities. The Mongol raids against Poland and to a lesser extent Hungary continued in the second half of the thirteenth century, but did not result in their permanent subjugation, as it did in Rus´.

The three polities developed different solutions to the problem of succession within the ruling dynasty. Rivalry for the succession in Hungary often led to instability and civil wars, and to the establishment of a duchy within the kingdom under a prince of the dynasty in the second half of the eleventh century. Yet the Hungarian kingdom did not disintegrate. In Poland, Duke Mieszko left power divided between his sons, but Boleslaw I (992–1025) managed to become sole ruler. Though Boleslaw II assumed the royal title in 1076, his successors were not crowned; and Boleslaw III in his testament divided the realm into principalities for his sons. Poland was often divided between heirs before that, but this time the division proved to be lasting: upon Boleslaw's death in 1138, Poland disintegrated into dukedoms. The law of seniority (first established in 1058) gave the oldest prince suzerainty, while younger members of the dynasty inherited independent provinces; these were to be hereditary in the various branches of the dynasty. In 1138 the ruler of Kraków was made the senior prince, but he rapidly lost any meaningful overall authority. Although the specific details of the arrangement were modified over time, a number of dukes, rather than a king, continued to rule over a growing number of independent duchies in the thirteenth century. Poland was reunified only in the fourteenth century. In Bohemia, the most senior member of the dynasty had the right to ascend the throne; but this could always be contested. Amidst constant challenges, no man without effective allies and military power, however legitimate his claim, could seize and hold power. Attempts to secure succession to the eldest son of the ruler recurred, and were finally realized in the thirteenth century. Přemysl Otakar I (1198–1230) succeeded in turning Bohemia into a hereditary kingdom, although ties to the empire were not severed; indeed, the Bohemian ruler became one of the seven electors of the emperor. Otakar II (1253–78), who was also duke of Austria, created unparalleled strong rulership in Bohemia, but failed in his bid to become German emperor, and lost his life in battle. In 1300, Václav II of Bohemia was also elected king of Poland; the two polities briefly came under the same ruler.

Two contrary trends—the consolidation of the ruler's power and forces of fragmentation—clashed in all three countries. Kings and dukes never had absolute power, but relied on a council of nobles and ecclesiastics; yet their powers became more centralized, and came to include the conduct of foreign diplomacy, decisions about warfare, and extensive or even monopolistic powers of jurisdiction. The basis of the rulers' power was their landed domain as well as services, payments for justice, tolls, taxes, and military service and construction work owed by the population. Dukes of Bohemia and kings of Hungary had a monopoly on the construction and custody of fortresses into the thirteenth century. Royal monopoly also extended to mining, minting coins, and the settling of immigrants, whose utility included technical expertise in agriculture or warfare and an increase in revenues. Rulers also tried to reinforce their power through Christianity; thus Bohemian dukes appropriated Saint Václav, saint and duke, as their patron, portraying him on their seals and coins.[6] However, nobles gradually gained previously royal rights in the thirteenth century. The high nobility increasingly took over political and judicial power, which undermined royal control. The nobility became the new challenge to royal power at the end of the period.

Over these centuries, society became more hierarchically structured. Initially it consisted of free warriors and workers of various degrees of unfreedom. The representative of the ruler such as the Hungarian *ispán**, Bohemian castellan, or the lord of the castle town in Poland held military, administrative, judicial, and fiscal powers in his district. They were appointed by the ruler and did not acquire independent power. The unfree provided agricultural labour and other services, and in all three central European countries there were villages that communally owed a certain type of service, reflected in the name of the village, a system that disappeared during the twelfth and thirteenth centuries. In Poland, for example, historians have counted artisans and servants of up to forty different crafts, such as cobblers, bakers, cooks, and beaver-hunters, attested by placenames such as Kuchary ('cooks') or Bartodzieje ('honey-collectors'), which survived after the system itself disappeared. While the various conditions of unfreedom increasingly coalesced into serfdom, the freemen slowly became stratified and in the twelfth and thirteenth centuries a separate nobility started to emerge. At the same time, knighthood and chivalry appeared in central Europe, though they did not gain prominence during the period. Also beginning in the twelfth century, peasants were becoming directly dependent on lords. Although ecclesiastics and high-ranking members of the rulers' entourage were frequently immigrants from western Europe already in the first century of Christianization, mass immigration increased only in the twelfth and thirteenth centuries. Immigrant communities of

[6] Photographs in L. Wolverton, *Hastening toward Prague: Power and Society in Medieval Czech Lands* (Philadelphia, 2001), figs. 3, 4, 5, 6.

Germans, Jews, and Romance-speakers lived in Bohemia and Poland; so did, in addition to such groups, Turkic nomads and Muslims in Hungary. These groups played a variety of roles. Peasant settlers were important in agricultural expansion. Turkic groups and Muslims, as members of the light cavalry in Hungary, and Western immigrants, as members of the heavy cavalry, had a significant military role. Westerners were involved in trade, mining, and urbanization—for instance, German merchants and miners and Walloon weavers were important in thirteenth-century Poland.

An agrarian subsistence economy was transformed by the end of the period through 'internal' colonization (the expansion of agricultural cultivation), the increased importance of trade, urbanization, and monetarization. The clearing of forests and draining of marshes started in the twelfth century, increasing the area of cultivated land, while new agricultural tools and methods were also introduced. Although the process was driven by the initiative of rulers and the nobility, Cistercians, Premonstratensians, and foreign settlers played a key role in it. The latter received privileges in order to bring new areas under cultivation. The influx of German settlers increased in the thirteenth century; rural and urban settlement under *ius theutonicum* or 'German law' (often even for natives) guaranteed personal freedom, juridical immunities, and fixed rent. Urbanization also took off in the twelfth and thirteenth centuries. The new legal status of cities emerged as immigrant immunities based on Western law developed into municipal law. German law, especially Magdeburg law, was the most significant model of the new urban law in Bohemia and Poland, while in Hungary a law developed for 'Latins' (French, Flemish, and Italian settlers) was also used. The minting of coins appeared at the same time as Christian rulership, but a monetarized economy became widespread only during the thirteenth century, although it has been argued that the Bohemian economy was already based on money in the eleventh century.[7]

Although eastern Europe and the Balkans were not part of Latin Christendom, it is important to signal that many of the major trends in these regions were similar to those found in central and northern Europe. The Christianization of Kievan Rus´ was roughly contemporaneous with that of central Europe (in 988), and was

[7] Ibid. 25–7, 166–7.

similarly initiatiated by a ruler, Vladimir, who accepted Byzantine Christianity. Taking advantage of Byzantine weakness, new polities emerged in the Balkans at the end of the twelfth and during the thirteenth centuries. These copied many of the Byzantine administrative structures, and the population adhered to Byzantine Christianity. Serbia was mostly under Byzantine control until Stephen Nemanja established an independent polity around 1170. His son, Stephen Nemanja II, adopted the royal title in 1217. Bulgaria, annexed in the early eleventh century by the Byzantine emperor, gained independence through a rebellion led by Peter and Asen in 1185 (the so-called second Bulgarian empire), and subsequently incorporated a large part of the Balkans. Patterns of religious and administrative adaptation coupled with political independence from the major power, Byzantium, were similar to the relations of central European polities to the German Empire.

The new polities of northern Europe

Scandinavia's history in its broad outline was in many ways similar to that of central Europe: Christianization and the formation of polities roughly coincided from the tenth century onwards. Yet the development of the Scandinavian kingdoms significantly diverged even from each other. Scandinavian Vikings raided in many parts of Europe between the ninth and eleventh centuries; at the same time settlements in or links to the British Isles, Francia, and the Empire also led to cultural borrowing, partly via missions. Early eleventh-century voyages to and settlement in North America did not last. The Christian kingdoms emerged through warfare between various claimants to each throne as well as between rulers of different territories; many areas changed hands frequently—for example, the lands around Oslo Fjord. None of these kingdoms covered the same areas as the modern states with identical names. Scandinavian kings initially had limited powers. They increased royal authority based on their landholdings with rights to labour service and fines, their personal guard, the monopoly to summon naval power for war, and often through Christianization. They also held a monopoly over building fortified places until the thirteenth century (in Norway even longer). Local rulers entered into royal service. The first recorded coronation, an ecclesiastical contribution to royal power, took place in Norway in 1163–4, in Denmark in 1170, and in Sweden in 1210.

The Danish kingdom, based on naval power and trade, existed by the late eighth century, but underwent numerous drastic territorial changes. In the second half of the tenth century Harald Bluetooth and his successor ordered the construction of forts, probably in order to subjugate the local population. Danish royal power increasingly centred on Lund and Roskilde, and under Sven Forkbeard (d. 1014) and Cnut the Great (d. 1035) Danish overlordship was extended to a large part of Scandinavia and England. With the disintegration of this empire, other Scandinavian kingdoms emerged. Denmark, through its contacts to England and western Europe, borrowed most from the West. The growth of monarchical power did not put an end to rivalry for the throne or to civil wars in the first half of the twelfth century. Indeed, some of the parties turned to the German emperor for aid in return for paying homage to him. In the second half of the century, a royal court and administration, including the chancery, were established. Nonetheless, laws, written down from the middle of the thirteenth century, were regional rather than unified for the entire kingdom. Norway briefly came under Danish rule in the early eleventh century, and rivalries for the throne were rife. Royal power increased substantially during Harald Hardrada's reign through the subjugation of chieftains and the growing importance of the administration of royal domains. Civil wars for succession were so violent that between 1130 and 1162 none of the eight kings of Norway died natural deaths. By the mid-thirteenth century, however, Norway was the most stable Scandinavian kingdom. This was partly due to luck; after 1227 most Norwegian kings left only one legitimate son as heir. In the late thirteenth century rules of succession were laid down. Yet another crucial factor contributed to stability: because of their relative poverty, Norwegian magnates were unable to challenge royal power. Instead, they became royal agents in order to achieve prestige and wealth, thus strengthening the king's authority. In the late thirteenth century territorial changes reshaped the kingdom. In 1266 King Magnus VI of Norway gave the overlordship of the Isle of Man and Hebrides to the Scottish king in return for payment and the recognition of Norwegian sovereignty over Orkney and Shetland. From 1262 Iceland started to pay a tax to the Norwegian king, as had Greenland, similarly organized, some years previously; in the 1260s Iceland formed a personal union with Norway. As with Christianization, political consolidation took longest in Sweden. Between the mid-eleventh and mid-thirteenth centuries, the rivalry of two powerful families for the throne often culminated in civil war and murders, and impeded the development of central monarchical power. This enabled provinces to retain their local autonomy into the thirteenth century. Provincial law codes were recorded in writing during the thirteenth century. Then nobles and the king's chief minister (jarl) dominated political life and opposed the royal officials' participation in local affairs.

Local assemblies (*thing*) were distinctive features of Scandinavian society. They included free farmers, and were the main institutions of government. They initially had political, social, and religious roles, then by the thirteenth century a legal one with royal agents gaining influence in them. These public meetings became representative institutions. A successful candidate to the throne had to be recognized in public assemblies. From the thirteenth century, political assemblies for entire countries arose, as well as councils dominated by the aristocracy that began to take on several of the assemblies' functions. In Norway centralized monarchy replaced the authority of local assemblies in law, jurisdiction, and administration. The Norwegian *King's Mirror* (c.1250) stated that rulership was determined by inheritance and the king ruled by divine right as God's representative. Iceland throughout the period retained a political system based on public assemblies that made political and judicial decisions. No king ruled over a society of freemen, although by the thirteenth century a few families held power as chieftains.

Early Scandinavian society consisted of slaves, freedmen, tenants, and landowning freemen. A farming and pastoral economy predominated, with many isolated farms. Denmark was the most fertile Scandinavian land, favourable to agriculture. Villages grew in the twelfth and thirteenth centuries in areas of open plains, where landlords formed large estates. At the same time, the proportion of free but dependent tenants increased. An aristocracy also emerged as a distinct military class of armoured knights, in Denmark in the second half of the twelfth century, in Sweden in the late thirteenth century. Taxation was introduced, but nobles were exempt because they provided military service; the legal differentiation of freemen thus began in the thirteenth century. Urbanization was well under way in Denmark by 1000, in Norway during the eleventh century, and in Sweden from the twelfth century. Many Scandinavian towns had a role in the Baltic trade, which from the thirteenth century was dominated by German merchants, exporting fish, fur, iron, walrus tusk (ivory), and falcons among other goods.

The rest of northern Europe, although frequented by missionaries and German merchants, became a fighting ground between the various powers set to conquer it. During the twelfth century, the Obodrites were conquered by the Saxons; Pomerania came under Polish suzerainty and was converted; West Pomerania under its own Slav dynasty became increasingly Germanized. Saxons and Danes participated in the Wendish crusade. Germans and Scandinavians launched a 'perpetual crusade' in the Baltic, which was indistinguishable from warfare for conquest. The main targets until around 1230 were Livonia and Estonia; then Finland (for the Swedes) and Prussia, where a state was eventually organized by the Teutonic Order. Following missions to the Livonians on the Dvina, crusaders from Germany led by the Order of the Sword Brothers, founded in 1202 by Albert of Buxhövden, bishop of Livonia, conquered Livonia by 1230. The local inhabitants were subjugated, and the order (which became a branch of the Teutonic Order in 1237) and the bishop divided the revenues, resisting papal pressure to establish the direct dependence of the area on the papacy. The Danes attacked Finland, Estonia, Saaremaa (Ösel), and Prussia at the end of the twelfth and early thirteenth centuries. King Valdemar II (1202–41) briefly occupied Holstein and Hamburg in the early thirteenth century and in 1219 invaded northern Estonia and established a stronghold at Tallinn (Reval). This led to conflict with the Germans, but King Valdemar achieved the recognition of Danish control over Estonia, even though most settlers were Germans. The Teutonic Order became involved in the region when Conrad of Mazovia invited them in 1226 to defend his territories against raids by the pagan Prussians (Pruthenians), and to convert them. Having received imperial and papal protection, they quickly took on the task of conquering Prussian territories. Despite Prussian revolts (1242, 1260s), the Order subjugated or killed the local inhabitants and created their own state, founded towns, and settled German burghers. The Order's further territorial expansion eastwards at the expense of the principality of Novgorod was checked by Alexander Nevsky in

1242. The Cours (of Western Latvia) and their neighbours the Semigallians were conquered in the late thirteenth century. By the end of the period most of northern Europe was subjugated by force and Christianized, with Germans settling throughout the region. The exception was Lithuania. It successfully resisted Christianization despite a brief period between its ruler Mindaugas's conversion and his turning against Christians (1251–61), and it defended itself against the Teutonic Knights. Pagan Lithuania became a highly organized and powerful political entity with an organized pagan religion, proving that political structure rather than religion was the key to survival.

Iberia

After the Arab–Berber conquest of the Iberian peninsula (starting in 711) and against the background of a shifting political landscape, warfare was endemic. War characterized relations both among Christians and Muslims as well as between Christians and Muslims; it was opportunistic rather than religious. Although the political legitimation of being heirs of the Visigoths was formulated in the late ninth century at the court of Alfonso III of León, the idea of religious war emerged only in the late eleventh century and became the prevalent Christian ideology in the twelfth and thirteenth centuries. It was only then that Christian advances came to be seen as a 'reconquest' from Muslims of lands rightfully belonging to Christians. This transformation can be illustrated through the example of Rodrigo Díaz de Vivar, better known as El Cid (c.1043–99). During his lifetime, Rodrigo was one of the many warlords looking for booty and building his own power. A Christian, Rodrigo served Kings Sancho II, then Alfonso VI of Castile until he was exiled (1081), when he went into the service of the Muslim ruler of Saragossa. He exacted tribute and exploited military opportunities; eventually he conquered Valencia for himself. By the early thirteenth century, legend turned him into a zealous Christian hero, fighting for the faith (see Chapter 5). The context was the crystallization of Iberian Christian identity, at least in royal and ecclesiastical circles.

   The Umayyad caliphate lost effective power after 1008, and gradually Muslim principalities (Taifas* or 'party-kings') took its place.

Christian rulers from the north exploited the lack of strong Muslim central power, and exacted tribute (*parias*) as protection money. Rulers of the Christian kingdom of Navarre and soon of the emerging León, Castile, and Aragon also enlarged their territories. They incorporated empty lands contiguous to their realms, and led invasions into Muslim territories. Christian advances, helped by tribute from Muslim rulers, were followed by periods of consolidation and reverses caused by Muslim triumphs. The capture of Toledo in 1085 by Alfonso VI of Castile and the beginnings of crusading to the Levant opened the way for a new understanding of local warfare. At the start of the crusades, Pope Urban II (1088–99) pronounced Muslims in Iberia to be just as much the enemies of Christians as Muslims in the Levant. Subsequently the papal grant of crusader privileges to Iberian crusaders fluctuated, sometimes postulating an equal, other times a lesser status to crusades to Jerusalem, designating only some of the wars there as crusades; nevertheless, crusader thought undoubtedly left a deep impact on interpretations of Iberian warfare. Spanish military orders were created and received papal approval: Calatrava (1164), San Julián del Pereiro (Alcántara) (1175), and Santiago (1176).

During the twelfth century the religious understanding of these wars was consolidated, a process to which French influence at court, pilgrims to the shrine of Saint James at Compostela, crusaders arriving from other parts of Europe (especially the Languedoc and Burgundy), and most importantly the popes all contributed. For Iberian kings the ideology of the *Reconquista* became an important diplomatic tool, especially in relation to the papacy as a basis for demands of funds and privileges. This ideology, however, did not put an end to peaceful relations between adherents of the two religions in either everyday coexistence or alliances.

Christian–Muslim interaction was influenced not only by Christian ideology and practice but also by Muslim activities. In response to the Christian conquest of Toledo, Almoravids from Morocco were invited into the peninsula in 1086 and defeated Alfonso VI. They once again centralized Muslim rule, establishing control over Taifa kings. When the Christian conquests started again in the mid-twelfth century, the Almohads invaded from North Africa (1146), subjugated the Almoravids and went on to attack the Christians. Muslim victory at Alarcos in 1195 checked the Christian advance. In its aftermath, Pope

Innocent III called for a crusade and, as its necessary precondition, for peace among the Christian kings of Iberia. A significant turning point came with the Christian victory of Las Navas de Tolosa (1212), celebrated as a victory for the whole of Christendom. It opened Andalucia to conquest, as Muslim Iberia fragmented once again into rival principalities. The first half of the thirteenth century increasingly provided material for Christian celebration. James I of Catalonia–Aragon (1213–76) and Ferdinand III of Castile (1217–52, from 1230 also king of León) conquered most of the peninsula by the mid-thirteenth century, notably Valencia (1238) by the Aragonese, and Córdoba (1236), Seville (1248), and Cadiz (1262) by the Castilians. After 1264, only Granada remained in Muslim hands, despite attacks by the Marinids of Morocco after 1275 and revolts of subject Muslims in the newly conquered areas. Over 400,000 sq. km. were incorporated into Christian Iberia.

Conquest was not achieved by sheer force alone. Military confrontation was accompanied by negotiation; Muslims capitulated in many cases, and surrender treaties were drawn up granting rights to the Muslim population. Yet the life of the Muslims changed even when these were honoured. Symbolic of this was the transformation of the main mosques of large cities such as Valencia, Córdoba, or Seville into churches after Christian conquest as a sign of victory. Muslims under Christian rule (*mudéjars*) progressively lost their freedoms. Learned elites often emigrated, and by the early sixteenth century Muslims were forced to convert or leave. Nonetheless, during the thirteenth century they contributed to the consolidation of Christian states—for example, by continuing to work the agricultural irrigation system in Valencia, or by testifying to the existing boundaries of estates.

It was not only Muslim Iberia that changed owing to the progress of Christian conquests: the eleventh, twelfth, and thirteenth centuries were formative for the Christian states themselves. Iberia's political map underwent radical changes over 300 years. Asturias, then the Asturo-Leonese kingdom where finally León took the leading role, Navarre, Aragon, Catalonia, Castile, and finally Portugal emerged. With its conquest of Toledo, Castile gained ascendancy over León; the two were united first temporarily in the early twelfth century until 1157, then permanently in 1230, thus forging a powerful Christian polity. The dynastic union of Aragon and the counties of Catalonia in the late 1130s created the other major power of the peninsula, the Crown of Aragon. Navarre lost access to further conquests from the Muslims, and in the treaty of Tudillén (1151) rulers of Aragon and Castile even decided to divide Navarre itself, but this project failed. In the late thirteenth century, the French king became the ruler of Navarre. Counts of Portugal strengthened their power during the twelfth century; in 1137 the count's autonomy was accepted by Alfonso VII of Castile-León. Count Afonso Henriques started to call himself king and gained *de facto* independence from León when he declared himself the vassal of the Holy See in 1143 (the pope started to address him by the royal title in 1179). Thus a new kingdom emerged, enlarging its territory by continued conquests from Muslims: in 1147 Lisbon was annexed, followed by the incorporation of Alcácer do Sal (1158) and Badajoz (1169). The French king had claims to Catalonia until 1258, the Aragonese king to many lands in Languedoc and Provence, a conflict of interests only partially resolved in the late thirteenth century. Overall, rulers strengthened their own power as they expanded and consolidated the frontiers of their kingdoms.

Iberia differed from northern and central Europe: this was not a new society to be converted and incorporated into Christendom. Existing Christian kingdoms at the beginning of the period were the locus of expansionary will. Although there was an influx of warriors from north of the Pyrenees, the *Reconquista* was increasingly manned by locals. The church in Iberia funded the reconquest, especially during the thirteenth century. Political structures were not identical in the different kingdoms. The Castilian king had a centralized administration and held more effective power than his counterpart in Aragon, who was the head of a confederation with separate institutions and without jurisdictional unity. During the twelfth and thirteenth centuries, royal courts were transformed into specialized departments staffed by professionals; local administration also developed in the conquered areas, often borrowing Muslim practices and officials. *Cortes*, assemblies of the estates, developed in Catalonia and Castile from the late twelfth century, in Aragon and Navarre during the thirteenth century. They included nobles, ecclesiastics, and representatives of towns, and started to participate in government. In the late thirteenth century, kings began to formulate legislation based on Roman law, which gave rise to the nobility's opposition to royal power. Nobility was based on descent, and was divided into two or three strata, the lowest often resembling peasants in their economic circumstances. Despite huge economic differences, nobles were juridically equal, and exempt from taxation. Cities in the newly conquered areas were often given charters of privileges (*fueros**) in exchange for consent to taxation and the city militias' participation in defence. Cities also became the allies of kings in political life against the nobility in thirteenth-century Castile, thus receiving urban autonomy. Economic differences between kingdoms were partly linked to the size of the population. Castile had a large sector of extensive agriculture, based on animal raising. Agricultural irrigation and the mercantile sector were important in the Crown of Aragon.

Historians have intensely debated the interpretation of Iberia's socio-economic characteristics: was Iberia a 'frontier society', shaped primarily by military expansion and unregulated conditions, or a 'feudal' one, moulded by relations between lords and men, kingship, and the tenure of land in exchange for service? In fact, Iberia resembled other medieval European kingdoms, while displaying some local specificities. The key issues in the debate are the militarization of Iberian society and the consequences of the process of expansion. Although it is true that warfare was an important feature of life in Iberia, medieval society was heavily militarized in the whole of Europe. The settlement of conquered areas in Iberia was a constant problem. The lack of population and thus of manpower led to the promulgation of privileges to draw settlers. A variety of solutions was adopted. In Castile, conquered lands were divided into units where the king's delegates exercised administrative, judiciary, and military functions. In Aragon in the eleventh and early twelfth centuries the grant of large estates attracted nobles to settle. The creation of cities, even through granting pardons to murderers if they settled, and of military orders was an equally important means of repopulation. Muslims played an important part, especially in Valencia, where they far outnumbered Christians; indeed, Muslim immigration was encouraged, even by military orders, to sustain the region's agriculture. Yet attracting settlers by privileges occurred in many other areas of Europe, including France. Cultural exchange with Muslims and Jews influenced Christian culture, as architecture, and translations of Greek works via Arabic, attest (see Chapter 5). At the same time, however, ecclesiastical structures were expanded into the newly conquered areas. Ecclesiastics served kings in the chancery, in diplomacy, and by composing chronicles recording the deeds of kings. The vernacular was already widely used in the thirteenth century for literary compositions as well as for charters. Finally, significant differences occurred between the development of different Iberian kingdoms. 'Frontier society' therefore does not work as a blanket explanatory concept for medieval Iberian history.

The conquest of the peninsula also paved the way for further maritime expansion. The Crown of Aragon eventually created a maritime empire in the western Mediterranean, the first step of which was the Catalan conquest of the Balearic Islands (1229–35). It opened the way for Atlantic exploration by Portuguese and Castilians in the fourteenth century. Castilians and Aragonese planned but failed to conquer Morocco and North Africa in the late thirteenth century, but Europeans continued to trade with North Africa, having contact only with coastal areas, not the interior.

Another area of the Mediterranean was incorporated into Latin Christendom early in the period. Normans displaced Byzantine rule in southern Italy, conquering Calabria and Apulia; they also conquered Sicily from the Muslims (1061–91) and created a centrally organized powerful kingdom. Roger II (1105–54, crowned king 1130) established the superiority of the ruler's justice, created an effective administrative system, and extended the range of royal control over diverse aspects of government, including the collection of revenues from trade and the local Church. He brought part of North Africa under his power, from political and economic, rather than religious, motives. He employed Muslim mercenaries, and drew on Greek, Muslim, Latin, and French traditions. A variety of peoples mixed in the kingdom; their religious observance, local institutions, and culture including language were left undisturbed. Historians have debated the nature of Byzantine and Muslim influence: whether it just had an impact on externals or fundamentally determined the nature of the polity. Rogers's heirs faced a variety of external threats and internal rebellions. In 1194 Sicily was conquered by Emperor Henry VI, whose son Frederick II eventually established strong monarchy in the kingdom of Sicily.

Crusades

The crusading movement emerged at the end of the eleventh century, when Pope Urban II raised an army to help the Byzantine Emperor Alexius I (1081–1118) against the Turks, who were conquering Asia Minor. Crusaders received indulgence*, protection, and even exemptions from taxes. Armies left in 1096, and the first crusaders unexpectedly created new states, first the county of Edessa, then the principality of Antioch, and in 1099 they conquered Jerusalem, which became the centre of a kingdom. These crusader states expanded, especially by capturing seaports. In 1109 the county of Tripoli was established, and the rulers of Edessa and Tripoli became vassals of the king of Jerusalem. The crusader states reached their greatest extent in the mid-twelfth century, but still consisted of a relatively narrow coastal strip. Over time, crusading became more organized. A maritime, rather than an overland, route to the East developed. Rulers became involved in leading crusades. In 1199 the first direct taxation of the Church (a fortieth) was introduced, which became a regular way to finance the crusades. Organized preaching recruited crusaders, and non-combatants (including women and even the dying) were encouraged to redeem crusade vows for payment from 1213 onwards.

Yet most crusaders returned home; there was very little population transfer from Europe to the East. At their most extensive, crusader states are estimated to have contained 250,000 Europeans (mainly Franks). The majority of the population were natives: Muslims, a variety of eastern Christians, and Jews. Many of the administrative traditions of the Romans and Byzantines had been incorporated into the Muslim system, and were in turn, enriched by Muslim innovations, integrated into the crusader states. The new rulers continued to levy the same taxes that the Muslims had collected, and used sophisticated accounting practices. In general, instruments of government and the bureaucratic system were adopted, while European practices, such as land and money fiefs in exchange for military service, were also introduced. The king of Jerusalem had some authority in the entire Latin East, shown, for example, in his role as arbiter in disputes between the other Frankish rulers and his leadership in defensive wars. His riches also distinguished him: he held vast lands and taxed trade, and could give money fiefs to vassals and hire mercenaries. The high court (*parlement*) debated political matters and extraordinary taxation. Historians once saw the kingdom of Jerusalem as a strong monarchy in the first half of the twelfth century, but the more recent consensus is that political fragmentation was present from the beginning. Although great lords were royal vassals, they exercised full authority in their principalities, constituting a 'confederation of lordships'.[8] The nobility of the crusader states differed from each other: for example, in Edessa it was primarily Armenian, in Jerusalem northern French. By the second half of the twelfth century it was difficult for newcomers, with a few exceptions, to rise into the nobility; about ten families held the twenty-four most important lordships. They also had rights to mint coins, legislate, and control the ports. Many lesser lords held money fiefs. Military service could not be commuted for payment. During the thirteenth century nobles relied on laws (which were remembered, as either laws had not been written down or written texts had been lost when Jerusalem fell to the Muslims once more in 1187) to strengthen their own power against that of the king; many nobles were skilled lawyers.

The recruitment of warriors to the Latin East caused a constant problem. This was partially alleviated by an innovation: military orders. The Knights Templar, a religious community founded in 1118–19, led this transformation. Within a few years of its foundation, the order's members combined taking monastic vows with fighting against the Muslims. In 1129 the Templar rule was drawn up. The Order of the Hospital of St John of Jerusalem, founded in the second half of the eleventh century, was reorganized along the same lines, and other military orders were established. They became important in providing permanently committed fighters and garrisoning castles built for defence. Orders established in the Latin East eventually moved into Europe; and new orders were founded there, most importantly in Iberia.

Warfare was not the only concern the settlers had in the Latin East. Agricultural life continued. The native inhabitants of the villages could not leave their land, and paid dues based on traditional Islamic ones. Very little land belonged directly to the lord (as demesne) on which peasants owed labour services. A headman and a council of

---

[8] J. Riley-Smith, *The Crusades: A Short History* (London, 1987), 69.

elders oversaw the functioning of villages. Franks also lived in some villages and manor houses. In the twelfth century, planned villages were established. Free peasants who came from Europe received privileges, including personal freedom, the right to alienate land, and to give a fixed percentage of produce to the local lord. These communities also had their own system of justice. Most Europeans lived in towns; the majority were burgesses. Burgess privilege—personal freedom, paying rent and no servile dues, having their own courts and law—was extended to attract settlers, including craftsmen, contrary to practices in most of Europe. Ports developed into major international commercial centres, used by Italian and other merchants (see Chapter 2).

The number of Catholics was small, even including converts from local Eastern Christian communities. At first Greek Orthodox clerics were recognized, although, in cases of vacancy or areas with no Christian hierarchy, Catholic bishops were installed. From the early twelfth century on, Latins aggressively intruded into offices, and a Latin hierarchy increasingly replaced the Greek Orthodox one. Rulers and laymen retained a large measure of control over the Church well into the twelfth century. Adherents of different faiths were distinguished in law. At the top were Catholic Franks, then Eastern Christians, and at the bottom Muslims and Jews. Only the testimony of Catholics was fully valid in court. Nonetheless, after initial massacres of local non-Christians, because of the need for manpower and trade, peaceful interaction grew. Non-Christians were allowed to practise their own faith; they also continued to participate in trade and the production of goods. Sources provide examples of friendship with Muslims and intermarriage with Eastern Christians. Art also shows the mingling of Frankish and Eastern Christian: from the second generation (1130s), strong Byzantine influence transformed art; Greek and Latin inscriptions were used. Existing urban architectural styles were also adopted.

Debate about the nature of society in the crusader states continues. According to the traditional model, the crusader settlements, often called a 'colonial' society, were characterized by a complete separation between Franks and locals. Yet there was no political direction from or economic exploitation for the benefit of the homeland, as in other colonial societies; on the contrary, these states were economically dependent on the homeland. The term 'religious colonization' has also been used. Another view posits the multi-ethnic character of the new society. This emphasizes the orientalization of the Franks, the merging of Muslim, Eastern Christian, and Latin Christian elements, pointing especially to accounts of friendships and intermarriage between Franks and locals (including Muslims), and the adoption of Muslim customs by the Franks. A third, most recent, analysis maintains that these states consisted of a 'Franco-Syrian' society that did not include Muslims. Based on settlement by Frankish immigrants— rather than on 'crusader settlement'—that concentrated in the areas inhabited by local Christians, it was agricultural in character. The population was increasingly locally born, consisting of farmers who raised families and did not see war as a priority; and the Franks interacted only with Eastern Christians (although the latter did not have the same legal status), not Muslims.

Spiritual benefits, a new legitimacy conferred on warriors through the exercise of warfare, the conquest of new areas, leading to land-holding and even rulership for some, all combined to attract crusaders, while trading advantages for the Venetians, Genoese, and Pisans ensured that their fleets were deployed for transport and the capturing of seaports. This attraction, however, was not constant, as attested by the ebb and flow of response to crusading calls. From the mid-twelfth century, Muslim counter-attack became effective, and the concept of *jihad** (holy war) developed in relation to Jerusalem. After Edessa had been recaptured by Muslims in 1144, the Second Crusade was called, but proved to be a failure. Saladin, who became the ruler of Egypt and parts of Syria in the late twelfth century, was victorious at Hattin in 1187. He conquered Jerusalem and many other lands from the crusaders. Yet Western rule over part of the territory was prolonged: the Third Crusade, led by the German Emperor Frederick Barbarossa, Kings Philip Augustus of France and Richard I of England, conquered Acre (1191) and Jaffa. The city of Jerusalem did not return to Christian control again, except for a brief period as a result of the negotiations between Frederick II and Sultan Al-Kamil of Egypt in 1229; it fell in 1244 to a Central Asian army in the service of Egypt. In the thirteenth century crusaders attempted to proceed through the conquest of Egypt to regain lost lands. In 1218–21 and 1248–50, they mounted large-scale attacks, but ultimately failed in both cases. The second time, Louis IX of France, the leader of the crusade, was taken captive. Sultan Baibars of Egypt started to capture crusader fortresses in 1265. Western reinforcements failed to arrive or were ineffective; among them was the disastrous attempt led by Louis IX of France, ending in the king's death at Tunis in 1270. Muslim reconquest continued until 1291, when the last crusader strongholds fell, and Latin control came to an end. The crusades thus demonstrated an expansionist drive, but did not result in a lasting contribution to the expansion of Latin Christendom in the East.

Latin states were also established elsewhere in the eastern Mediterranean, in regions where the majority population consisted of Eastern Christians. Expansion and conquest there were inextricably linked to the growth of Italian trade. Richard I of England conquered Cyprus in 1191; he gave lordship over the island to Guy of Lusignan in 1192, whose heir established a kingdom that lasted for almost 300 years. The Lusignan ruler became a vassal of the German emperor Henry VI in 1195, an overlordship that lasted until 1247, when the kingdom came directly under the Holy See. The native population was Greek; as settlers from the Latin states arrived, the Latin Church was established. Royal power was strong: no fortified places could be held by lay nobles. Cyprus exported agricultural produce, and Italian, especially Genoese merchants, used it as a stop-off point in international trade. Westerners settled in Cilician Armenia as well, and transformed some of its institutions and laws. Frankish Greece emerged as a result of the Fourth Crusade. Participants responded to an invitation from Alexius Angelus to intervene in Byzantine politics and restore him to the throne. Although they succeeded, relations quickly deteriorated between Alexius IV and the crusaders, and the latter finally subjugated the empire. After the conquest of Constantinople (1204), Count Baldwin IX of Flanders was elected to rule one-quarter of the territory, creating the Latin Empire of Constantinople, while the rest was divided between the Venetians and other crusaders. Historians have argued over who was responsible for 'corrupting' the crusade; rather, the events demonstrated the flexibility of crusading as a military venture. The Franks adopted the Byzantine tax system and officials, but introduced a hierarchical social structure reflected in the law. Latin settlers arrived, were granted fiefs, and a French-speaking court was established. Latin bishops replaced Orthodox ones. The Greek inhabitants were unfree, except the great lords. Greek nobles began to be incorporated into the elite by the second half of the thirteenth century. The Venetians centralized their government and bureaucracy, which directly depended on Venice. Byzantine power did not disappear, with rival rulers established in some areas, most notably Epiros in the Balkans and Nicaea in Asia Minor. From the latter base, Emperor Michael Palaeologus reconquered Constantinople in 1261, and only the principality of Achaea, the duchies of Athens and Naxos, and several islands remained under Latin occupation.

Crusading spread to different areas: during the twelfth century Iberia and the Baltic were important theatres of crusading warfare. For example, in 1147 English, Scottish, Norman, and Flemish participants of the Second Crusade *en route* to the East helped capture Lisbon in the fight against Muslims. In the same year, a German and Danish crusade against the Wends was part of the fight against pagans. Crusades in both areas continued during the thirteenth century, contributing to the expansion of Latin Christendom. Christian legitimation for these crusades centred around the notion of retaking land (just as the 'Holy Land' was deemed to be Christ's heritage, the Iberian war was a 'reconquest', and Livonia was the 'Virgin Mary's land'); of facilitating missions and the spread of the faith against pagans who resisted or hindered others from converting; or of defending Christian converts persecuted by pagan neighbours (in northern Europe). Crusades were often indistinguishable from other forms of warfare in these territories; the same expansionist warfare was sometimes called a crusade and at other times not. Finally, the crusade could be a useful tool, used independently of some of its founding elements such as pilgrimage, against heretics and political enemies of the papacy. Crusades were subsequently also called against non-Christians who attacked Europe: the Mongols in the mid-thirteenth century, seen as monsters, or even inhabitants of Hell, and the Ottomans from the fourteenth century onwards.

Some historians see only expeditions to the 'Holy Land' as true crusades, while others, basing their arguments on such criteria as a papal declaration, privileges given to warriors, and the taking of crusade vows, see crusades to all areas as equal. There was clearly no uniformity in contemporary attitudes. Sometimes popes, such as Innocent III in 1213 or Honorius III in 1219, promoted crusades to Jerusalem at the expense of other areas. For example, they gave lesser indulgences to crusaders headed for Iberia than to those bound for Jerusalem; they prohibited the commutation of crusading vows promising a journey to Jerusalem into one for fighting in other areas, or restricted European crusades to locals or those unable to travel to the 'Holy Land'. At other times popes expressly equated the merits of, and indulgence for, undertaking crusades to different areas. Urban II ordered Catalans not to go to Jerusalem but to stay and fight the Muslims in Iberia. One can find criticism of crusades directed to areas other than the Levant, but also of crusades to the Levant, deemed in the thirteenth century by many as much less important for the well-being of Christendom than European territories threatened by pagans or Mongols. Neither did popular understanding of the crusades always mesh with the papal message. Groups who were judged unfavourably by ecclesiastics yet were not intended to become the targets for violence, the Jews and Byzantines, became targets of crusaders.

Travels, mission, and discoveries

Mobility and long-distance travel grew from the eleventh century onwards. Pilgrimage to Jerusalem increased, overland via Hungary, the Balkans, and Byzantine Asia Minor, and soon across the sea from Italy. Travel to European shrines was also becoming popular. It is important to point out that there was no sharp distinction between the different categories of travellers and their motivation: trade or mission equally led to discoveries and the expansion of knowledge by Europeans.

Missionaries travelled as far as Persia and China. The mendicant orders, founded in the thirteenth century, made it one of their main aims to proselytize among pagans, Muslims, and other non-believers. After the conversion of Scandinavia and central Europe, missionaries became active in northern (Baltic) and eastern Europe. The Dominican Julian of Hungary in 1236–7 travelled from Hungary towards Siberia in the hope of finding the still pagan remnants of Hungarian tribes. Missionaries also wished to convert Muslims in the Levant, including Egypt and Damascus, and proselytized among indigenous Christians under Muslim rule. Soon the Mongols, and areas under Mongol control, became their primary target. Mission and diplomacy, including spying, were intertwined in the travels of John of

Plano Carpini, sent as an envoy to the Mongols by Pope Innocent IV in 1245, and William of Rubruck, supported by Louis IX of France in 1253. Their aim was to convert the Mongols, and find out as much as they could about Mongol customs and military strength; William of Rubruck was also to try to forge an alliance against Muslims. They produced fascinating accounts of their travels to Karakorum, the Mongol capital, and of the knowledge they gained about the Mongols. The consolidation of Mongol rule encouraged missionaries and merchants to travel to Asia from the mid-thirteenth century on. In the second half of the century missionaries penetrated western Asia (Iran, Mesopotamia), then under the rule of Mongol Il-khans*. There were persistent rumours in Europe that the Il-khans were preparing to accept baptism, fostered by their tolerant treatment of Eastern Christians (especially Nestorians) living under their rule. At the end of the century, the Dominican Ricold of Montecroce tried to preach in Muslim Baghdad, and the Franciscan John of Monte Corvino travelled to China to establish a missionary base there. The Chinese missions continued in the first half of the fourteenth century; and following a brief visit to India in the 1290s, friars started to proselytize there. In the late thirteenth century mendicant missionaries were also active in North Africa, trying to convert Muslims. Language schools were set up, and training for missionaries developed to make them more knowledgeable in the local beliefs and languages of their audience. More contact did not necessarily mean more realistic knowledge throughout Europe; stereotypes of Muslims as cruel, effeminate, idolatrous, sexual perverts continued to exist, while new ones of the chivalrous, brave Muslim soldiers emerged.

European discoveries about the rest of the world had unspectacular origins in attempts to have direct links to gold- and spice-producing areas. Expansion in the Atlantic first started as the extension of Mediterranean exploration. Navigation techniques developed through experience and the observation of the stars, the sun, and coastlines. The antecedents of later conquests were the Catalan exploration and conquest of the Balearics in the Mediterranean; the establishment of trading posts in North Africa; and the installation of Italian merchant colonies. Italian, especially Venetian and Genoese, involvement in the southern and eastern Mediterranean was already significant during the eleventh century, even leading to an attack against Mahdiya (Tunisia) in 1087. These Italians provided shipping for the crusader states in return for trading privileges. Venetians installed merchant quarters around the Mediterranean, including Constantinople and Crete. The Genoese established trading colonies across the Mediterranean and beyond, including Antioch, Acre, Chios, Cyprus, Pera (across from Constantinople), and Caffa on the Black Sea. Between 1262 and 1269, the Venetians Niccolò and Maffeo Polo travelled to China; they were the first Westerners to reach it since antiquity. Marco Polo, who initially went to China as part of a Venetian merchant venture, ended up living at the court of the Great Khan Kublai at Shangtu, Khanbalik (Peking), and other Chinese cities, probably employed on official business. He dictated an account of his life there to a fellow prisoner in Genoa in 1298, which became very popular.

Over the three centuries, the formation of new polities and the peaceful or forced incorporation of new areas radically changed the territory of Latin Christendom. Different solutions were found to attract settlers and to ensure the coexistence of locals and newcomers, be they immigrants or conquerors. Although some of this expansion was checked or reversed, Europe no longer consisted of western Europe alone. The expansion of Latin Christendom resulted in the integration of northern and central Europe and Iberia, and shaped European history for centuries to come.

Conclusion

Daniel Power

The Europe of 1320 was very different from the continent of three-and-a-half centuries earlier. After hundreds of years of Latin Christian expansion at the expense of Islam, Eastern Christianity, and pagan cultures, almost the whole continent apart from Russia and the southern and eastern Balkans now formed part of Latin Christendom. The candidacy of two Bohemian kings for the throne of the Holy Roman Empire in 1273 (Otakar II) and 1292 (Václav II) demonstrates the degree to which the kingdoms of east-central Europe had come to form an integral part of Latin Christendom. The extent of 'Frankish' aristocratic migration to the more remote parts of Europe may be seen in the fact that all the kings of Scots after 1292 were descended in the male line from French immigrants to England since 1066. Internal expansion had also transformed European society, which now enjoyed networks of towns, villages, parish churches, and roads that far surpassed their tenth-century counterparts; the growth in the number and complexity of settlements was especially far-reaching in northern and central Europe and in the interior of the Iberian peninsula, although hardly any part of Europe was unaffected.

Yet by the late thirteenth century the expansion of Latin Christendom was largely coming to a halt. Its end was most visible in the collapse of the 'crusader states' in the Eastern Mediterranean (see Chapters 3 and 6) in the face of resurgent Islamic power. Although the Mongols posed a terrible threat to Islamic power for a time, their defeat by the Mamluk rulers of Egypt near Nazareth in 1260 allowed the Mamluks to overthrow the surviving principalities established by the early crusades. Antioch fell in 1268 and Acre, the chief town of the 'kingdom of Jerusalem', in 1291. Meanwhile, the Latin Empire of

Constantinople came to a virtual end in 1261 thanks to a modest and short-lived resurgence of Byzantine power, and the Frankish colonies that clung on in mainland Greece were increasingly feeble. Thereafter the only significant Latin possessions in the Eastern Mediterranean were the islands conquered from the Byzantines, notably Crete and Cyprus.

Not all the eastern borders of Latin Christendom were in retreat: in the 1260s the Genoese took over Caffa in the Crimea and the Venetians acquired Tana in the Sea of Azov, in the fourteenth century both groups of Italians tightened their grip over the Aegean islands, and between 1306 and 1310 the Hospitallers (Knights of Saint John) attempted to compensate for their eviction from the 'Holy Land' by seizing Rhodes. Although the Scandinavian connection with Green-land was declining, sailors were venturing further and further afield elsewhere in the Atlantic, especially down the north-west African coast. In north-east Europe, the short-lived conversion to Christianity of the Lithuanian grand duke in 1251–3 foreshadowed the long-prepared conversion of his successors in 1386, which would bring the boundaries of Latin Christendom to within 250 miles of Moscow. Yet here, too, Latin Christian expansion suffered setbacks: the (Orthodox) Russian prince Alexander Nevsky halted the eastward advances of the Swedes and Teutonic Knights in 1240–2. Only in Spain did Latin Christendom continue to make substantial gains. The Muslim rulers of Seville were appealing to Morocco for aid in 1247–8, much as the Levantine Franks sent many pleas to the West for help throughout the thirteenth century; neither group was saved from defeat. Taking the Mediterranean as a whole, Christianity and Islam were broadly in equilibrium at the end of the period. There was as yet no hint that the Ottoman Turks, who began seizing Byzantine possessions in Anatolia in 1301, would establish one of the greatest Islamic empires in history, taking Constantinople in 1453 and reaching Morocco and the gates of Vienna by 1529.

Demographic growth within much of Europe was also slowing down or even ceasing altogether by the end of the thirteenth century, and there is widespread evidence that population growth was placing great pressure upon available resources. Then from 1315 to 1322 a series of natural disasters struck the northern part of the continent. A succession of exceptionally wet summers, harsh winters, and failed harvests combined with devastating outbreaks of livestock diseases to cause a substantial fall in human population as well as ruinous increases in food prices. These natural problems were compounded by the disruption of dynastic wars in Scandinavia, the Empire, Flanders, and the British Isles. It is unclear how far the demographic decline of the 1310s and early 1320s was a temporary blip or the beginnings of a long-term phenomenon. What is certain is that demographic growth ceased to be the chief factor shaping the European economy; that within a generation Europe's population would suffer a much more substantial blow from the plague known to history as the Black Death (1347–51); and that recovery after 1351 was hindered by recurring plague epidemics as well as endemic warfare, with profound implications for European society, economy, and culture. It is one of the ironies of the central Middle Ages that its external expansion inadvertently sparked the end to internal growth, for the Black Death reached Italy in ships from one of Latin Christendom's furthest outposts, the Genoese colony of Caffa in the Crimea. West European commercial expansion had imported a terrible commodity.

Yet, despite the continent's economic stagnation, the profound commercial, religious, and political achievements of the period survived intact. The fourteenth-century European economy remained far more monetarized than in 950, its commercialization continued, and economic advances such as the development of long-distance banking and trading networks and the use of large-denomination coinage were not overturned. The phenomenal increase in the use of the written word was also sustained: the number of documents produced on behalf of the papacy and most monarchs, prelates, and urban associations continued to increase exponentially; by 1300 a sizeable proportion of these written instruments were in vernacular languages rather than in Latin. In the early fourteenth century European society was more culturally sophisticated, more literate, and wealthier than three-and-a-half centuries earlier.

Within Latin Christendom, however, the energies that had driven external expansion seem increasingly turned inwards. Even in the twelfth century the kings of Aragon had devoted as much concern to their claims in southern France and Provence as to their Muslim frontier; from 1282 the War of the Sicilian Vespers embroiled them in conflict with the kings of France and Sicily and the pope, who sponsored a French crusade against this Christian kingdom. 'Holy' wars proclaimed against other Christians were not a new phenomenon, but in the thirteenth century they gained in prominence compared with expeditions against non-Christians: other examples include the Albigensian Crusade, which affected the Catholic nobles and townspeople of southern France even as it sought to crush the Cathar heresy, and the wars sponsored by Pope Innocent IV against Emperor Frederick II. The sudden and brutal suppression of the Templars (1307–14), when the French crown systematically denigrated and destroyed an order of knights renowned for its warfare on the frontiers of Christendom, was a different but equally dramatic manifestation of growing Latin Christian introversion; so was the wholesale expulsion of the Jews from England in 1290 and from the French royal domain in 1306. Nevertheless, many European warriors were still prepared to fight traditional non-Christian enemies. Throughout the fourteenth century the Teutonic Knights continued to attract recruits for their campaigns against the pagans of Lithuania. Holy wars against the Muslims continued until the eighteenth century, while the Templars' fellow religious warriors and rivals, the Hospitallers, remained integral to the defence of Christian territory in the Mediterranean until Napoleon Bonaparte evicted them from Malta in 1798.

Conventional dynastic wars within Latin Christendom, which remained as prevalent in the fourteenth as in the tenth century, also provide indications that European society was entering a new era. Chief amongst these was the resurgence of infantry in battle. Cavalry had never been invincible, as several Anglo-Norman battles (see p. 36) as well as imperial defeats by the Saxons (1080) and the Lombards (1176, 1237) revealed; nor did mounted warriors now cease to play a major role on the battlefield. However, the convincing defeats of French cavalry by Flemish militias at Courtrai (1302), of English cavalry by Scottish infantry at Stirling Bridge (1297) and Bannockburn (1314), of the Latin knights of Athens by the mercenary Catalan Company at Halmyros (1311), and of Austrian men-at-arms by the Swiss at Mortgarten (1315), together seem to usher in a new phase in European history—even though in each case the losers had made crucial tactical errors.

None of these infantry victories was due to technological innovation; indeed, the increased use of plate armour from c.1250 afforded greater protection to wealthier knights, while gunpowder, although first used in European warfare in the 1320s, would not play an important part until later in the century. Instead, ancient weapons such as the longbow and the pike were being used in new ways, in much greater numbers, and with more effective organization. The significance of these battles was primarily social. Stirling Bridge, Courtrai, Halmyros, and Mortgarten all demonstrate the ability of commanders of humble birth and infantry united by a common cause to overcome better armed warriors of high rank; such plebeian victories were, in Norman Housley's words, 'an affront to the age's sense of social order'.[1] Moreover, noble attitudes themselves were changing: noble commanders were increasingly willing to use their low-born infantry to defeat—and kill—fellow nobles. Some of the most dramatic victories involving massed infantry, notably Bannockburn and Crécy (1346), were possible only because a royal or noble general—in these instances, King Robert I (Bruce) of Scotland and King Edward III of England respectively—was prepared to countenance the slaughter of enemy noblemen by his own common soldiers. Just when the nobility was coming to enjoy greater legal definition across much of Europe (see pp. 37–40), its military pre-dominance was being challenged by the very rulers whose laws were conferring that same legal protection; noble economic power was also being undermined (see p. 60).

Pitched battles remained a rare occurrence, and sieges, which were far more common, had always relied heavily upon infantry of all ranks; the chief technological innovation in siege warfare, the type of catapult known as the counterweight trebuchet, occurred in the middle of the period in question, around 1200. Yet the way that warfare was organized was fundamentally different in 1320 compared with 950. Rulers were now able to fund large armies on a regular basis, using their increased powers of taxation. As Björn Weiler has shown in Chapter 3, they did so at considerable political cost; the more formal character of political relations, for instance, through regularized representative assemblies, was one of the legacies of the central Middle Ages. Bolstered by such powers of exploitation, the monarchies of western Europe were well prepared for more sustained confrontation; and in 1294, renewed Plantagenet–Capetian war in south-west France and the Low Countries, after half a century of

[1] N. Housley, 'European Warfare, c.1200–1320', in M. Keen (ed.), *Medieval Warfare: A History*. (Oxford, 1999), 113–35, at 114.

peace, was a prelude for the series of Anglo-French conflicts known to history as the Hundred Years War (1337–1453). Ostensibly fought because of the claims of Edward III of England and his successors to the French throne, these wars also embroiled Scotland and most Iberian kingdoms and occasionally threatened to engulf the Empire as well; their impact upon late-medieval European society and culture would be profound. They had more immediate consequences for the direction of European 'high' politics. Thanks to the chronic dynastic conflicts within the Empire following the death of the great emperor Frederick II (1250) and the demise of his Hohenstaufen dynasty soon after, the Capetian kings of France had emerged the most powerful rulers in Europe under Louis IX (1226–70) and Philip IV (1285–1314); they had also begun probing imperial territory in Lorraine and on the east banks of the Rivers Saône and Rhône, traditionally the eastern borders of the Capetian kingdom. Renewed conflict with the kings of England may therefore have averted a Franco-Imperial contest for the leadership of Christendom; that struggle would have to await the rise of the Habsburgs in the fifteenth century.

Meanwhile, monarchical power was undergoing qualititative changes either side of 1300. Its ideological foundations were being strengthened by the revival of interest in Roman Law, notably the precept 'What pleases the prince has the force of law'. Its effectiveness was increasing because of the rise of professional lawyers and bureaucrats, which epitomized the shift in this period from mediation within local communities to their external direction by agents of superior authority. A different shift was in the treatment of political protest. Despite, or perhaps because of, the development of representative institutions, armed protest against the ruler was becoming less acceptable. Nowhere is this clearer than in the increasing severity of punishment for rebellion. In 1268 the Hohenstaufen prince Conradin, grandson of Emperor Frederick II, tried and failed to gain his grandfather's kingdom of Sicily. His vanquisher, Charles of Anjou, the reigning king of Sicily, had him publicly tried and beheaded. Such an event would have been unthinkable two centuries earlier: there was nothing new about rulers doing away with rebels or dynastic rivals, and the politics of the Italian cities in particular had always been murderous, but the increasing use of law to destroy men of noble blood before public tribunals represented an ominous extension of monarchical power. Conradin's execution was the first of many such judicial murders: King Edward I of England condemned to death Dafydd, last prince of Gwynedd in Wales, in 1283, and three brothers of Robert Bruce, claimant to the Scottish throne, in 1306–7. Still more significant was the increasing resort to public execution as a punishment for simple political failure: victims included Enguerrand de Marigny, grand chamberlain of Philip IV, sacrificed by Louis X to a rival court faction in 1315, and Piers Gaveston, the favourite of Edward II of England, the target for the wrath of rebel earls in 1312. Such events were becoming common across Europe, amongst urban oligarchies as much as royal courts; they heralded the vindictive factionalized politics of the late Middle Ages and early modern period.

The consolidation of monarchical power was the most common trend in Europe in the opening years of the fourteenth century, from Spain to Scandinavia and Hungary, but there were significant exceptions. In 1320 noble power varied enormously in strength across the continent. The western emperors continued to pursue universalist ambitions, although strife between rival claimants to the throne, especially during the so-called Interregnum (1256–73), seriously undermined their authority; it is telling that no fewer than four 'kings of the Romans' perished in battle between 1256 and 1308. In particular, imperial weakness south of the Alps after the death of Frederick II encouraged the rise of the signori* (often rather inaccurately translated as 'despots'), dynasts who wrested power from the city communes or subverted them, and whose regional hegemonies would evolve into the little states of Renaissance Italy; in the 1310s Dante immortalized many of the most notorious signori by placing them amongst the inhabitants of Hell. North of the Alps, the chronic rivalries for the imperial crown (chiefly, moreover, between dynasties with few domains in central or northern Germany) thrust power into the hands of the princes, the most powerful of whom increasingly formed a coterie of 'electors'*. Meanwhile, the flourishing cities of north Germany, buoyed by their growing monopoly of Baltic trade, were laying the foundations for the Hanseatic League.

The end of the period witnessed the decline of not only imperial but also papal leadership. While Julia Barrow challenges the concept of a single 'reform' movement (above, Chapter 4), the energy and scope of Innocent III's Fourth Lateran Council (1215) outshone all succeeding councils until the Counter-Reformation in the sixteenth century. The Council of Lyon (1274) effected a brief reunion with the Greek Orthodox Church but pales in comparison with its predecessor of 1215. In some ways the papacy still appeared to be occupying the heights to which the firm leadership of Urban II, Alexander III, and Innocent III had raised it. The quarrels of John XXII with Louis IV (Ludwig of Bavaria) in the 1320s appear very traditional in many respects, for it pitted a strident pope against an emperor who yearned to revive imperial power in Italy and was prepared to depose the pope if need be; each cultivated supporters amongst the peninsula's cities and nobles and attracted strident propagandists such as Louis's adherent Marsilius of Padua. However, increasing royal control of clerical taxation to fund internecine dynastic warfare signalled the weakening of the liberties for which successive popes and prelates had fought so hard. The papacy had never fully extricated itself from the mire of Italian politics, but the chief threat to its independence came from a different quarter. Boniface VIII's quarrel with Philip IV of France even led to a French attempt to kidnap him in 1303, and was swiftly followed by the removal of the papacy to Avignon in Provence, on the very borders of the kingdom of France (although it technically lay in an imperial county held by the king of Naples). The 'Babylonian Captivity' at Avignon lasted until 1377.

The difficulties of the Catholic Church around 1300 were not confined to the papacy. Most of the monastic orders founded in the 'long twelfth century' witnessed a decline in benefactions from the late thirteenth century onwards; the friars continued to thrive, but internal crises within the Franciscan Order led to harsh papal persecution of the 'Spiritual Franciscans', and several friars were even executed as heretics in 1318. The sense of crisis should not be exaggerated: in 1300 the first papal 'jubilee' was celebrated, apparently because of spontaneous popular demands, and new orders emerged in response to lay aspirations, such as the 'double' communities of men and women of the Brigittine Order founded by Saint Bridget (Birgitta) of Sweden (1346–50). Other forms of religious observance or endowment such as confraternities and chantry chapels would continue to grow in popularity. New forms of church architecture continued to flourish, not least at parish level, and Giotto's frescos in Assisi, Padua, and Florence attest in a different fashion to the vibrancy of the Church at the end of the period. Nevertheless, the strong direction that characterized ecclesiastical organization from the mid-eleventh to the mid-thirteenth century had weakened by the 1330s.

Any final assessment of the central Middle Ages must recognize that the various national traditions or myths treat the period very differently from one another, and these have contributed heavily to differing interpretations of the period. French historiography has conventionally viewed it as the age in which a unitary French monarchical state emerged, forerunner of the modern French republic. English national tradition has depicted it as the age when English identity and national institutions, especially the triple blessings of the Common Law, Magna Carta, and Parliament, were forged in reaction to 'foreign' kings; for the Scots, the central Middle Ages witnessed the unification of the kingdom in preparation for its 300-year resistance against English dominance from 1296 onwards. The period has occupied a comparable place in the historical memory of the peoples of Scandinavia and east-central Europe: each major kingdom was established and each of the main peoples was converted to Christianity— the medieval equivalent of entry to the European Union, perhaps, but with the promise of eternal salvation as an extra inducement. For some of these peoples, notably the Danes and the Hungarians, the central medieval kingdom occupied a far larger territory than the equivalent modern state and so the period has sometimes evoked a particular pride. For the Spanish, the central Middle Ages traditionally marked the age of the *Reconquista*, or 'reconquest' of the Iberian peninsula from Muslim rule—a concept that historians have largely repudiated but that lingers in the popular imagination. In the same vein, some other national historical traditions regard the central Middle Ages far less positively. The Welsh and Irish have customarily seen it as a period of cruel repression when their ancient liberties were lost to the English; Slovakians and Croatians have regarded the period in the same light, but with the Hungarians as the oppressor. For the Greeks, haunted by dim memories of Byzantine greatness, this age of the Crusades is still recalled with horror. Above all, the fragmentation of the Holy Roman Empire has generally been regarded as a tragedy for Germany, since it appeared to prevent its emergence as a nation state before the nineteenth century; on the other hand, that same imperial disunity has been regarded more favourably by the Italians since it made possible the glories of the Italian Renaissance, which was fostered by the rivalries of the independent city states.

Such national traditions have proved very durable, despite being challenged by the more nuanced findings of modern scholarship. Yet both crude national myths and meticulous research demonstrate the fundamental place of the central Middle Ages in the history of most European countries, even though the vast majority of their citizens are unaware how much their culture and outlook owe to those distant centuries. Equally telling is the view from outside. For outsiders looking in, the period represents above all the age of the Crusades, when barbaric 'Franks' from western Europe brutally ravaged, pillaged, and attempted to conquer the more venerable and sophisticated civilizations that were unfortunate enough to live in proximity. 'Franks' became the generic term for Europeans in languages as dispersed as Greek, Arabic, Ethiopian, Iranian, and Chinese. It is the supreme irony of the period 950–1320 that it witnessed both the welding of a common 'European' culture, and the hardening of the continent's chief divisions along national lines.

Further Reading

General

The following recommendations are primarily intended to help English-speaking students to delve more deeply into the topics discussed in the chapters above: works written in other languages are therefore cited in translations into English wherever possible. The following abbreviations are used below:

MW	Peter Linehan and Janet L. Nelson (eds.), *The Medieval World* (London, 2001)
NCMH iii	*The New Cambridge Medieval History*, iii. c.*900*–c.*1024*, ed. T. Reuter (Cambridge, 1999)
NCMH v	*The New Cambridge Medieval History*, v. c.*1198*–c.*1300*, ed. D. Abulafia (Cambridge, 1999)
RR	R. L. Benson, G. Constable, and C. D. Lanham (eds.), *Renaissance and Renewal in the Twelfth Century* (Oxford, 1982)

The New Cambridge Medieval History volumes are multi-authored collections of articles that offer excellent, detailed treatment of most themes in this work, with very extensive bibliographies. Readers are also referred to *The New Cambridge Medieval History*, iv. c.*1024*–c.*1198*, ed. D. Luscombe and J. Riley-Smith (2 vols., Cambridge, 2004), which appeared too late for specific chapters to be recommended here; and, for the early fourteenth century, to *The New Cambridge Medieval History*, vi. c.*1300*–c.*1415*, ed. M. Jones (Cambridge, 2000). *The Medieval World* is more selective in its topics but still breathtaking in its scope (see below for specific articles).

Three important recent interpretative essays concerning the central Middle Ages are Robert Bartlett, *The Making of Europe: Conquest, Colonisation and Cultural Change, 950–1350* (Harmondsworth, 1993); William Chester Jordan, *Europe in the High Middle Ages* (Harmondsworth, 2001); and, concerning a shorter period, R. I. Moore, *The First European Revolution c.970–1215* (Oxford and Malden, MA, 2000). Malcolm Barber, *The Two Cities: Medieval Europe 1050–1320*

(2nd edn., London, 2004), is a very useful reference work. A rather different approach in the French *Annaliste* tradition, emphasizing 'mentalities' and the influence of the environment upon human development, is provided by J. Le Goff, *Medieval Civilization*, trans. J. Barrow (Oxford and Cambridge, MA, 1988). Also still of interest is R. W. Southern, *The Making of the Middle Ages* (London, 1953), a venerable and idiosyncratic introduction to the period. M. Bentley (ed.), *The Companion to Historiography* (London, 1997), part II, contains useful introductions to medievalists' approaches to their period. Atlases include A. MacKay and D. Ditchburn (eds.), *Atlas of Medieval Europe* (London, 1997); Paul Robert Magocsi (ed.), *Historical Atlas of East Central Europe* (Seattle and London, 1993); and J. Riley-Smith (ed.), *Atlas of the Crusades* (London, 1991).

Sources

The number of primary sources in translation for this period is rapidly increasing, and many are now available on university websites. Amongst the numerous collections of source extracts, *Readings in Medieval History*, ed. Patrick J. Geary (3rd edn., 2 vols, Peterborough, Ontario, 2003), is one of the most comprehensive.

For the Empire, important narratives include *Ottonian Germany: The* Chronicon *of Thietmar of Merseburg*, trans. D. A. Warner (Manchester, 2001), and Otto of Freising's two works, *The Two Cities*, trans. C. C. Mierow (New York, 1928, repr. 2002), and *The Deeds of Frederick Barbarossa*, trans. C. C. Mierow (New York, 1953); see also the selected texts in *Medieval Monarchy in Action: The German Empire from Henry I to Henry IV*, trans. B. H. Hill (London and New York, 1972), and *Imperial Lives and Letters of the Eleventh Century*, ed. R. L. Benson, trans. T. E. Mommsen and K. F. Morrison (2nd edn., New York, 2000). Two important Norman narratives are *The* Gesta Normannorum Ducum *of William of Jumièges, Orderic Vitalis, and Robert of Torigni*, ed. and trans. E. M. C. van Houts (2 vols., Oxford, 1992–5), and *The Ecclesiastical History of Orderic Vitalis*, ed. and trans. M. Chibnall (6 vols., Oxford, 1969–80). Other French regions are less well served by English translations; exceptions include *Feudal Society in Medieval France: Documents from the County of Champagne*, trans. T. Evergates (Philadelphia, 1993); Rodulfus Glaber, *The Five Books of the Histories*, ed. and trans. J. France (Oxford, 1989); *Self and Society in Medieval France: The Memoirs of Abbot Guibert of Nogent*, trans. J. F. Benton (New York, 1970); Suger, *The Deeds of Louis the Fat*, trans. R. C. Cusimano and J. Moorhead (Washington, 1992); and Jean de Joinville, 'The Life of Saint Louis', *Chronicles of the Crusades*, trans. M. R. B. Shaw (Harmondsworth, 1963), 164–353. For Flanders, see Galbert of Bruges, *The Murder of Charles the Good, Count of Flanders*, trans. J. B. Ross (New York, 1967).

Many of the vast numbers of translated sources concerning England are collected in *English Historical Documents*, i. *500–1042*, ed. D. Whitelock (2nd edn., London, 1979); ii. *1042–1189*, ed. D. C. Douglas and G. W. Greenway (2nd edn., London, 1981); iii. *1189–1327*, ed. H. Rothwell (London, 1975). Amongst important narratives are *The Anglo-Saxon Chronicle*, trans. D. Whitelock *et al.* (London, 1961); William of Malmesbury, *Gesta Regum Anglorum*, ed. R. A. B. Mynors *et al.* (2 vols., Oxford, 1998–9); and Henry of Huntingdon, *Historia Anglorum*, ed. and trans. D. Greenway (Oxford, 1996). Sources from other parts of the British Isles include *Early Sources of Scottish History A.D. 500–1286*, ed. A. O. Anderson (2 vols., 1922, repr. 1990); *Brut y Tywysogyon or the Chronicle of the Princes: Red Book of Hergest Version*, ed. and trans. T. Jones (2nd edn., Cardiff, 1973); and Gerald of Wales, *Expugnatio Hibernica: The Conquest of Ireland*, ed. and trans. A. B. Scott and F. X. Martin (Dublin, 1978). For one of the most influential of all medieval texts, see Geoffrey of Monmouth, *History of the Kings of Britain*, trans. L. Thorpe (Harmondsworth, 1966).

Other regional collections include *Medieval Iberia: Readings from Christian, Muslim, and Jewish Sources*, ed. Olivia Remie Constable (Philadelphia, 1997); *The World of El Cid: Chronicles of the Spanish Reconquest*, trans. S. Barton and R. Fletcher (Manchester, 2000); *The Towns of Italy in the Later Middle Ages*, trans. T. Dean (Manchester, 2000); and *The Normans in Europe*, ed. and trans. E. van Houts (Manchester, 2000); see also 'Hugh Falcandus', *The History of the Tyrants of Sicily 1154–69*, trans. G. Loud and T. Wiedemann (Manchester, 1998). For east-central Europe, see Gallus Anonymous, *Gesta Principum Polonorum: The Deeds of the Princes of the Poles*, trans. Paul W. Knoll and Frank Schaer (Budapest and New York, 2003); Simon of Kéza, *Gesta Hungarorum (The Deeds of the Hungarians)*, trans. László Veszprémy and Frank Schaer (Budapest and New York, 1999); and *The Origins of Christianity in Bohemia: Sources and*

Commentary, ed. Marvin Kantor (Evanston, IL, 1990). The best-known Byzantine narrative is *The Alexiad of Anna Comnena*, trans. E. R. A. Sewter (Harmondsworth, 1969).

Great vernacular literary or historical works include *The Song of Roland*, trans. D. Sayers (Harmondsworth, 1957); *The Poem of El Cid*, trans. R. Hamilton and J. Perry (Harmondsworth, 1984); Chrétien de Troyes, *Arthurian Romances*, trans. W. W. Comfort (Everyman, repr. 1968); *The Songs of Bernart de Ventadorn*, ed. and trans. S. G. Nichols and J. A. Galm (Chapel Hill, NC, 1962); *The Courtly Love Tradition*, ed. B. O'Donoghue (Manchester, 1982); *The History of William Marshal*, ed. A. J. Holden and D. Crouch, trans. S. Gregory (2 vols. to date, London, 2002–4); Dante's *The Divine Comedy* (many translations); *The Book of Deeds of James I of Aragon*, trans. D. Smith and H. Buffery (Aldershot, 2003); and *The Jewish Poets of Spain*, ed. D. Goldstein (Harmondsworth, 1971). Source collections for specific themes include *Women's Lives in Medieval Europe: A Sourcebook*, ed. E. Amt (London and New York, 1993), and *Love, Marriage, and Family in the Middle Ages: A Reader*, ed. J. Murray (Peterborough, Ontario, 2001). Legal texts include *The Établissements de Saint Louis: Thirteenth-Century Law Texts from Tours, Orléans, and Paris*, trans. F. R. P. Akehurst (Philadelphia, 1996); *The Treatise on the Laws and Customs of the Realm of England commonly called Glanvill*, ed. and trans. G. D. G. Hall (2nd edn., Oxford, 1993); and *The Usatges of Barcelona*, trans. D. J. Kegay (Philadelphia, 1994). For Andreas Capellanus, see *The Art of Courtly Love*, trans. J. J. Parry (New York, 1941).

For religious orders, see *The Cistercian World: Monastic Writings of the Twelfth Century*, trans. P. Matarasso (Harmondsworth, 1993); *St Francis of Assisi: Writings and Early Biographies*, trans. M. A. Habig (4th edn., Chicago, 1983); and *The Templars: Selected Sources*, trans. Malcolm Barber and Keith Bate (Manchester, 2002). *The Letters of St Bernard of Clairvaux*, trans. B. S. James (Stroud, 1953), provides the leading source for the most famous twelfth-century monk. For Abelard and Heloise, see below (Intellectual and Cultural History). *The Register of Pope Gregory VII 1073–1085*, trans. H. E. J. Cowdrey (Oxford, 2002), provides insights into the period's most controversial pope. Examples of sources concerning religious practice are *The Miracles of Our Lady of Rocamadour*, trans. M. Bull (Woodbridge, 1999); *The Pilgrim's Guide to Santiago de Compostela*, trans. W. Melczer (New York, 1993); and *Medieval Popular Religion, 1000–1500:*

A Reader, ed. John Shinners (Peterborough, Ontario, 1997). Sources for heresy include *The Birth of Popular Heresy*, ed. R. I. Moore, (London, 1975); *Heresy and Authority in Medieval Europe: Documents in Translation*, ed. E. Peters (London, 1980); *Heresies of the High Middle Ages*, ed., W. L. Wakefield and A. P. Evans (2nd edn., New York, 1991); Peter of Les-Vaux-de-Cernay, *The History of the Albigensian Crusade*, trans. W. A. and M. D. Sibly (Woodbridge, 1998); and *The Song of the Cathar Wars*, trans. J. Shirley (Aldershot, 1996).

Amongst translated crusading narratives are *The First Crusade: The Chronicle of Fulcher of Chartres and Other Source Materials*, ed. and trans. E. Peters (2nd edn., Philadelphia, 1998), and *Gesta Francorum: The Deeds of the Franks and the other pilgrims to Jerusalem*, ed. R. Hill (London, 1972); for the Second Crusade, Odo of Deuil, *De profectione Ludovici VII in Orientem*, ed. and trans. V. G. Berry (New York, 1948), and *The Conquest of Lisbon*, ed. and trans. C. W. David, rev. J. Phillips (New York, 2001); for the Third, *The History of the Holy War: Ambroise's Estoire de la Guerre Sainte*, ed. and trans. M. Ailes and M. Barber (2 vols., Woodbridge, 2003); *Chronicle of the Third Crusade*, trans. H. Nicholson (Aldershot, 1997); and *The Rare and Excellent History of Saladin*, trans. D. S. Richards (Aldershot, 2002). For later crusades, see *Joinville and Villehardouin: Chronicles of the Crusades*, trans. M. R. B. Shaw (Harmondsworth, 1963), and *Christian Society and the Crusades 1198–1229*, ed. and trans. E. Peters (Philadelphia, 1971). See also *Arab Historians of the Crusades*, trans. F. Gabrieli and E. J. Costello (New York, 1969), and *The Jews and the Crusaders: The Hebrew Chronicles of the First and Second Crusades*, ed. and trans. S. Eidelberg (Madison, 1977). For the most famous of all medieval travellers' texts, see *The Travels of Marco Polo*, trans. R. Latham (Harmondsworth, 1958).

Introduction

There is a plethora of fine studies concerning the kingdoms and regions of Europe. For Iberia, southern Italy and Sicily, east-central and northern Europe, and the 'crusader states', see the recommendations for Chapter 6 below. For Byzantium, see M. Angold, *The Byzantine Empire, 1025–1204: A Political History* (2nd edn., London and New York, 1998). Useful works concerning Germany include T. Reuter, *Germany in the Early Middle Ages c.800–1056* (London and New York, 1991), chs. 6–9; Alfred Haverkamp, *Medieval Germany 1056–1273*, trans. H. Braun and R. Mortimer (2nd edn., Oxford, 1992); B. Arnold, *Princes and Territories in Medieval Germany* (Cambridge, 1991), and *Medieval Germany 500–1300* (Basingstoke, 1997). For prophecies concerning the 'last emperor', see B. McGinn, *Visions of the End: Apocalyptic Traditions in the Middle Ages* (New York, 1979). For Italy, see *Italy in the Central Middle Ages*, ed. D. Abulafia (Oxford, 2004), and D. Abulafia, *The Western Mediterranean Kingdoms 1200–1500* (London and New York, 1997). For France, see J. Dunbabin, *France in the Making, 843–1180* (2nd edn., Oxford, 2000); E. Hallam, *Capetian France, 987–1328*, rev. J. A. Everard (London, 2001); *France in the Central Middle Ages*, ed. M. Bull (Oxford, 2002); and, for the south, L. Paterson, *The World of the Troubadours* (Cambridge, 1993). Many studies in English concern regions ruled by the Norman and Plantagenet kings: see, most recently, C. Harper-Bill and E. M. C. van Houts (eds.), *Companion to the Anglo-Norman World* (Woodbridge, 2003), and J. Gillingham, *The Angevin Empire* (2nd edn., London, 2001). For the British Isles, see D. Carpenter, *The Struggle for Mastery: Britain 1066–1284* (London, 2003), and the many works of R. R. Davies, including *The First English Empire: Power and Identities in the British Isles 1093–1343* (Oxford, 2000); surveys of individual countries include M. T. Clanchy, *England and Its Rulers, 1066–1307* (2nd edn., Oxford, 1998); R. Bartlett, *England under the Norman and Angevin Kings, 1075–1225* (Oxford, 2000); R. R. Davies, *The Age of Conquest: Wales 1063–1415* (Oxford, 1991); G. W. S. Barrow, *Kingship and Unity: Scotland 1000–1306* (2nd edn., London, 1989); B. Webster, *Medieval Scotland: The Making of an Identity* (Basingstoke, 1997); A. Cosgrove (ed.), *New History of Ireland*, ii. *1169–1534* (2nd edn., Oxford, 1993); and S. Duffy, *Ireland in the Middle Ages* (Basingstoke, 1997). For identities and for Europe as a geographical concept, see Bartlett, *Making of Europe*, 269–91; S. Forde, L. Johnson, and A. V. Murray (eds.), *Concepts of National Identity in the Middle Ages* (Leeds, 1995); and A. P. Smyth (ed.), *Medieval Europeans: Studies in Ethnic Identity and National Perspectives in Medieval Europe* (Basingstoke, 1998).

For 'mutationism', the epoch-making work was Georges Duby, *La Société aux XIe et XIIe siècles dans la région mâconnaise* (Paris, 1953); translated extracts are in Fredric L. Cheyette (ed.), *Lordship and*

Community in Medieval Europe (New York, 1968), 137–55. More controversial is G. Bois, *The Transformation of the Year One Thousand*, trans. J. Birrell (Manchester, 1992); for critiques (in French), see the articles collected in *Médiévales*, 21 (Autumn 1993). For recent debates concerning the 'transformation of the year 1000', see T. Bisson, 'The "Feudal Revolution" ', *Past and Present*, 144 (1994), 6–42; the comments by D. Barthélemy, S. D. White, T. Reuter, and C. Wickham, and Bisson's rejoinder, in ibid. 152 (1996), 196–223; 155 (1997), 177–225; also J.-P. Poly and E. Bournazel, *The Feudal Transformation 900–1200*, trans. C. Higgitt (New York, 1991); D. Barthélemy, *La Mutation de l'an mil: A-t-il eu lieu?* (Paris, 1997); D. Bates, 'England and the "Feudal Revolution" ', in *Il feudalesimo nell'alto medioevo* (Spoleto, 2000), ii., 611–49; and Warren C. Brown and Piotr Górecki (eds.), *Conflict in Medieval Europe* (Aldershot, 2003) (articles by Stephen D. White and Fredric L. Cheyette). For the *mutation documentaire* ('transformation of the sources'), see P. Geary, *Phantoms of Remembrance* (Princeton, 1994), and O. Guyotjeannin, ' "*Penuria scriptorum*": Le Mythe de l'anarchie documentaire dans la France du nord (X^e–première moitié du XIe siècle)', *Bibliothèque de l'École des Chartes*, 155 (1997), 11–44.

For the expansion of Latin Christendom, see the recommendations for Chapter 6 below; for 'frontiers', see R. Bartlett and R. MacKay (eds.), *Medieval Frontier Societies* (Oxford, 1989); D. Power and N. Standen (eds.), *Frontiers in Question: Eurasian Borderlands 700–1700* (Basingstoke, 1999), especially 1–12; D. Abulafia and N. Berend (eds.), *Medieval Frontiers: Concepts and Practices* (Aldershot, 2002); and, for 'internal' colonization, William H. TeBrake, *Medieval Frontier* (College Station, TX, 1985). William C. Jordan, *The Great Famine: Northern Europe in the Early Fourteenth Century* (Princeton, 1996), addresses the relationship between society and the environment far more generally than for the events of 1315–22 alone.

Society

Three works, now regarded as classics, serve as introductions to central medieval society: M. Bloch, *Feudal Society*, trans. L. A. Manyon (London, 1961; first published 1939–40); J. Le Goff, *Medieval Civilization*, trans. J. Barrow (Oxford, and Cambridge, MA, 1988); and

R. Fossier, *La Société médiévale* (Paris, 1991). For the nobility, in addition to the articles of Georges Duby, *The Chivalrous Society*, trans. Cynthia Postan (Berkeley and Los Angeles, 1977), see D. Crouch, *The Image of Aristocracy in Britain, 1000–1300* (London, 1992); M. Aurell, *La Noblesse en Occident (Ve–XVe siècle)* (Paris, 1996); A. Duggan (ed.), *Nobles and Nobility in Medieval Europe*, (Woodbridge, 2000); S. Barton, *The Aristocracy in Twelfth-Century León and Castile* (Cambridge, 1997); J. Green, *The Aristocracy of Norman England* (Cambridge, 1997); and J. B. Freed, 'Reflections on the Medieval German Nobility', *American Historical Review*, 91 (1986), 553–75. For noblewomen, see T. Evergates (ed.), *Aristocratic Women in Medieval France* (Philadelphia, 2001), and S. Johns, *Noblewomen, Aristocracy, and Power in the Twelfth-Century Anglo-Norman Realm* (Manchester, 2003).

For medieval social structures, see G. Duby, *The Three Orders: Feudal Society Imagined*, trans. A. Goldhammer (Chicago, 1980); S. Reynolds, *Fiefs and Vassals: The Medieval Evidence Reinterpreted* (Oxford, 1994); and N. Fryde, P. Monnet, and G. Oexle (eds.), *Présence du féodalisme et présent de la féodalité* (Göttingen, 2002). Thomas N. Bisson, 'La Terre et les hommes: A Programme Fulfilled?', *French History*, 14 (2000), 322–45, provides a useful overview and list of regional studies of French and Mediterranean society. The numerous studies of knighthood include J. Flori, *Chevaliers et chevalerie au Moyen Age* (Paris, 1998); B. Arnold, *German Knighthood, 1050–1300* (Oxford, 1985); and C. B. Bouchard, *Strong of Body, Brave and Noble: Chivalry and Society in Medieval France* (Ithaca, NY, 1998); those about warfare include R. C. Smail, *Crusading Warfare 1097–1193* (Cambridge, 1956); Matthew Strickland (ed.), *Anglo-Norman Warfare* (Woodbridge, 1992); John France, *Western Warfare in the Age of the Crusades 1000–1300* (Ithaca, NY, 1999); Richard W. Kaeuper, *Chivalry and Violence in Medieval Europe* (Oxford, 1999); M. Keen (ed.), *Medieval Warfare: A History* (Oxford, 1999); and A. Forey, *The Military Orders* (Basingstoke, 1992). Amongst the many works concerning medieval castles, the most comprehensive is C. L. H. Coulson, *Castles in Medieval Society: Fortresses in England, France, and Ireland in the Central Middle Ages* (Oxford, 2003); see also M. Bur (ed.), *La Maison forte au Moyen Âge* (Paris, 1986), and A. Debord, *Aristocratie et pouvoir: Le Rôle du château dans la France médiévale* (Paris, 2000). See also M. Keen, *Chivalry* (New Haven, 1984); M. Strickland, *War and Chivalry: The Conduct and Perception of War in England and Normandy, 1066–1217* (Cambridge, 1996); Joachim Bumke, *Courtly Culture: Literature and Society in the High Middle Ages* (Berkeley and Los Angeles, 1991); and C. Stephen Jaeger, *The Origins of Courtliness* (Philadelphia, 1985).

The numerous studies concerning aristocratic kinship include M. Aurell, 'La Parenté en l'an mil', *Cahiers de Civilisation Médiévale*, 43 (2000), 125–42; K. S. B. Keats-Rohan (ed.), *Family Trees and the Roots of Politics* (Woodbridge, 1997); and C. B. Bouchard, *'Those of My Blood': Constructing noble Families in Medieval Francia* (Philadelphia, 2000). For naming patterns, see G. Beech *et al.* (eds.), *Personal Names Studies of Medieval Europe: Social Identity and Familial Structures* (Kalamazoo, MI, 2002); for the social significance of clothing, see F. Piponnier and P. Manne, *Se vêtir au Moyen Âge* (Paris, 1995). For childhood, see D. Alexandre-Bidon and D. Lett, *Les Enfants au Moyen Age* (Paris, 1997); studies concerning marriage include G. Duby, *The Knight, the Lady, and the Priest*, trans. B. Bray (London, 1984), and C. Brooke, *The Medieval Idea of Marriage* (Oxford, 1989).

Recent collective works concerning urban oligarchies include *Le Marchand au Moyen Âge* (Paris, 1992); *Les Élites urbaines au Moyen Âge* (Paris and Rome, 1997); and J. Aurell (ed.), *El Mediterráneo medieval y renacentista, espacio de mercados y culturas* (Pamplona, 2002) (see also the recommendations for the Economy below); ecclesiastical attitudes to mercantile wealth are discussed in J. Baldwin, *Masters, Princes and Merchants: The Social Views of Peter the Chanter and his Circle* (Princeton, 1970), and R. De Roover, *San Bernardino de Siena and Sant'Antonino of Florence, the Two Great Economic Thinkers of the Middle Ages* (Cambridge, MA, 1967). For the peasantry, there are several classics from British historiography: E. Miller and J. Hatcher, *Medieval England: Rural Society and Economic Change, 1066–1348* (London, 1978); H. E. Hallam, *Rural England, 1066–1272* (Brighton, 1980); and P. R. Hyams, *King, Lord, and Peasants in Medieval England* (Oxford, 1980); more recent works include R. Fossier, *Peasant Life in the Medieval West*, trans. J. Vale (Oxford, 1988); W. Rösener, *Peasants in the Middle Ages*, trans. A. Stutzer (Cambridge, 1992); P. Freedman, *Images of the Medieval Peasant* (Stanford, 1999); R. Faith, *The English Peasantry and the Growth of Lordship* (Leicester, 1997); M. Bourin and P. Freedman (eds.), *La Servitude dans les pays de la Méditerranée occidentale chrétienne au XIIe siècle et au-delà* (Rome, 2000); and

A. Champagne, *L'Artisanat rural en Poitou au Moyen Age* (Rennes, forthcoming). For the poor and those at the margins of society, see D. Flood (ed.), *Poverty in the Middle Ages* (London, 1975), and M. Mollat, *Les Pauvres au Moyen Âge* (Paris, 1978).

Economy

Several good general histories of the European economy during the central Middle Ages are available. A fundamental work remains M. M. Postan *et al.*, *The Cambridge Economic History of Europe*, i. *The Agrarian Life of the Middle Ages* (2nd edn., Cambridge, 1966); ii. *Trade and Industry in the Middle Ages* (2nd edn., Cambridge, 1987); iii. *Economic Organization and Policies in the Middle Ages* (Cambridge, 1965). Each volume contains excellent bibliographies.

The best treatment of the medieval economy in a single volume is Norman J. G. Pounds, *An Economic History of Europe* (2nd edn., London, 1994). Also useful are Carlo M. Cipolla (ed.), *The Middle Ages* (The Fontana Economic History of Europe; London, n.d.); R. H. Bautier, *The Economic Development of Medieval Europe* (New York, 1971); and Guy Fourquin, *Histoire économique de l'Occident medieval* (Paris, 1969). The older accounts of M. M. Postan, *The Medieval Economy and Society: An Economic History of Britain 1000–1500* (London, 1972), Gino Luzzatto, *An Economic History of Italy from the Fall of the Roman Empire to the Beginning of the Sixteenth Century* (London, 1961), and J. A. Van Houtte, *An Economic History of the Low Countries, 800–1800* (London, 1977) are regionally focused and remain valuable. Georges Duby, *The Early Growth of the European Economy: Warriors and Peasants from the Seventh to the Twelfth Century* (Ithaca, NY, 1974), bridges the chronological divide between this volume and its predecessor.

For the population curve, see J. C. Russell, 'Population in Europe 500–1500', in Cipolla, *The Middle Ages*, 25–70; J. C. Russell, *Late Ancient and Medieval Population* (Philadelphia, 1958); and more generally Carlo M. Cipolla, *The Economic History of World Population* (Harmondsworth, 1969). For studies incorporating more recent literature, see Pounds, *Economic History*, 125–63. Although countless local studies have questioned Russell's figures, his remains the only synthesis in English.

For more specialized work on the agrarian economy, see Georges Duby, *Rural Economy and Country Life in the Medieval West* (Columbia, SC, 1968); Werner Rösener, *Peasants in the Middle Ages* (Urbana, 1992); J. Z. Titow, *English Rural Society, 1200–1350* (London, 1969); Lynn White Jr., *Medieval Technology and Social Change* (Oxford, 1962); J. Z. Titow, *Winchester Yields: A Study in Medieval Agricultural Productivity* (Cambridge, 1972); and B. H. Slicher Van Bath, *The Agrarian History of Western Europe, A.D. 500–1850* (London, 1963).

On the towns and the commercial and urban economies, see in general David Nicholas, *The Growth of the Medieval City: From Late Antiquity to the Early Fourteenth Century* (London, 1997), with bibliography; also Adriaan Verhulst, *The Rise of Cities in North-West Europe* (Cambridge, 1999); André Chédeville, Jacques Le Goff, and Jacques Rossiaud (eds.), *La Ville en France au Moyen Âge, des Carolingiens à la Renaissance* (*Histoire de la France Urbaine*, ed. G. Duby, vol. II; Paris, 1980); Carlo M. Cipolla, *Before the Industrial Revolution: European Society and Economy, 1000–1700* (2nd edn., New York, 1980); and Jacques Rossiaud, 'The City-Dweller and Life in Cities and Towns', in Jacques Le Goff (ed.), *The Medieval World* (London, 1990), 138–179. Numerous treatments on individual city economies have been published; see particularly Frederic C. Lane, *Venice: A Maritime Republic* (Baltimore, 1973); and David Herlihy, *Medieval and Renaissance Pistoia* (New Haven, 1967) and *Pisa in the Early Renaissance: A Study of Urban Growth* (New Haven, 1958).

On the growth of trade and commerce, see Robert S. Lopez, *The Commercial Revolution of the Middle Ages, 950–1350* (Cambridge, 1976); Kathryn L. Reyerson, 'Commerce and Communications', *NCMH* v, 50–70; and Jean Favier, *Gold and Spices: The Rise of Commerce in the Middle Ages* (New York, 1998). Richard H. Britnell, *The Commercialization of English Society, 1000–1500* (2nd edn., Manchester, 1996), and James Masschaele, *Peasants, Merchants, and Markets: Inland Trade in England, 1150–1350* (New York, 1997), are valuable in illustrating the extent to which commercial relations penetrated the agrarian economy.

For commercial techniques, see Edwin S. Hunt and James M. Murray, *A History of Business in Medieval Europe, 1200–1550* (Cambridge, 1999), and Thomas Noonan, *The Scholastic Analysis of Usury* (Cambridge, MA, 1967). On the Hanse, see Philippe Dollinger, *The German Hansa* (Stanford, 1970). The essays in *The Dawn of*

Modern Banking (New Haven, 1979) have much of value. Two superb collections of documents remain *Medieval Trade in the Mediterranean World*, ed. Robert S. Lopez and Irving W. Raymond, rev. O. R. Constable (New York, 2001), and *A Source Book for Medieval Economic History*, ed. Roy C. Cave and Herbert H. Coulson (New York, 1936).

The monetary revolution has received excellent treatment in Peter Spufford, *Money and Its Use in Medieval Europe* (Cambridge, 1988). On the fairs, see Elizabeth Chapin, *Les Villes de foires de Champagne des origins au début du XIVe siècle* (Paris, 1937); Rosalind K. Berlow, 'The Development of Business Techniques Used at the Fairs of Champagne from the End of the Twelfth Century to the Middle of the Thirteenth Century', *Studies in Medieval and Renaissance History*, 8 (1971), 3–32; Peter Johanek and Heinz Stoob (eds.), *Europäische Messen und Märktesysteme in Mittelalter und Neuzeit*, (Cologne, 1996); and Ellen Wedemeyer Moore, *The Fairs of England: An Introductory Survey* (Toronto, 1985).

Politics

In addition to the chapters in *NCMH* iii–v, see, for more specific introductions, the specific histories of kingdoms and regions listed for the Introduction above; also, for Iberia and Sicily, those listed for Chapter 6. Stimulating interpretations of medieval politics, relevant well beyond their immediate chronological context, are provided by Karl Leyser, *Rule and Conflict in an Early Medieval Society* (London, 1979), and his collected essays, edited by Timothy Reuter, *Communications and Power in Medieval Europe* (2 vols., London, 1994), as well as Gerd Althoff, *Family, Friends and Followers* (Cambridge, 2004), and the essays collected in Bernhard Jussen (ed.), *Ordering Medieval Society* (Philadelphia, 2001). Also helpful are the chapters in *MW*, especially those by Timothy Reuter, Susan Reynolds, Philippe Buc, and Magnus Ryan, as well as the essays in Gerd Althoff, Johannes Fried, and Patrick J. Geary (eds.), *Medieval Concepts of the Past* (Cambridge, 2002). Janet Nelson is currently preparing the publication of Timothy Reuter's collected papers, which will provide a wealth of stimulating insights. The variety of networks linking men and women of the central Middle Ages are highlighted by Susan

Reynolds, *Kingdoms and Communities, 900–1300* (2nd edn., Oxford, 1997); Donald Matthew, *The English and the Community of Europe in the Thirteenth Century* (Reading, 1997); and Björn Weiler and Ifor Rowlands (eds.), *England and Europe in the Reign of Henry III (1216–1272)* (Aldershot, 2002). Some of the key institutions and elite groupings in medieval politics are explored by the essays edited by Anne J. Duggan in *Kings and Kingship in Medieval Europe* (London, 1993), *Queens and Queenship in Medieval Europe* (Woodbridge, 1995), and *Nobles and Nobility in Medieval Europe* (Woodbridge, 1997). For key questions surrounding the ideals and practice of knighthood and chivalry, see the recommendations for Chapter 2, especially the works by Crouch, Bumke, Jaeger, and Bouchard; and for the main aspects of warfare, see the works of Matthew Strickland and John France cited there.

The rise of pragmatic literacy has been investigated by M. T. Clanchy, *From Memory to Written Record: England, 1066–1307* (2nd edn., Oxford and Cambridge, MA, 1993), with implications well beyond its immediate geographical focus, as illustrated by Adam J. Kosto and Anders Winroth (eds.), *Charters, Cartularies and Archives* (Toronto, 2002). On the ideology and practice of justice, see William Ian Miller, *Bloodtaking and Peacemaking* (Chicago, 1990), and Theodore Ziolkowski, *The Mirror of Justice* (Princeton, 1997).

Religion

For general overviews of Christianity and its institutions in this period, see R. W. Southern, *The Making of the Middle Ages* (London, 1953); *id., Western Society and the Church in the Middle Ages* (Harmondsworth, 1970); Colin Morris, *The Papal Monarchy: The Western Church from 1050 to 1250* (Oxford, 1989); and Joseph Lynch, *The Medieval Church: A Brief History* (Harlow, 1992). For the period before *c.*1050, see Heinrich Fichtenau, *Living in the Tenth Century: Mentalities and Social Orders*, trans. P. J. Geary (Chicago, 1991), esp. 30–49, 181–216, 217–41, 262–83; Timothy Reuter, *Germany in the High Middle Ages, 800–1056* (Harlow, 1991), 183–252; Sarah Hamilton, *The Practice of Penance, 900–1050* (Woodbridge, 2001); and R. McKitterick, 'The Church', *NCMH* iii. 130–62. On the evolving role of the papacy, see Gerd Tellenbach, *The Church in Western Europe from the Tenth to the Early Twelfth Century*, trans. T. Reuter (Cambridge, 1993); Southern, *Western Society*, esp. 91–133; Uta-Renate Blumenthal, *The Investiture Controversy: Church and Monarchy from the Ninth to the Twelfth Century* (Philadelphia, 1988); I. S. Robinson, *The Papacy, 1073–1198* (Cambridge, 1990); and J. A. Watt, 'The Papacy', *NCMH* v. 107–63. On bishops and clergy, see Southern, *Western Society*, 170–213, and Robert Bartlett, *England under the Norman and Angevin Kings, 1075–1225* (Oxford, 2000), ch. 8, esp. 377–402. For the impact of Christianity on the laity, see J. Blair (ed.), *Minsters and Parish Churches: The Local Church in Transition, 950–1200* (Oxford, 1988); C. N. L. Brooke, *The Medieval Idea of Marriage* (Oxford, 1989); D. M. Hadley, *Death in Medieval England: An Archaeology* (Stroud, 2001); James A. Brundage, *Law, Sex and Christian Society in Medieval Europe* (Chicago, 1987); M. C. Mansfield, *The Humiliation of Sinners: Public Penance in Thirteenth-Century France* (Ithaca, NY, and London, 1995); Bartlett, *England*, 442–81; André Vauchez, 'The Church and the Laity', *NCMH* v. 182–203. On popular religion, see Rosalind and Christopher Brooke, *Popular Religion in the Middle Ages: Western Europe 1000–1300* (London, 1984); for magic at the outset of our period, see V. I. J. Flint, *The Rise of Magic in Early Medieval Europe* (Oxford, 1991), and K. L. Jolly, *Popular Religion in Late Saxon England: Elf Charms in Context* (Chapel Hill, 1996), and for the central Middle Ages, see Charles Burnett, *Magic and Divination in the Middle Ages: Texts and Techniques in the Islamic and Christian Worlds* (Aldershot, 1996).

On saints' cults, the following are useful entries into a prolific field of study: Benedicta Ward, *Miracles and the Medieval Mind: Theory, Record and Event, 1000–1215* (London, 1982); David Rollason, *Saints and Relics in Anglo-Saxon England* (Oxford, 1989); André Vauchez, *Sainthood in the Later Middle Ages*, trans. Jean Birrell (Cambridge, 1997); and Jonathan Sumption, *Pilgrimage* (London, 1975). On the Peace of God, see Thomas Head and Richard Landes (eds.), *The Peace of God: Social Violence and Religious Response in France around the Year 1000* (Ithaca, NY, and London, 1992). On monasticism throughout this period, see Southern, *Western Society*, 214–99; C. H. Lawrence, *Medieval Monasticism: Forms of Religious Life in Western Europe in the Middle Ages* (2nd edn., Harlow, 1989); Janet Burton, *Monastic and Religious Orders in Britain, 1000–1300* (Cambridge, 1994); for the tenth century, see Patrick Wormald, 'Æthelwold and his Continental

Counterparts: Contact, Comparison, Contrast', in Barbara Yorke (ed.), *Bishop Æthelwold: His Career and Influence* (Woodbridge, 1988), 13–42, and Barbara Rosenwein, *To be the Neighbor of St Peter* (Ithaca, NY, and London, 1989); on the new orders, see Henrietta Leyser, *Hermits and the New Monasticism* (London, 1984); on the spread of new orders to Europe's periphery, see Bartlett, *The Making of Europe*, 243–68, esp. 255–60; on thirteenth-century monasticism, see Herbert Grundmann, *Religious Movements in the Middle Ages*, trans. Steven Rowan (Notre Dame, IN, 1995), and André Vauchez, 'The Religious Orders', *NCMH* v. 220–55. For the Cistercians, see L. J. Lekai, *The Cistercians: Ideals and Reality* (Kent, OH, 1977); A. Bredero, *Cluny et Cîteaux au douzième siècle* (Amsterdam and Maarssen, 1985); and I. Alfonso, 'Cistercians and Feudalism', *Past and Present*, 133 (1991), 3–30. For Sempringham, see Brian Golding, *Gilbert of Sempringham and the Gilbertine Order, c.1130–c.1300* (Oxford, 1995). On anchorites, see Ann K. Warren, *Anchorites and their Patrons in Medieval England* (Berkeley and London, 1985), and, on Beguines, see Grundmann, *Religious Movements*. On the Friars, see C. H. Lawrence, *The Friars: The Impact of the Early Mendicant Movement on Western Society* (London, 1994), and works on thirteenth-century monasticism mentioned above. For suggestions for new angles on the study of monasticism, see J. L. Nelson, 'Medieval Monasticism', *MW* 576–604.

On heretics, see Malcolm Barber, *The Cathars: Dualist Heretics in Languedoc in the High Middle Ages* (Harlow, 2000); Bernard Hamilton, 'The Albigensian Crusade and Heresy', *NCMH* v. 164–81; R. I. Moore, *The Formation of a Persecuting Society* (Oxford, 1987); B. M. Kienzle, *Cistercians, Heresy and Crusade in Occitania, 1145–1229* (York, 2001); Peter Biller, *The Waldenses, 1170–1530: Between a Religious Order and a Church* (Aldershot, 2001). There are several recent regional studies of the Jews in medieval Europe: see especially Norman Golb, *The Jews in Medieval Normandy: A Social and Intellectual History* (Cambridge, 1998); Yom Tov Assis, *The Golden Age of Aragonese Jewry: Community and Society in the Crown of Aragon, 1213–1327* (London and Portland, OR, 1997); and Patricia Skinner (ed.), *The Jews in Medieval Britain: Historical, Literary and Archaeological Perspectives* (Woodbridge, 2003). See also Kenneth R. Stow, *Alienated Minority: the Jews of Medieval Latin Europe* (Cambridge, MA, 1992). On the Muslims in Spain, see Rachel Arié, *España musulmana (siglos VIII–XV)* (Barcelona,

1982); Richard Fletcher, *Moorish Spain* (London, 1992); David Abula-fia, 'The Nasrid Kingdom of Granada', *NCMH* v. 636–43; and David Nirenberg, 'Muslims in Christian Iberia, 1000–1526: Varieties of Mudejar Experience', *MW* 60–76.

Intellectual and Cultural Creativity

Essential overviews are provided in *RR*, and M. L. Colish, *Medieval Foundations of the Western Intellectual Tradition 400–1400* (New Haven and London, 1997), from which Chapter 5 draws much material for its sections on education and learning and literate ver-nacular culture. R. N. Swanson, *The Twelfth-Century Renaissance* (Manchester and New York, 1999), is useful too. The *Lexikon des Mittelalters* (Munich and Zurich, 1977–99) is a first-class reference work. On the question of individualism, see C. Morris, *The Discovery of the Individual 1050–1200* (London, 1972), J. F. Benton's article in *RR*, 263–95, and C. Walker Bynum, 'Did the Twelfth Century Discover the Individual?', in her *Jesus as Mother: Studies in the Spirituality of the High Middle Ages* (Berkeley and Los Angeles, 1982).

R. W. Southern's article on Paris and Chartres in *RR* is very good on the development of the schools, as are the two volumes of his *Scholastic Humanism and the Unification of Europe* (Oxford, 1995, 2001). His *Saint Anselm: Portrait of a Landscape* (Cambridge, 1990) is a work of art. For a different view on scholastic humanism, see John Marenbon, 'Humanism, scholasticism, and the School of Chartres', *International Journal of the Classical Tradition* 6 (2000), 569–77. See also G. R. Evans, *Anselm* (Outstanding Christian Thinkers Series; London, 1989), and Anselm of Canterbury, *The Prayers and Meditations of St Anselm with the Proslogion*, trans. B. Ward (Harmondsworth, 1973). Colish, *Medieval Foundations*, is excellent on all aspects of education and learning, as is her two-volumed *Peter Lombard* (Leiden, 1994). Beryl Smalley, *The Study of the Bible in the Middle Ages* (3rd edn., Oxford, 1983), remains essential. For the concept of reason and the position of Jews in the twelfth century, see A. Sapir Abulafia, *Jews and Christians in the Twelfth-Century Renais-sance* (London, 1995). Herrad of Hohenbourg is studied by F. J. Griffiths, 'Herrad of Hohenbourg: A Synthesis of Learning in *The*

Garden of Delights', in C. Mews (ed.), *Listen Daughter: The* Speculum Virginum *and the Formation of Religious Women in the Middle Ages* (Basingstoke, 2001), 221–343. See also V. I. J. Flint, *Honorius Augustodunensis of Regensburg* (Aldershot, 1995). On the translation of the Aristotelian Corpus, see B. G. Dod, 'Aristoteles latinus', in *The Cambridge History of Later Medieval Philosophy*, ed. N. Kretzmann, A. Kenny, and J. Pinborg (Cambridge, 1982), 45–79. John Marenbon provides the latest assessment of Abelard's philosophy in his *The Philosophy of Peter Abelard* (Cambridge, 1997); M. T. Clanchy, *Abelard: A Medieval Life* (Oxford, 1997), says more about Abelard's social setting and his relationship with Heloise, for which the main source is *The Letters of Abelard and Heloise*, ed. B. Radice (Harmondsworth, 1974). See also C. J. Mews, *The Lost Love Letters of Abelard and Heloise: Perceptions of Dialogue in Twelfth-Century France*, with translation by N. Chiavaroli and C. J. Mews (New York, 1999); F. J. Griffiths, Brides and *Dominae*: Abelard's *Cura monialium* at the Augustinian Monastery of Marbach', *Viator* 34 (2003), 57–88, and ' "Men's duty to provide for women's needs": Abelard, Heloise, and their negotiation of the *cura monialium*', *Journal of Medieval History* 30 (2004), 1–24. For Peter the Chanter, see J. W. Baldwin, *Masters, Princes, and Merchants. The social views of Peter the Chanter and his Circle* (Princeton, 1970). On the development of science, see T. Stiefel, *The Intellectual Revolution in Twelfth-Century Europe* (London and Sydney, 1985). Studies on the development of the universities include S. C. Ferruolo, *The Origins of the University: The Schools of Paris and their Critics, 1100–1215* (Stanford, 1985); O. Pedersen, *The First Universities*, trans. R. North (Cambridge, 1997); H. De Ridder-Symoens (ed.), *Universities in the Middle Ages* (A History of the University in Europe, ed. W. Rüegg, vol. 1; Cambridge, 1992); and J. van Engen (ed.), *Learning Institutionalized: Teaching in the Medieval University* (Notre Dame, IN, 2000), in which the articles by J. Verger (syllabus and degrees) and J. A. Brundage (canon law) are particularly useful. See also J. Verger, 'The Universities and Scholasticism', *NCMH* v. 256–76. Anders Winroth, *The Making of Gratian's* Decretum (Cambridge, 2000) has revolutionised all thinking on the study of law in general and Gratian in particular. For Aquinas, J. A. Weisheipl, *Friar Thomas D'Aquino: His Life, Thought, and Works* (Oxford, 1974), is still a good read. For Grosseteste, see R. W. Southern, *Robert Grosseteste: The Growth of an English Mind in Medieval Europe* (2nd edn., Cambridge, 1992). In general, see also G. Leff, *Medieval Thought from St Augustine to Ockham* (Harmondsworth, 1985).

On historical writing, see Peter Classen's article in *RR*. D. Hay, *Annalists and Historians: Western Historiography from the Eighth to the Eighteenth Centuries* (London, 1977), is also useful. R. W. Southern's four-part overview, 'Aspects of the European Tradition of Historical Writing', *Transactions of the Royal Historical Society*, 5th series, 20 (1970), 173–96; 21 (1971), 159–79; 22 (1972), 159–80; 23 (1973), 243–63, is full of valuable insights. See also P. J. Geary, *Phantoms of Remembrance: Memory and oblivion at the end of the First Millennium* (Princeton, NJ, 1994); H. W. Goetz, *Geschichtsschreibung und Geschichtsbewusstsein im Mittelalter* (Berlin, 1999); E. van Houts *Local and Regional Chronicles*. Typologies des Sources du Moyen Âge Occidental 74 (Turnhout, 1995), and *Memory and Gender in Medieval Europe 900–1200* (Basingstoke, 1999); and R. Chazan, *God, Humanity and History: The Hebrew First Crusade Narratives* (Berkeley and Los Angeles, 2000).

On vernacular culture, see Colish, *Medieval Foundations*, and the works she lists there. R.W. Southern's treatment of epic and romance in *The Making of the Middle Ages* (London, 1953) continues to be important. J. Bumke, *Courtly Culture: Literature and Society in the High Middle Ages*, trans. T. Dunlap (Berkeley and Los Angeles, 1991), is essential reading. Elisabeth van Houts, 'The State of Research: Women in Medieval History and Literature', *Journal of Medieval History*, 20 (1994), 277–92, gives a good overview of publications about women and literature. Peter Dronke's work on Latin and vernacular literature is seminal: among his many publications see his article in *RR* and his books *The Medieval Lyric* (2nd edn., London, 1978) and *Women Writers of the Middle Ages: A Critical Study of Texts from Perpetua (d. 203) to Marguerite Porete (d. 1310)* (New York, 1984). See also S. Kay, *The Chansons de Geste in the Age of Romance: Political Fictions* (Oxford, 1995), and D. H. Green, *The Beginnings of Medieval Romance: Fact and Fiction, 1150–1220* (Cambridge, 2002). On the concepts of 'Renaissance' and 'humanism', see *RR* and R. W. Southern, *Medieval Humanism and other Studies* (Oxford, 1970). For art and architecture, useful introductions include G. Zarnecki, *Art of the Medieval World* (New York, 1975); V. Sekules, *Medieval Art* (Oxford, 2001); H. E. Kubach, *Romanesque Architecture* (New York, 1975); C. Wilson, *The Gothic Cathedral* (London, 1990); and N. Coldstream,

Medieval Architecture (Oxford, 2002), which offers a thought-provoking challenge to the conventional schemes of architectural history. For the various texts mentioned in this chapter, see also the recommendations above (Sources).

The Expansion of Latin Christendom

Malcolm Barber, *The Two Cities: Medieval Europe 1050–1320* (2nd edn., London, 2004), provides a general account with chapters on the areas covered here. Robert Bartlett, *The Making of Europe: Conquest, Colonisation and Cultural Change, 950–1350* (Harmondsworth, 1993), focuses on the process of expansion. Literature in English does not provide full coverage of central and northern Europe. Jean W. Sedlar, *East Central Europe in the Middle Ages 1000–1500* (Seattle and London, 1994), is an overall introduction, including the Balkans. On Bohemia, Marvin Kantor, *The Origins of Christianity in Bohemia* (Evanston, IL, 1990), provides primary sources in translation, and Lisa Wolverton, *Hastening toward Prague: Power and Society in the Medieval Czech Lands* (Philadelphia, 2001), analyses political and social development. On Hungary, Pál Engel, *The Realm of St Stephen: A History of Medieval Hungary, 895–1526*, trans. A. Ayton (London, 2001), offers a comprehensive introduction; see also Nora Berend, *At the Gate of Christendom: Jews, Muslims and 'Pagans' in Medieval Hungary, c.1000–c.1300* (Cambridge, 2001). On Poland, the relevant chapters of Aleksander Gieysztor *et al.*, *History of Poland* (Warsaw, 1968), and W. F. Reddaway *et al.*, *The Cambridge History of Poland* (Cambridge, 1950), are still the most useful general introductions, while Tadeusz Manteuffel, *The Formation of the Polish State: The Period of Ducal Rule 963–1194* (Detroit, 1982), is a thorough analysis of early political history. For Lithuania, see S. C. Rowell, *Lithuania Ascending: A Pagan Empire within East-Central Europe 1295–1345* (Cambridge, 1994), and for Rus´, see Jonathan Shepard and Simon Franklin, *The Emergence of Rus´ 750–1200* (London, 1996), and John Fennell, *The Crisis of Medieval Russia 1200–1304* (London and New York, 1983).

On Scandinavia, Birgit and Peter Sawyer, *Medieval Scandinavia: From Conversion to Reformation circa 800–1500* (Minneapolis, 1993), provides a good overview with bibliography; *The Cambridge History of Scandinavia*, i (*Prehistory to 1520*), ed. Knut Helle (Cambridge, 2003), offers in-depth thematic chapters; and Phillip Pulsiano (ed.), *Medieval Scandinavia: An Encyclopedia* (New York, 1993), is a useful reference work. For Latin Christian expansion in the Baltic, see Eric Christiansen, *The Northern Crusades: The Baltic and the Catholic Frontier 1100–1525* (2nd edn., London, 1997); William Urban, *The Baltic Crusade* (2nd edn., Chicago, 1994); and Alan V. Murray (ed.), *Crusade and Conversion on the Baltic Frontier 1150–1500* (Aldershot, 2001), 3–20. Literature on Iberia is proliferating, but for overviews Joseph F. O'Callaghan, *A History of Medieval Spain* (Ithaca, NY, and London, 1975); Derek W. Lomax, *The Reconquest of Spain* (London and New York, 1978); and Angus MacKay, *Spain in the Middle Ages: From Frontier to Empire 1000–1500* (London, 1977), remain the most useful; see also T. N. Bisson, *The Medieval Crown of Aragon* (Oxford, 1986). For southern Italy and Sicily, see Graham A. Loud, *The Age of Robert Guiscard: Southern Italy and the Norman Conquest* (Harlow, 2000); Alex Metcalf, *Muslims and Christians in Norman Sicily* (London, 2002); and David Abulafia (ed.), *Italy in the Central Middle Ages* (Oxford, 2004).

Literature on the crusades is vast. The following books provide a comprehensive introduction and contain good bibliographies: Jonathan Riley-Smith, *The Crusades: A Short History* (London, 1987), and Jonathan Riley-Smith (ed.), *The Oxford Illustrated History of the Crusades* (Oxford, 1997). Norman Daniel, *Islam and the West: The Making of an Image* (2nd edn., Oxford, 1993), analyses interaction with Muslims. For the nature of 'Latin' society in the Levant, see Ronnie Ellenblum, *Frankish Rural Settlement in the Latin Kingdom of Jerusalem* (Cambridge, 1998); for Frankish settlement in Byzantium, see Peter Lock, *The Franks in the Aegean 1204–1500* (London, 1995), and Peter W. Edbury, *The Kingdom of Cyprus and the Crusades 1191–1374* (Cambridge, 1991). On travels, missions, and discoveries, see J. R. S. Phillips, *The Medieval Expansion of Europe* (2nd edn., Oxford, 1998), and Felipe Fernandez-Armesto, *Before Columbus: Exploration and Colonisation from the Mediterranean to the Atlantic 1229–1492* (Basingstoke, 1987).

Chronology

A more detailed chronology for the tenth century may be found in the previous volume of The Short Oxford History of Europe (Rosamond McKitterick (ed.), *The Early Middle Ages* (Oxford, 2001), 274–7). It should be noted that dating medieval events precisely is often very difficult, and sources often contradict one other.

910	Foundation of the abbey of Cluny.
919	The election of Henry I ('the Fowler') as king ends Carolingian rule in East Francia.
929	'Abd al-Rahmān III, ruler of al-Andalus (Muslim Spain and Portugal), formally establishes the Umayyad Caliphate.
933	Henry the Fowler defeats the Hungarians (Magyars) at the Riade.
954	Death of Erik Bloodaxe ends Viking kingdom of York; unification of England under the West Saxon kings.
955	Otto I, king of the East Franks, defeats the Magyars at the Lechfeld and a number of Slav tribes at the Recknitz.
962	Otto I is crowned as emperor in Rome by Pope John XII.
965	Conversion to Christianity of Harold Bluetooth, king of the Danes.
966	Conversion of Miezko I, king of Poland.
968	Foundation of the archbishopric of Magdeburg, a base for the conversion of the western Slavs.
c.972	Destruction of the Muslim base at La Garde-Freinet in Provence by William, count of Arles, and Arduin, marquis of Turin.
973	Death of Otto I; accession of his son Otto II.
983	Death of Otto II, leaving his young son Otto III under the regency of his widow, the Byzantine princess Theophano; major uprising of Slavs against imperial rule.
985	Beginnings of Scandinavian settlement in Greenland.
c.986	Resumption of Danish raids upon England.
987	Election of Hugh Capet as king of the West Franks: end of Carolingian rule in Frankia.

*c.*988	Baptism of Prince Vladimir of Kiev.
997	Al-Mansūr, effective ruler of the Umayyad Caliphate, sacks the shrine of Santiago de Compostela. Martyrdom of St Adalbert (Vojtěch), bishop of Prague, in Prussia.
*c.*1000	Scandinavian discovery of the North American coast.
*c.*1001	(St) Stephen (Vajk), ruler of the Hungarians, receives a royal crown from Pope Sylvester II.
1002	Brian Bóruma (Boru), king of Munster, makes himself high-king of Ireland.
1009	Al-Hākim, the Fatimid caliph of Egypt, destroys the Church of the Holy Sepulchre in Jerusalem; the news provokes persecution of Jews in several French cities.
1013–14	Swein, king of the Danes, conquers England from Æthelred II (the Unready).
1014	Death of Brian Bóruma during his victory over the Vikings at Clontarf. Death of Swein of Denmark.
1016	Cnut (III, the Great), son of Swein of Denmark, becomes king of the English; he succeeds to the kingdom of the Danes in 1017.
*c.*1017	Norman war bands begin to arrive in Southern Italy.
1018	The Byzantine Emperor Basil II completes the annexation of Bulgaria.
1020s	Sancho Garcés III (the Great), king of Navarre, subjugates Gascony.
1022	Heresy trials at Orleans under Robert II of France: first great persecution of heretics in western Europe for several centuries.
1024	Death of Henry II, last of the Ottonian emperors; succession of Conrad II establishes the Salian dynasty.
1025	Death of Emperor Basil II inaugurates dynastic instability in Byzantium (until 1081).
1028–30	Cnut conquers Norway from King (St) Olaf Haroldsson, who perishes in battle. Sancho Garcés III of Navarre annexes Castile and León.
1031–2	Collapse of the Umayyad Caliphate in al-Andalus. Dynastic struggle between Henry I of France and his brother Robert, who is supported by their mother Constance.
1032	Death of Rudolf III, king of Burgundy, whose kingdom is absorbed into the Empire.

1035	Death of Sancho Garcés III, 'king of the Spains': collapse of Navarrese hegemony over Christian Spain and Gascony.
1037	Ordinance of Conrad II at Milan, later seen as crucial to the development of hereditable fiefs in the Western Empire.
1038–43	Failed Byzantine attempts to reconquer Sicily from the Muslims.
1042	Accession of Edward the Confessor ends Danish rule in England.
1044	Count Geoffrey Martel of Anjou takes Tours, securing Angevin control of the lower Loire.
1046	Council of Sutri: beginning of reform of papacy under the auspices of Emperor Henry III.
1047	Harold Hardrada, half-brother of Olaf Haroldsson, becomes king of Norway.
1049	Council of Reims: Pope Leo IX forces simoniacal bishops to renounce their sees.
1049–1109	Abbacy of (St) Hugh of Cluny: greatest period of Cluniac expansion.
1051–2	Revolt of Godwin, earl of Wessex, against Edward the Confessor.
1052	Diarmait mac Maíl na mBó, king of Leinster, captures Dublin from the Scandinavian 'Ostmen'.
1053	Battle of Civitate: Leo IX is defeated and captured by the southern Italian Normans.
1054	Mutual excommunications formally mark the Schism between the Roman and Greek Orthodox Churches.
1055	Seljuk Turks seize Baghdad, establishing Seljuk sultanate.
1056	Death of Emperor Henry III; accession of his young son, Henry IV, as king of Germany, under the regency of his mother Agnes of Poitou.
1058	Accession of Malcolm (III) Canmore as king of Scots.
1059	Codification of election of popes by cardinals. Pope Nicholas II formally grants southern Italy and Sicily to the Norman leader Robert Guiscard.
1061	Beginning of Norman conquest of Sicily.
1063	Death of Gruffydd ap Llywelyn ends brief period of Welsh unity.
1066	Harold, earl of Wessex, succeeds Edward the Confessor: he crushes the last major Scandinavian invasion of England,

killing Harold Hardrada of Norway, but is slain at Hastings by William (the Conqueror), duke of Normandy, who becomes king of England.

1071 Seljuk victory over the Byzantines at Manzikert opens the way for the Turkish subjugation of Byzantine Anatolia. Jerusalem falls under Turkish control. Fall of Bari, completing the Norman conquest of Byzantine southern Italy.

1072 Normans capture Palermo, the chief city of Sicily.

1073 Election of Cardinal Hildebrand as Pope Gregory VII. Outbreak of great Saxon revolt against Henry IV of Germany.

1074 Abortive attempt by Gregory VII to lead an expedition to support the Byzantines against the Turks.

1075 Gregory VII's *Dictatus Papae* sets out exceptionally broad claims for papal power.

1076 Henry IV seeks to depose Gregory VII, who excommunicates him. The Polish prince Bolesław II assumes a royal title.

1077 Henry IV does penance to Gregory VII after mediation by Abbot Hugh of Cluny and Matilda, marquise of Tuscany.

1078 Gregory VII's decree outlawing lay investiture.

1080 Gregory VII's second deposition by, and excommunication of, Henry IV, who promotes Guibert of Ravenna as (antipope) Clement III. Rudolf of Rheinfelden, Gregory's candidate to be king of Germany, is killed.

1081 Alexius Comnenus becomes Byzantine emperor, establishing the Comnenian dynasty (to 1185); he initially fails to repel Robert Guiscard's invasion of Albania, but (at an uncertain date) he makes valuable trading concessions to the Venetians.

1084 Henry IV captures Rome and is crowned emperor by Clement III. The Normans of Apulia rescue Gregory VII and sack Rome. St Bruno founds La Grande Chartreuse, mother house of the Carthusian Order.

1085 Alfonso VI of León-Castile captures Toledo from the Muslims. Deaths of Gregory VII in exile at Salerno and of Robert Guiscard in Greece. Fall of Antioch to the Seljuk Turks.

1086 Danish invasion threat spurs William the Conqueror into ordering the Domesday Survey. The Almoravids of Morocco seize al-Andalus.

1087	Death of William the Conqueror; division of England and Normandy between his sons (until 1106). Pisan and Genoese attack against Mahdia (Tunisia).
1088	Odo, prior of Cluny, becomes pope as Urban II.
1091–4	Victories of Alexius Comnenus over the Pechenegs and Cumans secure the Byzantine Balkans against nomad invasions.
1092	Death of Malik Shah: disintegration of the Seljuk empire.
1095	Council of Clermont: Pope Urban II calls the First Crusade. He also dedicates St Hugh of Cluny's great abbey church ('Cluny III').
1096	Massacre of Jews in the Rhineland and northern France by crusaders. Destruction of the 'People's Crusade' in Anatolia.
1097	Main crusading armies under Godfrey de Bouillon, Raymond of Toulouse, Robert Curthose of Normandy and Bohemond (son of Robert Guiscard) reach Constantinople and defeat a Turkish army at Dorylaion. Alexius Comnenus recovers western Anatolia for Byzantium.
1098	Baldwin of Boulogne establishes the county of Edessa, the first 'crusader state'. The crusaders capture Antioch; the Fatimids of Egypt take Jerusalem from the Turks. Foundation of Cîteaux by Robert of Molesme (beginning of the Cistercian Order). Council of Bari: Urban II bans clerics from doing homage to laymen.
1099	The crusaders capture Jerusalem from the Fatimids and defeat them at Ascalon. Godfrey de Bouillon becomes 'advocate of the Holy Sepulchre'.
1100	Death of Godfrey de Bouillon; his brother Baldwin, count of Edessa, becomes king of Jerusalem. Death of the antipope Clement III.
c.1100	Putative date for the *Song of Roland* in its extant form.
1101–2	New crusading expeditions ('crusade of 1101') destroyed at the battles of Heraclea and Ramleh.
1103–4	Establishment of the first Scandinavian archbishopric at Lund.
1106	Death of Emperor Henry IV after capture by his son, who succeeds as Henry V. Henry I of England reunites England and Normandy.
1106–8	Failed 'crusade' of Bohemond against the Byzantines in the Balkans.

1107	Concord of London: reconciliation of Henry I of England and Archbishop Anselm of Canterbury concerning royal rights over bishoprics.
1110	First evidence for the Exchequer in England.
1111	Paschal II is forced to concede that the Church will accept imperial claims and renounce all its temporal property, but soon rescinds his promises.
1112	Dynastic union of the counties of Provence and Barcelona (until 1245).
c.1113	Emergence of the Hospitallers as a separate order, later militarized as the Knights of St John.
1115	Death of Matilda of Tuscany, whose inheritance becomes the focus of later imperial ambitions. Foundation of Clairvaux under (St) Bernard.
1118	Death of Alexius I Comnenus.
1118–20	Major rebellions against Henry I in Normandy, supported by Louis VI and the counts of Flanders and Anjou.
c.1119	Foundation of the Order of Knights Templar by Hugh de Payns.
1120	William the Atheling, only legitimate son of Henry I, drowns in the wreck of the *White Ship*, the root of dynastic crises in England and Normandy until 1154.
1121	Council of Soissons: first condemnation of Peter Abelard for heresy. (St) Norbert of Xanten founds Prémontré, mother house of the Premonstratensian Order.
1122	Concordat of Worms: resolution of the papal-imperial conflict over episcopal investiture.
1124	Louis VI rallies support from many parts of the kingdom of France to resist invasion by Emperor Henry V.
1125	Death of Henry V ends the Salian dynasty of emperors; he is succeeded by Lothar (III) of Supplinberg.
1127–8	Civil war in Flanders following the assassination of Count Charles of Flanders.
1130	The antipope Anacletus crowns Count Roger II of Sicily as king, establishing the 'Norman' kingdom of Sicily.
c.1131	Peter Abelard composes the *Historia Calamitatum*.
1135	Death of Henry I of England, inaugurating a series of wars in England and Normandy between his daughter Matilda and his nephew, King Stephen of England. Roger II begins

the Sicilian occupation of parts of the North African coast (lasting until 1160).

1137   Death of Louis VI; his successor Louis VII marries Eleanor, heiress of Aquitaine. Death of Lothar III after a failed invasion of Roger II's lands in southern Italy. The Byzantine emperor John Comnenus asserts his lordship over Antioch. Union of Aragon and Catalonia.

1138   Election of Conrad III as first Hohenstaufen emperor. Death of King Bolesław II of Poland; the kingdom remains divided into numerous small duchies until 1300.

c.1138   Geoffrey of Monmouth completes his *History of the Kings of Britain*, chief source for Arthurian legends.

1139   Roger II's capture of Innocent II secures his position as ruler of southern Italy.

1140   Council of Sens: second condemnation of Peter Abelard for heresy.

c.1140   Gratian compiles the *Decretum*, henceforward the standard compilation of canon law.

1140s   Anna Comnena composes her biography of her father Alexius Comnenus (the *Alexiad*).

1144   Count Geoffrey V (Plantagenet) of Anjou completes the Angevin conquest of Normandy. Consecration of the choir of the abbey church of Saint-Denis, the first great Gothic structure in Europe. Fall of county of Edessa to Zengi, ruler of Mosul.

1148   The radical preacher Arnold of Brescia evicts the papacy from Rome.

1146–9   Second Crusade to Palestine by Conrad III and Louis VII, promoted by St Bernard. Regency in France of Abbot Suger of Saint-Denis.

1147   Capture of Lisbon by Count Alfonso Henriques of Portugal, assisted by English and Flemish crusaders. German-Danish crusade against the pagan Wends. The Almohads invade Spain from North Africa, taking Seville and Córdoba.

1148   An unsuccessful siege of Damascus by the Second Crusade and the army of Jerusalem is rebutted by Zengi's son Nur-ad Din.

1151   Hildegard of Bingen completes her prophetic work, the *Scivias*.

1152   Louis VII divorces Eleanor of Aquitaine, whose marriage to Henry of Anjou, duke of Normandy, establishes the Angevin

Empire. Death of Conrad III: election of his nephew
Frederick I Barbarossa. Reform of the Irish Church
establishes territorial dioceses and archbishoprics.

1153   Death of David I, king of Scots and ruler of much of
northern England.

1154   Death of King Stephen of England; Henry of Anjou succeeds
him as Henry II. Death of Roger II. Election of Nicholas
Breakspear as Pope Adrian IV (the only English pope in
history). End of the *Anglo-Saxon Chronicle.*

1155   Adrian IV grants Henry II the right to invade Ireland, and
crushes and executes Arnold of Brescia. Ordinance of
Soissons: Louis VII proclaims a general peace throughout
his kingdom.

1158   Frederick Barbarossa confirms the privileges of the School
(later University) of Bologna, and seeks to centralize
imperial power in Italy at the Diet of Roncaglia. Foundation
of the military Order of Calatrava in Castile.

1159   Election of Alexander III as pope; schism with imperial
candidates (until 1177). Louis VII forces Henry II to lift his
siege of Toulouse.

*c.*1160   Assassination of (St) King Eric (Jedvardsson) of Sweden.

1164   Thomas Becket, archbishop of Canterbury, is driven into
exile by Henry II. Establishment of the first Swedish
archbishopric at Uppsala.

1164–9   Campaigns of Amaury I, king of Jerusalem, in Egypt.

1166   Louis VII exerts his authority in Burgundy; Henry II
subdues Brittany. Assize of Clarendon, keystone of Angevin
legal developments in England. Death of William I of Sicily,
leaving an under-age heir, William II.

1167   North Italian cities form the Lombard League against
Frederick Barbarossa.

1169   Beginning of Anglo-Norman invasion of Ireland. Saladin
(Salah ad-Din Yusuf), a general of Nur ad-Din, takes over
Egypt.

1170   Reconciliation of Henry II and Thomas Becket, but followed
by the archbishop's murder in Canterbury Cathedral.

*c.*1170–*c.*1181   Main period for composition of the Arthurian romances
of Chrétien of Troyes.

1171   Richard fitzGilbert ('Strongbow') acquires Leinster, but
submits to Henry II, who adds Ireland to the Angevin

Empire. Saladin ends the Shīite Fatimid Caliphate and restores Sunni Islam in Egypt.

1172   Introduction of silver *grossi* (groats) at Genoa, the first larger-denomination European coin.

1173–4   First revolt against Henry II of his son Henry 'the Young King', supported by the kings of France and Scotland, affecting most parts of the Angevin Empire.

1174   Death of Nur ad-Din; Saladin soon makes himself Sultan of Egypt, establishing the Ayyubid dynasty.

*c.*1174   Cathar council at St-Félix-de-Caraman near Toulouse purportedly establishes Cathar bishoprics for Languedoc (and allegedly some other Mediterranean regions).

1176   Defeat of Frederick Barbarossa by the Lombard League at Legnano, and of Manuel Comnenus by the Turks at Myriokephalon.

1177   Frederick Barbarossa comes to terms with Alexander III and the Lombard League. John de Courcy establishes the Anglo-Norman lordship of Ulster (Ulaid).

1179   Third Lateran Council attempts to regulate the 'schools' (universities) and to control the Waldensian sect, and issues decrees against Cathars and Jews.

1180   Death of Louis VII; accession of his son Philip II 'Augustus'. Death of Manuel Comnenus. Frederick Barbarossa drives his greatest subject, Henry the Lion, the Welf duke of Saxony and Bavaria, into exile.

1181   Death of Alexander III.

1181–5   Philip Augustus greatly increases Capetian power in northern France at the expense of Count Philip of Flanders.

1182   Massacre of the Latin inhabitants of Constantinople by its citizens; seizure of power by Manuel II's cousin Andronicus Comnenus.

1183   Treaty of Constance between Frederick Barbarossa and the Italian cities. Second revolt and death of Henry the Young King.

1184   Proclamation of Pope Lucius III, with Frederick Barbarossa, setting out procedures for the persecution of heretics.

1185   Byzantine revolt leads to the overthrow and murder of Andronicus Comnenus. Vlacho-Bulgarian rebellion revives Bulgarian kingdom.

1186   Marriage of Henry, son of Frederick Barbarossa, and

Constance, aunt and heir of William II of Sicily; the papacy fears encirclement by the Hohenstaufen dynasty.

1187   Saladin routs the army of the kingdom of Jerusalem at Hattin and conquers most of the kingdom, including Jerusalem.

1188   The Third Crusade is called to reconquer Jerusalem. Alfonso IX of León summons the first representative assembly (*cortes*) in his kingdom.

1189   War between Henry II and his son Richard (the Lionheart), who is supported by Philip Augustus and succeeds as Richard I. Death of William II of Sicily ends legitimate male line of Norman kings of Sicily. Siege of Acre begins.

1190   Frederick Barbarossa is drowned during the Third Crusade. Foundation of the German Order (Teutonic Knights) at the siege of Acre (a military order from 1198).

1191   Fall of Cyprus and Acre to the Third Crusade under Richard I and Philip Augustus.

1192   Richard I is taken prisoner while returning from the Third Crusade and is handed over to Emperor Henry VI.

1193   Death of Saladin. Philip Augustus invades the Angevin Empire.

1194   Henry VI conquers the kingdom of Sicily in right of his wife Constance. Release of Richard I, who makes war against Philip of France.

1197   Death of Henry VI, leaving his 2-year-old son Frederick of Hohenstaufen as his heir: succession crisis in the Empire.

1198   Election of Lotario dei Conti di Segni as Pope Innocent III. Election as king of the Romans of Otto IV, son of Henry the Lion, but he soon loses ground to Philip of Swabia, brother of Henry VI. Duke Otakar I is acknowledged as king of Bohemia.

1199   Death of Richard I; war of succession between his brother John (who becomes king of England) and their nephew Arthur.

1200   Philip Augustus acknowledges John as Richard's successor in return for extensive concessions; he grants privileges to the University of Paris.

1201   The Italian sect of the Humiliati is reconciled to the Roman Church.

1202   Death of Joachim, abbot of Fiore, mystic and author of profoundly influential prophetic writings. Byzantine recognition of Bulgarian autonomy under the Vlacho-Bulgarian Ašen dynasty.

1202–4   Philip Augustus conquers Anjou, Maine, Normandy and much of Aquitaine from King John.

1203   The Byzantine pretender Alexius Angelus persuades the Fourth Crusade to besiege Constantinople, where he becomes Emperor Alexius IV.

1204   Murder of Alexius IV by the Byzantines. Second siege of Constantinople, which the crusaders capture, establishing the 'Latin Empire' under Count Baldwin IX of Flanders. Byzantine successor states emerge at Nicaea and Trebizond (Anatolia) and in Epiros (northern Greece). Death of Eleanor of Aquitaine.

1205   Vlacho-Bulgarian defeat of the crusaders of Constantinople at Adrianople; capture (and subsequent death) of Emperor Baldwin.

1207–14   England is placed under a papal interdict because King John refuses to accept Cardinal Stephen Langton as archbishop of Canterbury.

1208   Assassination of the papal legate Peter of Castelnau: *casus belli* for the Albigensian Crusade against the Cathars of Languedoc. Murder of Philip of Swabia revives Otto IV's cause.

1209   Albigensian Crusade massacres the inhabitants of Béziers. Innocent III excommunicates Otto IV (for invading Apulia) and King John.

1210   King John's expedition to Ireland. St Francis of Assisi receives papal endorsement for his community (origins of the Franciscan Order).

1211   King John imposes his will upon the Welsh princes.

1212   Spanish Christians defeat the Almohads at Las Navas de Tolosa. Frederick of Hohenstaufen, king of Sicily, bids for the imperial throne. Welsh revolt against King John. Simon de Montfort, leader of the Albigensian Crusade, becomes count of Toulouse. 'Children's Crusade' in Germany and France.

1213   Battle of Muret: Simon de Montfort defeats and kills Peter II of Aragon. Philip Augustus plans to invade England, prompting King John to submit to Innocent III.

1214   Philip Augustus routs Emperor Otto IV and the counts of Flanders and Boulogne at Bouvines; his son Louis repels King John in Anjou.

1215   The Fourth Lateran Council imposes annual communion and confession upon all Catholics, bans the foundation of new religious orders, and legislates against Jews and Cathars. King John concedes the charter of liberties known as Magna Carta, but it is soon annulled by Pope Innocent. Coronation at Aachen of Frederick of Hohenstaufen as Frederick II. (St) Dominic Guzman establishes the first Dominican house at Toulouse.

1215–17   Civil war in England: Louis of France fails to conquer England with the aid of English rebels.

1216   Death of King John; the regency of his son Henry III reissues Magna Carta to appease the rebels. Formal establishment of the first female Dominican house at Prouille.

1217   Stipan (Stefan) II, prince of Serbia, is crowned its first king.

1218   Simon de Montfort is killed while besieging Toulouse. Death of Otto IV ends the Hohenstaufen-Welf rivalry for the imperial crown.

1219   The Fifth Crusade captures Damietta, one of the chief ports of Egypt. Valdemar II of Denmark conquers Estonia.

1220   Frederick II issues a privilege for the German ecclesiastical princes.

c.1220   Death of Wolfram von Eschenbach. Eike of Regpow writes the *Sachsenspiegel*.

1221   The Egyptians recover Damietta and expel the Fifth Crusade from Egypt.

1221–2   First great Mongol invasion of Europe: defeat of the Christian kingdoms of the Caucasus (including Georgia) and southern Russia.

1222   Andrew II of Hungary grants the 'Golden Bull' to his nobles.

1223   Death of Philip Augustus; accession of his son as Louis VIII.

1224   Louis VIII conquers Poitou from Henry III.

1226   Death of Louis VIII while on Albigensian Crusade; accession of Louis IX and regency of his mother, Blanche of Castile (to 1234). Teutonic Knights established in Prussia. Italian cities revive the Lombard League to oppose Frederick II. Death of St Francis of Assisi.

1227   Citizens of Lübeck and Count Henry of Schwerin rout Valdemar II of Denmark, ending Danish supremacy in the Baltic and paving the way for the later German 'Hanse'.

1228–9   Crusade of Emperor Frederick II recovers Jerusalem from the Egyptians through negotiation.

1228–35	Conquest of the Balearic Islands from the Muslims by James I (the Conqueror) of Aragon.
1229	Treaty of Paris ends the Albigensian Crusade and establishes effective Capetian rule in Languedoc.
1230	Henry III campaigns in Brittany and Poitou but fails to recover Plantagenet lands in France from Louis IX. Final union of Castile and León under (St) Ferdinand III.
1231–2	Frederick II proclaims the Constitutions of Melfi (*Liber Augustalis*) for Sicily and the *Statute in Favour of the Princes* for Germany; his *augustalis* is the first gold coinage minted in Europe for several hundred years.
1231–3	Great persecution of heretics in Germany by Conrad of Marburg.
1233	Beginning of Inquisition's activities in Languedoc.
1234	Theobald IV, count of Champagne, becomes king of Navarre.
1235	Emperor Frederick II suppresses the rebellion of his son Henry and issues the imperial land peace of Mainz.
1236–48	Ferdinand III of Castile conquers Córdoba, Seville, and Murcia from the Muslims.
1237	Teutonic Knights take over Livonia (part of modern Latvia). Frederick II's forces defeat the Lombard League at Cortenuova.
1237–42	Second great Mongol invasion of Europe: destruction of the Russian principalities of Vladimir, Kiev, Chernigov, and Riazan (1237–40); defeat of the Poles and Teutonic Knights at Legnica and of the Hungarians at Muhi (1241).
1238	Fall of Valencia to James I of Aragon.
1239–41	'Barons' Crusade' of French and English nobles shores up the kingdom of Jerusalem.
1240	Alexander Nevsky, prince of Novgorod, defeats the Swedes at the Neva.
1242	Second Poitevin campaign of Henry III. Alexander Nevsky halts the advance of the Teutonic Knights at the battle of Lake Peipus. Burning of the manuscripts of the Talmud in Paris.
1244	Khwarismian Turks seize Jerusalem and destroy the Frankish army at La Forbie. Massacre of 200 Cathars at

Montségur delivers a decisive blow against the heresy in France.

1244–8 Journey of the Franciscan friar John of Piano Carpini to the court of Küyük, the Mongol Great Khan, at Karakorum in Mongolia.

1245 First Council of Lyon: Pope Innocent IV declares Frederick II deposed.

1247 The citizens of Parma defeat Frederick II at Vittoria.

1248–50 Seventh Crusade: defeat and capture of Louis IX in Egypt. Second regency of Blanche of Castile in France.

1250 Death of Emperor Frederick II ends Hohenstaufen greatness. The Mamluks (Turkic slave-warriors) displace the Ayyubid dynasty as rulers of Egypt.

1251 Conversion of Mindaugas of Lithuania (king 1253–63) to Christianity; he reverts to paganism by 1261. Popular religious uprising, the *Pastoureaux* ('Shepherds'), in northern France.

1251–69 Otakar II of Bohemia extends his rule over the imperial territories of Austria, Styria, and Carinthia.

1252 Death of Blanche of Castile. Gold coins begin to be minted in Florence and Genoa.

1253–5 Journey of the Franciscan William of Rubruck to the court of the Great Khan Möngke at Karakorum.

1254 Death of Conrad IV, son of Frederick II, ends Hohenstaufen rule in Germany; his illegitimate brother Manfred becomes ruler of Sicily (king from 1258). Great ordinance of Louis IX to reform abuses in his realm.

1255 Fall of Quéribus, last Cathar fortress in France.

1257 Election of Earl Richard of Cornwall, brother of Henry III of England, as king of the Romans.

1258 Murderous sack of Baghdad by the Mongols. English political crisis forces Henry III to concede the Provisions of Oxford. Franco-Aragonese treaty formally ends French rights over Catalonia and most Aragonese claims in southern France.

1259 Henry III renounces all Plantagenet claims to Normandy, Anjou, and Poitou.

1260 Battle of ʿAin Jālūt: the Mamluks of Egypt repel the Mongols.

1260–9	Journey of the Venetian merchants Niccolò and Maffeo Polo to Mongolia and China.
1261	Michael Palaeologus of Nicaea captures Constantinople, reviving the Byzantine Empire and reducing the 'Latin Empire' to a small part of Greece.
1262	Iceland comes under Norwegian rule.
1263	Battle of Largs: end of Norwegian supremacy over Hebrides.
1264	English rebels under Simon de Montfort (a son of the leader of the Albigensian Crusade) capture Henry III at Lewes. Major uprising of Muslims in southern kingdom of Castile.
1265	Simon de Montfort calls assembly traditionally regarded as the first English Parliament, but is defeated and killed at Evesham by Edward, eldest son of Henry III.
1266	Charles of Anjou, brother of Louis IX, defeats and kills Manfred of Sicily at Benevento; crowned as Charles I of Sicily.
1268	Charles of Anjou defeats Conradin, son of Conrad IV, at Tagliacozzo, and beheads him. Fall of Antioch to Baibars, Mamluk sultan of Egypt.
1270	Eighth Crusade led by Louis IX, who dies at Tunis after diversion there by Charles of Anjou.
1272	Death of Henry III of England; accession of his son Edward I.
1273	Election of Rudolf of Habsburg as Holy Roman Emperor.
1274	Second Council of Lyon, effecting reunion with the Greek Church (until 1283). Death of Thomas Aquinas, who leaves his *Summa Theologica* unfinished.
c.1275– c.1292	Residence of Marco Polo (with his father Niccolò) at the court of the Mongol Khan, Kublai, in China.
1276	Death of James I of Aragon: his younger son James established as king of Majorca.
1277–8	Edward I reduces Llywelyn the Last, prince of Gwynedd, to submission.
1278	Rudolf of Habsburg kills his rival Otakar II of Bohemia at Dürnkrut. Suppression of the Cathar Church of Desenzano near Lake Garda, undermining Italian Catharism.
1282	Revolt in Sicily against Charles of Anjou (the 'Sicilian Vespers'), supported by Peter III of Aragon. Revolt and death of Llywelyn the Last; end of independent Wales.

1284	Great marine victory of the Genoese over the Pisans at the sea battle of Mazoria ends Pisan sea power.
1285	Philip III of France leads a crusade against Peter III of Aragon in support of Charles of Anjou, but all three kings die. Navarre passes with Champagne to the French crown (until 1316).
1286	Death of Alexander III of Scotland inaugurates Scottish succession crisis.
1289	Qalawun, Mamluk sultan of Egypt, captures Tripoli.
1290	Death of Margaret of Norway, heiress of Scotland: first Scottish Interregnum. Edward I expels all Jews from England.
1291	Fall of Acre, Tyre, Sidon, and Beirut to Qalawun's successor al-Ashraf: end of the 'crusader states' in the 'Holy Land'. Departure of the Vivaldi brothers of Genoa in search of a sea route to India (their fate is not known). Foundation of the Swiss Confederation.
1292	Edward I promotes John Balliol to the Scottish throne.
1293–9	Great Genoese-Venetian war.
1294	Philip IV declares Gascony forfeit, renewing Anglo-French wars (until 1303).
1296	Edward I drives John Balliol into exile: beginning of second Scottish Interregnum and wars of Scottish independence.
1297	Scottish rebels under William Wallace defeat the English at Stirling Bridge. Costs of French and Scottish wars force Edward I to reissue Magna Carta.
1298	Adolf of Nassau, king of the Romans, is deposed and killed by the supporters of Albert I of Habsburg. Edward I defeats William Wallace at Falkirk.
1300	First papal 'jubilee' celebrated in Rome by Pope Boniface VIII. Václav II of Bohemia is elected as king of Poland.
1301	Death of Andrew III of Hungary ends the Árpád dynasty.
1302	Flemish rebellion against Philip IV: massacre of French at Bruges ('Matins of Bruges') and rout of French cavalry by Flemish urban militias at Courtrai (Kortrijk).
1302–10	The Ottoman Turks overrun most remaining Byzantine possessions in Anatolia.
1303	Philip IV attempts to have Boniface VIII seized at Anagni.
c.1303–6	Giotto paints the Scrovegni Chapel at Padua.

1305	Execution of William Wallace. Peace of Athis-sur-Orge ends Franco-Flemish war, largely in Philip IV's favour.
1306	Robert I (Bruce) seizes the Scottish throne. Philip IV expels all Jews from the French royal domain.
1307–12	Brutal suppression of the Order of Knights Templar in France by Philip IV.
1308–10	Accession to Hungarian throne of Charles Robert (Carobert), grandson of Charles II of Naples, establishes the Angevin dynasty of Hungarian kings.
1309	Avignon becomes the chief papal residence (until 1377). The Knights Hospitaller establish themselves in Rhodes.
1310–12	Philip IV annexes Lyon to the French royal domain.
1311	Edward II of England is forced to concede the Ordinances, constraining his authority. Catalan mercenaries conquer the Latin duchy of Athens.
1312	Execution of Piers Gaveston, favourite of Edward II, by rebel barons.
1314	Robert Bruce defeats Edward II at Bannockburn. Deaths of Philip IV of France and Clement V. Execution of Jacques de Molay, Grand Master of the French Templars, in Paris.
c.1314–21	Dante Alighieri completes the *Divine Comedy* (*Hell*, *Purgatory*, and *Paradise*).
1315	Louis X of France has Philip IV's minister Enguerrand de Marigny executed on charges of sorcery; he concedes charters of liberties to French provincial leagues. Defeat of Austrians at Mortgarten establishes Swiss autonomy.
1315–18	Scottish invasion under Edward, brother of Robert Bruce, inflicts a serious blow against English rule in Ireland.
1315–22	The 'Great Famine' devastates the northern European population.
1317–22	Persecution of the Spiritual Franciscans by Pope John XXII.
1320	Peasant uprising, the *Pastoureaux* ('Shepherds'), attacks the Jews of southern France. Declaration of Arbroath expounds Scottish claims to independence.
1321	Inquisition at Montaillou in the Pyrenees: effective end of Catharism. Massacres of lepers across France.
1324	Siege of Metz: first mention of gunpowder in European warfare. Marsilius of Padua completes his *Defensor Pacis*, an exceptionally detailed critique of ecclesiastical and temporal power.

1328	Edward III of England recognizes Scottish independence.
*c.***1336**	Christian 'discovery' of the Canary Islands.
1337	Beginning of Hundred Years War between the royal dynasties of France and England.
1347	The Black Death reaches western Europe.

Glossary

a(l)lod: property held free of service.

althing: (in Iceland) annual assembly of chieftains.

Angevin: from Anjou in western France, used (i) for the 'Plantagenet' dynasty, kings of England (1154–1399); (ii) for a junior branch of the Capetian dynasty, beginning with Charles I, count of Anjou and king of Sicily (1266–85), whose descendants were variously kings of Sicily, Naples, Hungary, and Poland.

antipope: pope not accepted as legitimate (frequently an imperial nominee).

Augustinian: concerning the works of St Augustine of Hippo (d. 430); the Augustinian Rule (eleventh–twelfth centuries) for regular canons was partly based upon his writings.

autarky: economic self-sufficiency.

ban: power of command over a district's people and resources.

bannal: (exactions, rights, etc.) concerning or resulting from the ban.

benefit of (the) clergy: legal privileges held by virtue of holy orders.

canon: (as noun) (i) (secular canon) senior member of a cathedral chapter, or member of the chapter of a collegiate church; (ii) (regular canon) member of a religious order of priests (cf. Augustinian); (iii) an ecclesiastical decree or law.

canon law: ecclesiastical law.

cartulary: register of charters, sometimes also containing narratives (e.g. a monastery's foundation story).

castellanus (castellan): lord (sometimes custodian) of a castle, and usually also of the surrounding area (castellany).

Chain of Being: the theory that all creation is linked in an unbroken chain extending from God to the most degenerate beings.

confraternity: religious or charitable association.

consolamentum: deathbed sacrament administered to Cathars.

contado: territory around an Italian city, usually under its political and economic control.

conversi: (in Cistercian monasteries) the lay brethren, whose chief duties were manual work.

cortes (Spanish), corts (Catalan): representative, consultative assembly, originally a plenary session of the royal council.

corvée: unpaid labour service, usually customary.

Curia (lit.: 'court'): (used especially for) the papal court and administration.

daughter-house: religious house dependent upon a superior monastery.

diet: (in the Holy Roman Empire) an occasional, representative assembly.

ealdorman: (in Anglo-Saxon England) a nobleman with regional military and judicial powers.

elector: (in the Holy Roman Empire) one of a group of princes claiming the right to choose the emperor.

encellulement (lit. 'breaking up into cells'): fragmentation of political power around castles (especially in eleventh-century France).

endogamy: marrying within one's own social group or kin group.

eschatology: study of the 'last things' (Death, the Last Judgement, Hell, and Heaven) and hence of the end of Time.

exegetical: concerning the explanation of the Bible (exegesis).

fief: a wide variety of types of aristocratic property; by 1200, usually held from a superior in return for honourable (normally military) service, and hereditarily.

fin'amors: the set of concepts loosely referred to as 'courtly love'; its nature (and indeed existence) is much disputed.

freies Eigen (lit. 'free possession'): (in Germany) piece of property held by a free or noble family.

fuero: (in Iberia) one of several types of charter, including municipal privileges and contracts between lords and their collective tenants.

hagiographer: author of a saint's life (hagiography).

hauberk: long mail coat, often a symbol of a knight's status.

homiletical: concerning a homily (sermon) or preaching.

humanist: (in medieval contexts) one who emphasizes human value rather than human depravity—sometimes through interest in classical learning.

Il-Khan: Mongol ruler of Persia from mid-thirteenth century to 1335.

incastellamento: (in eleventh-century southern Europe) resettlement of rural communities in fortified villages.

indulgence: (from Latin: 'to be kind') remission of temporal punishment granted by ecclesiastical authority to penitent sinners.

ispán: royal officer in charge of a county in medieval Hungary, with military, administrative, and judicial responsibilities.

jihad: (from Arabic for 'to strive') either inner spiritual struggle, or outward struggle or holy war to extend territories under Muslim rule.

lazarhouse: religious community and hospital for lepers.

lyric: (of poetry) expressing emotions, usually written in brief stanzas.

manumission: grant of freedom to an unfree peasant.

miles (lit.: 'soldier'; pl. *milites*): the usual word in medieval Latin for a knight.

ministerialis (pl. *ministeriales*): (in Germany) unfree knight.

Minnesänger (also *Minnesinger*): German poet (twelfth–thirteenth centuries), author of love songs (*Minne* = love).

Nicolaitism: (pejorative term for) clerical marriage or concubinage.

nominalist: one who holds philosophical doctrine that universal ideas are mere names, not realities.

Occitan: the chief language of southern France in this period (also called the *langue d'oc* or, less accurately, Provençal).

Old Church Slavonic: literary and liturgical language developed from a Slavic dialect by Saints Cyril and Methodius (ninth-century Byzantine missionaries).

ontological: concerning the nature of being.

ordo (lit. 'order'; pl. *ordines*): (i) religious order; (ii) 'order' of society; (iii) liturgical rite for specific occasion (e.g. coronation *ordo*).

patrilineality: descent in the male line.

patristic: concerning the writings of the 'Church Fathers' (early Christian theologians).

patronym: name referring to one's father or an ancestor in the male line.

Peace and Truce of God: attempts to restrict violence in France, *c.*990–*c.*1050 (no longer regarded as a coherent movement); the Peace council proclamations were later used to buttress princely authority.

portolan: type of map (from thirteenth century) depicting charted coastlines, usually marked with navigational directions.

prebend: stipend of a cathedral canon.

quadrivium: the second tier of the classical seven liberal arts (mathematics, astronomy, music, and geometry) (cf. trivium).

salvific: concerning divine salvation.

schism: formal rift within a religion, especially (in this period) between different branches of the Christian Church.

scriptorium: (in a monastery) room where manuscripts were written.

Shia, Shi'ism: one of two main branches of Islam, regarding Muhammad's son-in-law Ali as the Prophet's first legitimate successor; its medieval adherents included the Fatimids and the Assassins (cf. Sunni).

signori: (in thirteenth- and fourteenth-century Italy) masters of city states, usually enjoying informal but immense local power, and increasingly hereditary.

simony: purchase of spiritual gifts, especially clerical office.

sumptuary laws: legal codes forbidding people of lower status to wear high-status garments.

Sunni: branch of Islam, commonly regarded as 'orthodox', that rejects Muhammad's son-in-law Ali as the Prophet's first legitimate successor; its medieval adherents included the Seljuk Turks, Ayyubids, Mamluks, and most Iberian Muslims (cf. Shia).

taifa: (in Iberia, following the decline of the Umayyad Caliphate) local Muslim prince or 'party-king'.

Thomist: concerning the Dominican theologian Thomas Aquinas (d. 1274).

toponymic: (of a surname) derived from, or referring to, a place-name.

transhumance: seasonal migration of livestock to suitable pastures.

trivium: first tier of the classical seven liberal arts (grammar, rhetoric, and dialectic or logic) (cf. quadrivium).

troubadour: lyric poet in southern France (twelfth–thirteenth centuries), using Occitan.

trouvère: lyric poet in northern France (twelfth–thirteenth century), analagous to a troubadour but using the *langue d'oïl* (Old French).

usury: charging interest for a loan, regarded as sinful because of Old Testament prohibitions.

Maps

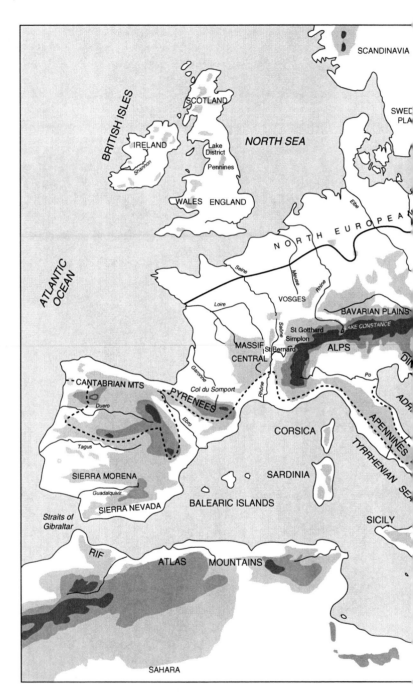

1 Europe: Physical

Source: Based upon J. Le Goff, *Medieval Civilization*, trans. J. Barrow (Oxford and Cambridge, MA: Blackwells, 1988), map 1.

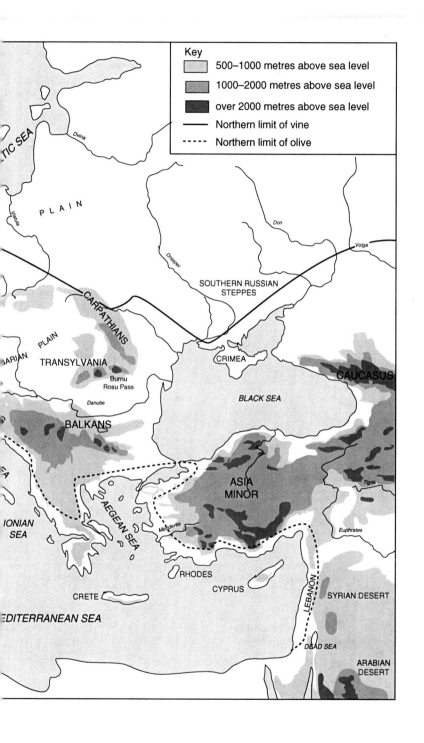

Key

- 500–1000 metres above sea level
- 1000–2000 metres above sea level
- over 2000 metres above sea level
- —— Northern limit of vine
- ---- Northern limit of olive

BALTIC SEA

Dvina

PLAIN

Vistula

Dnieper

Don

Volga

SOUTHERN RUSSIAN
STEPPES

CARPATHIANS

PLAIN

HUNGARIAN PLAIN

TRANSYLVANIA

Burnu
Rosu Pass

Danube

CRIMEA

BALKANS

BLACK SEA

CAUCASUS

SEA

IONIAN
SEA

AEGEAN SEA

ASIA
MINOR

Menderes

Tigris

Euphrates

RHODES

CYPRUS

CRETE

MEDITERRANEAN SEA

LEBANON

SYRIAN DESERT

DEAD SEA

ARABIAN
DESERT

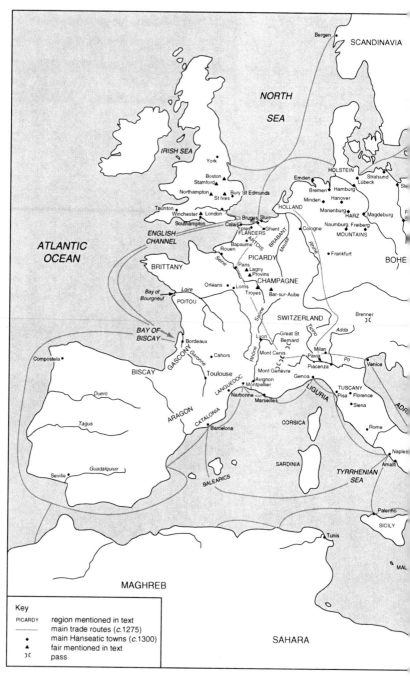

Key

PICARDY   region mentioned in text
- - - - - main trade routes (c.1275)
•   main Hanseatic towns (c.1300)
▲   fair mentioned in text
)(pass

2 Economic Change in the Central Middle Ages

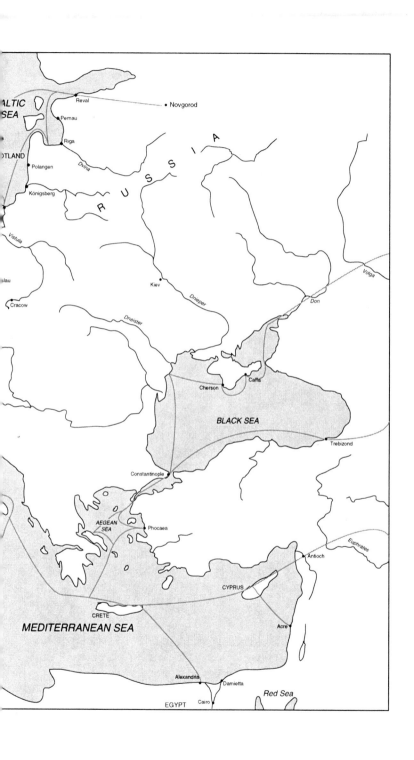

ALTIC
SEA

Reval

• Novgorod

Pernau

Riga

OTLAND

Polangen

Dvina

R U S S I A

Königsberg

Vistula

lau

Kiev

Volga

Cracow

Dnieper

Dniester

Don

Cherson

Caffa

BLACK SEA

Trebizond

Constantinople

AEGEAN
SEA

Phocaea

Euphrates

Antioch

CYPRUS

CRETE

Acre

MEDITERRANEAN SEA

Alexandria

Damietta

Red Sea

EGYPT

Cairo

NORWEGIANS

NORSE

KINGDOM
OF
SCOTS
(ALBA) • Edinburgh

STRATHCLYDE

ULSTER

CONNACHT

MUNSTER Dublin
LEINSTER

NORTHUMBRIA

SWED

DENMARK

SWE

Elbe

OBODRITES

Bremen •

SAXONY
Magdeburg •

SAXON MARCH

KINGDOM
OF YORK
York •
MERCIA

WELSH
KINGDOMS OF ENGLAND

WESSEX
Winchester • London •

FLANDERS
Cambrai •

KINGDOM OF

Aachen •

FRANCONIA

BOHE

NORMANDY
Rouen • Seine
Laon •
Paris •

LOTHARINGIA
Mainz •

Meuse

Rhine

GERMANY

BRETONS

DUCHY OF FRANCIA
Tours • • Orléans

SWABIA

BAVARIA
Augsburg •

Danu

**KINGDOM
OF THE
WEST
FRANKS**

Poitiers •

AQUITAINE

BURGUNDY
(DUCHY)

Loire

(EAST FRANKS)

KINGDOM
OF

Lyon •

Rhône

KINGDOM
Pavia • • Milan • Verona

Po

VENICE

Compostela • KINGDOM
OF LEÓN

Garonne

KINGDOM
OF PAMPLONA

Toulouse

BURGUNDY

Arles •

OF

Genoa •

OF

ITALY

Duero

CATALONIA

Tagus

COUNTY OF
ARAGON

Barcelona •

CORSICA

Rome •

LOMB

PRINCIPA

U M A Y Y A D

Cordoba •
Seville • Guadalquivir

BALEARICS

SARDINIA

Amalfi

Palermo

SICILY

C A L I P H A T E

F A T I M I D

C A L I P H A T E

M

Key

.... Main borders *c*.950 (approx.)
⬛⬛⬛⬛⬛ Extent of Carolingian Empire, *c.* 814
▬ ▬ ▬ ▬ Extent of Byzantine Empire, *c.* 1025

3 Europe (political) *c*.950

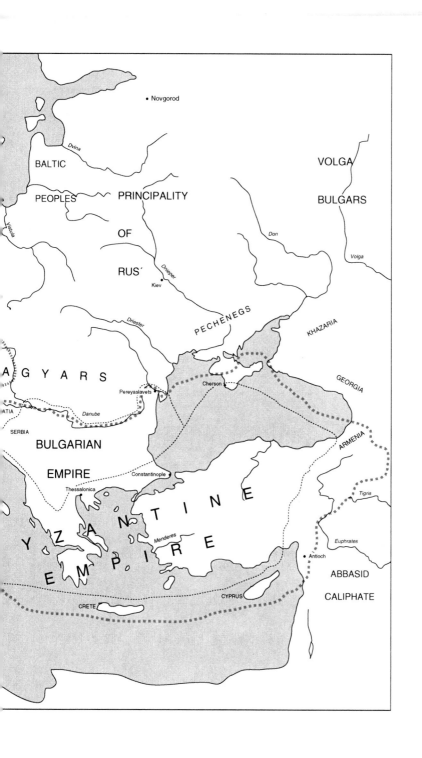

- Novgorod

BALTIC

PEOPLES

PRINCIPALITY

OF

RUS´

Dvina

Vistula

VOLGA

BULGARS

Don

Volga

Dnieper

Kiev

Dniester

PECHENEGS

KHAZARIA

GEORGIA

A G Y A R S

Pereyaslavets

Cherson

ATIA

SERBIA

Danube

BULGARIAN

EMPIRE

Thessalonica

Constantinople

ARMENIA

B Y Z A N T I N E

E M P I R E

Menderes

Tigris

Euphrates

Antioch

ABBASID

CALIPHATE

CRETE

CYPRUS

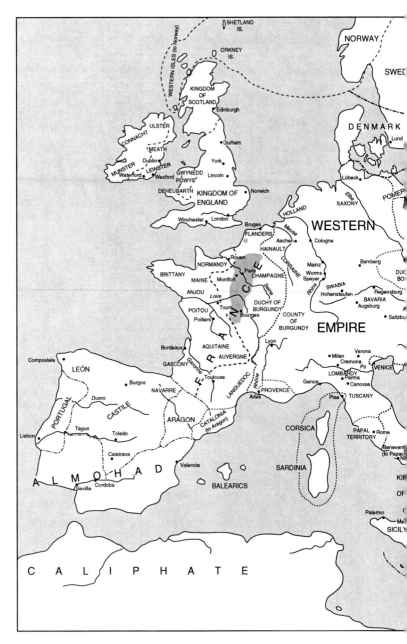

4 Europe (political) *c.*1180

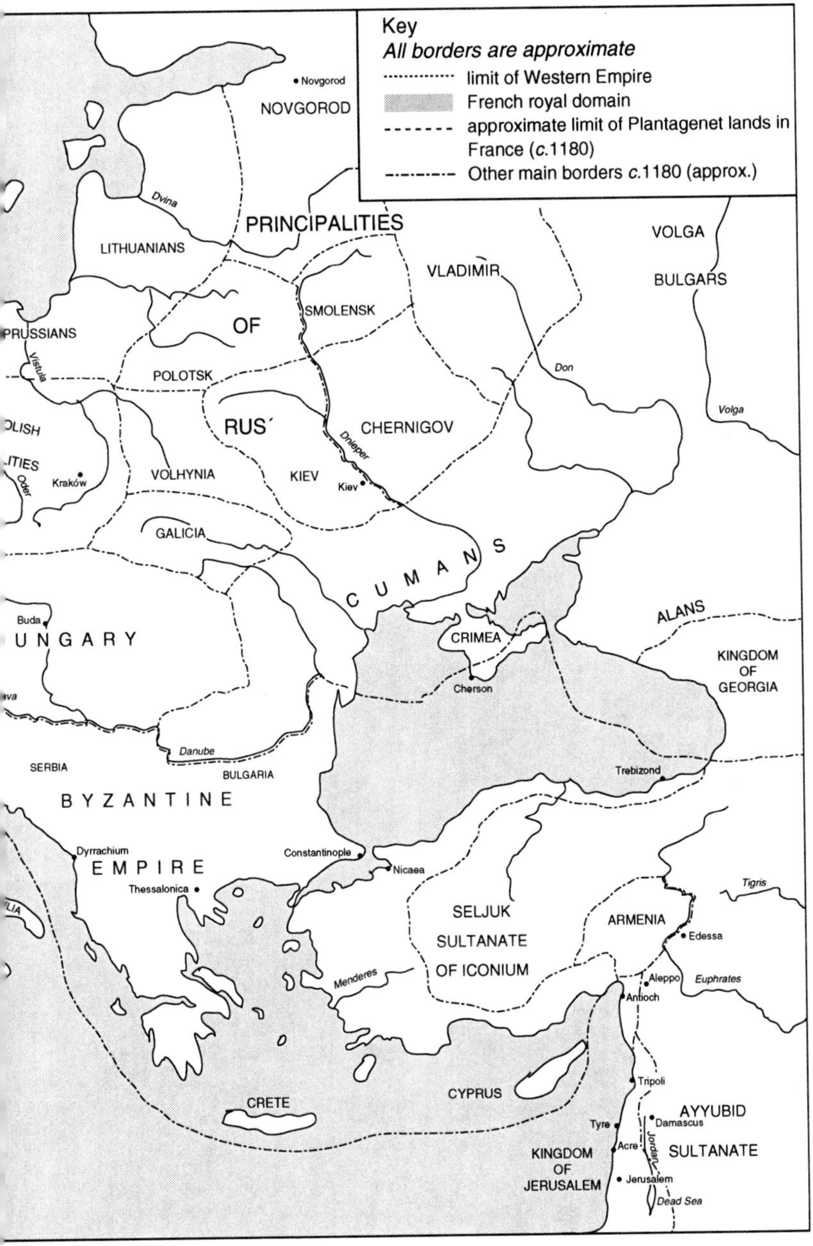
Key
All borders are approximate
limit of Western Empire
French royal domain
approximate limit of Plantagenet lands in France (c.1180)
Other main borders c.1180 (approx.)
Novgorod
NOVGOROD
Dvina
PRINCIPALITIES
OF
RUS´
LITHUANIANS
PRUSSIANS
Vistula
POLOTSK
SMOLENSK
VLADIMIR
VOLGA
BULGARS
Don
Volga
CHERNIGOV
Dnieper
KIEV
Kiev
VOLHYNIA
Kraków
Oder
GALICIA
CUMANS
Buda
UNGARY
ALANS
KINGDOM OF GEORGIA
CRIMEA
Cherson
Danube
SERBIA
BULGARIA
BYZANTINE
EMPIRE
Trebizond
Dyrrachium
Constantinople
Nicaea
Thessalonica
SELJUK SULTANATE OF ICONIUM
ARMENIA
Tigris
Edessa
Euphrates
Aleppo
Antioch
Menderes
CYPRUS
CRETE
Tripoli
Tyre
Damascus
AYYUBID SULTANATE
Acre
Jordan
KINGDOM OF JERUSALEM
Jerusalem
Dead Sea

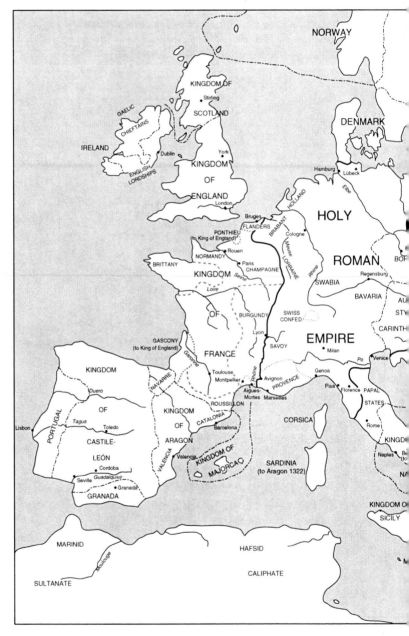

5 Europe (political) c.1320

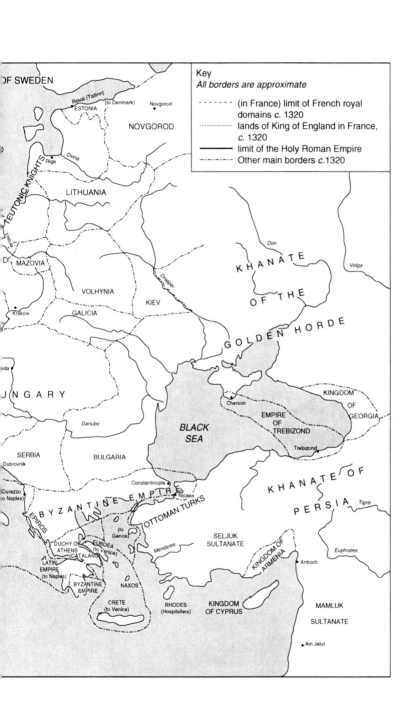

OF SWEDEN

Reval (Tallinn)
(to Denmark)
ESTONIA
Novgorod

NOVGOROD

Key
All borders are approximate

------ (in France) limit of French royal domains *c.* 1320
.... lands of King of England in France, *c.* 1320
—— limit of the Holy Roman Empire
—·—·— Other main borders *c.*1320

Riga
Dvina

LITHUANIA

TEUTONIC KNIGHTS

Vistula

D·

MAZOVIA

Don

KHANATE

Volga

OF THE

VOLHYNIA

Dnieper

KIEV

Kraków

GALICIA

GOLDEN HORDE

·da

NGARY

KINGDOM

Cherson

OF

GEORGIA

Danube

EMPIRE
OF
TREBIZOND

BLACK
SEA

SERBIA

Dubrovnik

BULGARIA

Trebizond

Durazzo
(to Naples)

Constantinople

KHANATE OF

BYZANTINE EMPIRE

Nicaea

Tigris

OTTOMAN TURKS

PERSIA

EPIROS

(to
Genoa)

SELJUK
SULTANATE

DUCHY OF
ATHENS
(CATALANS)

EUBOEA
(to Venice)

Menderes

KINGDOM OF
ARMENIA

Euphrates

Antioch

LATIN
EMPIRE
(to Naples)

BYZANTINE
EMPIRE

NAXOS

CRETE
(to Venice)

RHODES
(Hospitallers)

KINGDOM
OF CYPRUS

MAMLUK

SULTANATE

Ain Jalut

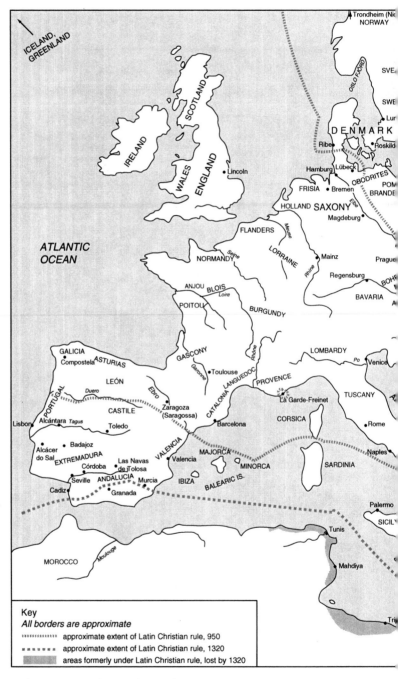

6 The expansion of Latin Christendom

FINLAND

GULF OF FINLAND
Tallinn (Reval)

• Novgorod

SAAREMAA
(ÖSEL)

ESTONIA *LAKE PEIPUS*

GULF OF RIGA

Riga *Dvina*

LIVONIA

•LAND

COURS

SEMIGALLIANS

SIA

LITHUANIA

S

MAZOVIA

•AND

Don

Volga

R

Dnieper

• Kiev

Kraków

JC

• Esztergom

HUNGARY

TRANSYLVANIA

Danube

TIA

SERBIA

•Dubrovnik

BULGARIA

IA

•Durazzo

EPIROS

Thessalonica

THESSALY

'ONIAN
RIA
SEA

ACHAEA
(MOREA)

AEGEAN SEA

Athens

Chios

Menderes

Naxos

RHODES

DITERRANEAN SEA

CRETE

• Tana

SEA OF AZOV

CRIMEA

Caffa

BLACK SEA

•Trebizond

GREATER

ARMENIA

Constantinople

• Nicaea

ANATOLIA

LESSER ARMENIA

Tigris

CILICIA

• Edessa

MESOPOTAMIA

• Aleppo

Antioch

Euphrates

SYRIA

• Tripoli

CYPRUS

Acre

• Damascus

• Jerusalem

• Damietta

EGYPT

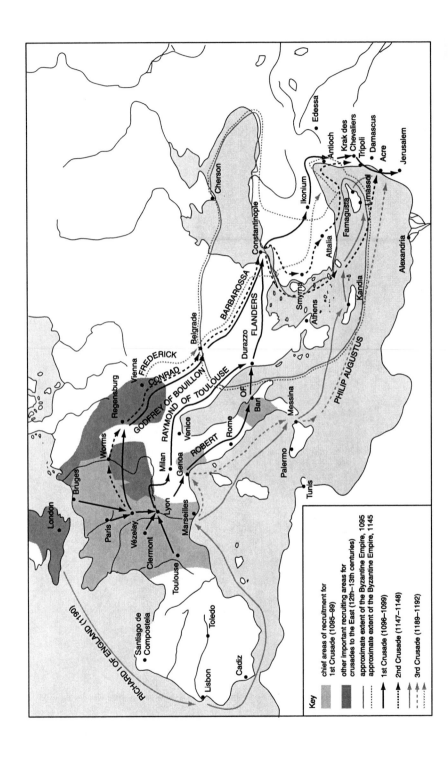

Key

chief areas of recruitment for
1st Crusade (1095–99)

other important recruiting areas for
crusades to the East (12th–13th centuries)

approximate extent of the Byzantine Empire, 1095
approximate extent of the Byzantine Empire, 1145

1st Crusade (1096–1099)
2nd Crusade (1147–1148)
3rd Crusade (1189–1192)

RICHARD I OF ENGLAND (1190)

PHILIP AUGUSTUS

BARBAROSSA

FREDERICK

CONRAD

GODFREY OF BOUILLON

RAYMOND OF TOULOUSE

OF FLANDERS

ROBERT

London
Bruges
Paris
Vézelay
Clermont
Toulouse
Santiago de Compostela
Toledo
Cadiz
Lisbon
Marseilles
Lyon
Worms
Regensburg
Vienna
Milan
Genoa
Venice
Rome
Bari
Belgrade
Durazzo
Palermo
Messina
Tunis
Athens
Smyrna
Attalia
Kandia
Famagusta
Limassol
Constantinople
Cherson
Ikonium
Edessa
Antioch
Krak des Chevaliers
Tripoli
Damascus
Acre
Jerusalem
Alexandria

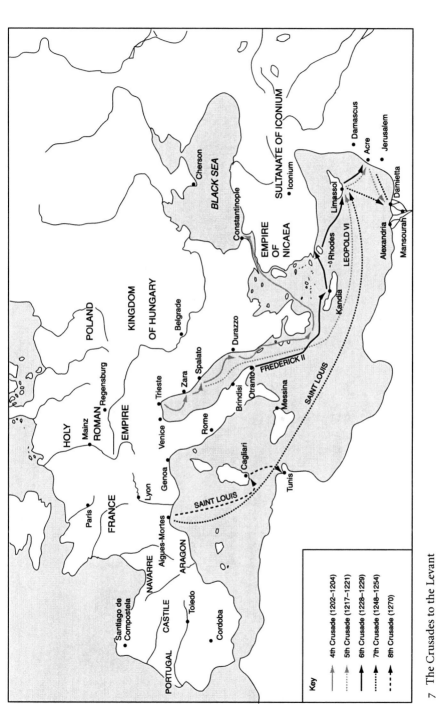

7 The Crusades to the Levant

Source: Partly based upon Le Goff, *Medieval Civilization*, maps 12–13.

Key

□ **Rome**	Patriarchate
◆ RAVENNA	Metropolitan see
● St Andrews	Episcopal see
○ *Bamberg*	Episcopal see immediately subject to Rome

Areas under Muslim domination

Areas under Pagan dominaiton

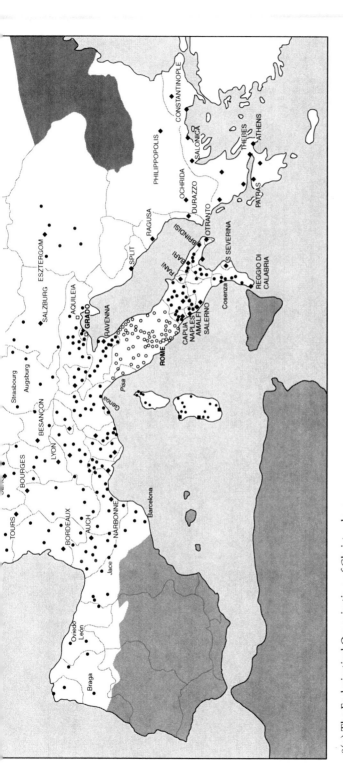

8(a) The Ecclesiastical Organisation of Christendom, c. 1000

Source. Based upon A. MacKay and D. Ditchburn (eds.), *Atlas of Medieval Europe* (London, 1997), 48–9.

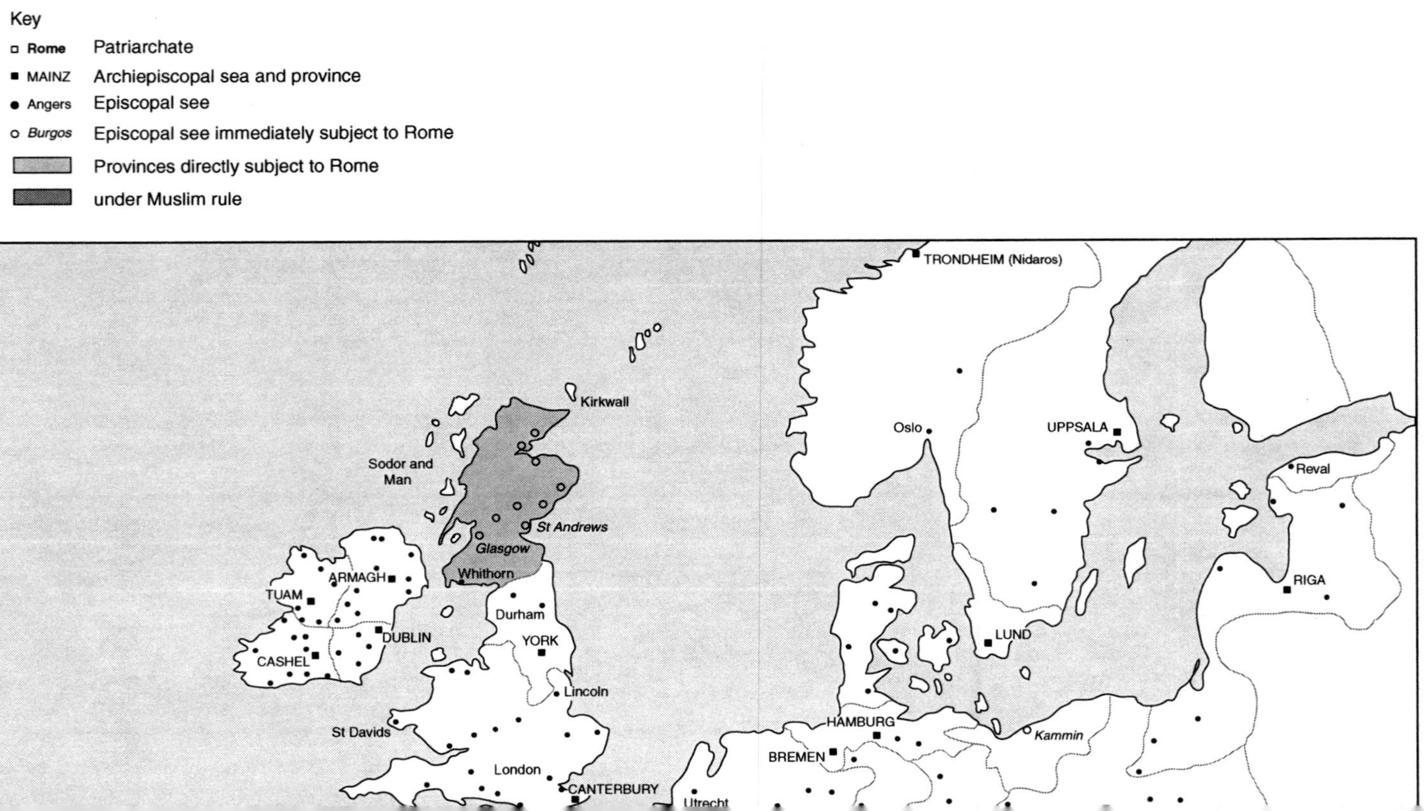

Key

Rome   Patriarchate

■ MAINZ   Archiepiscopal sea and province

● Angers   Episcopal see

○ Burgos   Episcopal see immediately subject to Rome

          Provinces directly subject to Rome

          under Muslim rule

TRONDHEIM (Nidaros)

UPPSALA

Reval

RIGA

Kammin

LUND

Oslo

HAMBURG

BREMEN

Utrecht

Kirkwall

St Andrews

Glasgow

Whithorn

Sodor and Man

Durham

YORK

Lincoln

London

CANTERBURY

St Davids

ARMAGH

DUBLIN

TUAM

CASHEL

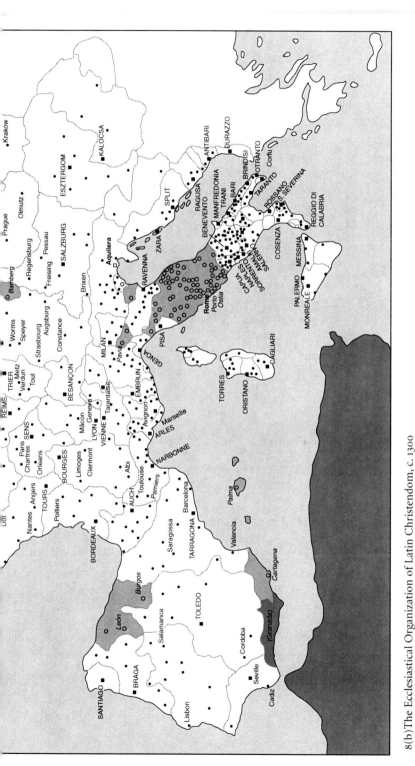

8(b) The Ecclesiastical Organization of Latin Christendom, c. 1300

Source. Based upon A. MacKay and D. Ditchburn (eds.), *Atlas of Medieval Europe* (London, 1997), 112–13, 188. Latin sees in Greece are not depicted.

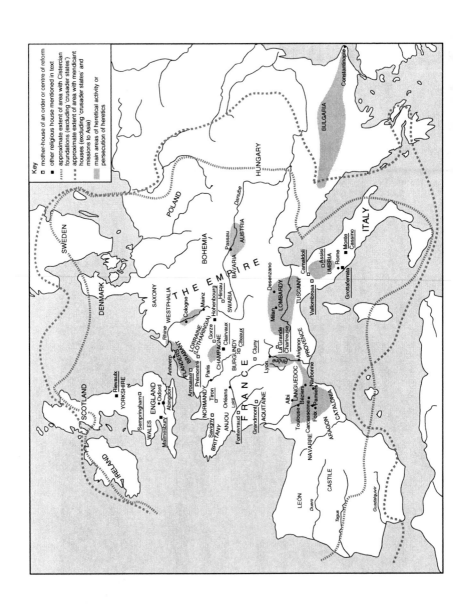

Key

□ mother-house of an order or centre of reform

■ other religious house mentioned in text

approximate extent of area with Cistercian foundations (excluding 'crusader states')

∗∗∗ approximate extent of area with mendicant houses (excluding crusader states and missions to Asia)

▨ main areas of heretical activity or persecution of heretics

SWEDEN

DENMARK

SCOTLAND

IRELAND

YORKSHIRE
Rievaulx ■

ENGLAND
Sempringham □
Malmesbury ■   Abingdon □   Oxford □

WALES

POLAND

BOHEMIA

SAXONY

WESTPHALIA

Cologne □   Mainz ■
Hirsau ■   Hohenbourg ■

Rhine

FLANDERS   BRABANT

Antwerp □

LORRAINE (LOTHARINGIA)
Gorze ■

THE EM P I R E

HUNGARY

BULGARIA

AUSTRIA
Passau ■

BAVARIA

SWABIA

Danube

Arrouaise □   Prémontré □
Paris ■   Clairvaux ■
Cîteaux □

Tiron □

NORMANDY

BRITTANY

Orléans ■

ANJOU

Savigny □

CHAMPAGNE

BURGUNDY

Cluny ■

FRANCE

Fontevraud □

Grandmont □

AQUITAINE

Lyon ■

Rhône

La Grande
Chartreuse □

Avignon ■
PROVENCE

LANGUEDOC
Albi ▪
Toulouse ■   Béziers ■
Carcassonne ■   Narbonne ■
Foix ■   Pamiers ■

NAVARRE

ARAGON

CATALONIA

LEÓN

CASTILE

Duero

Tague

Guadalquivir

Desenzano ▪

Milan ■
LOMBARDY

Vallombrosa ■

TUSCANY

Camaldoli □

Grottaferrata ■

UMBRIA
Assisi ■
Rome ■
Monte
Cassino ■

ITALY

Constantinople ▪

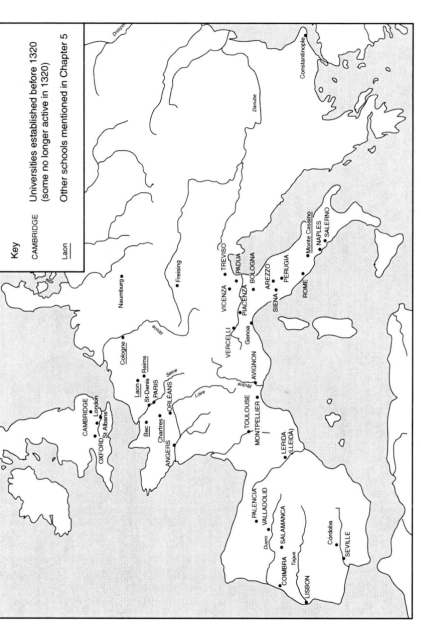

Key

CAMBRIDGE   Universities established before 1320 (some no longer active in 1320)

Laon   Other schools mentioned in Chapter 5

10 Schools and universities in the central Middle Ages

Index

Medieval personal names are organized by first name, not surname or nickname.

Lightning Source UK Ltd.
Milton Keynes UK

177281UK00008B/4/P